Risk, Disaster and Crisis Reduction

Valerie November • Yvan Leanza

Risk, Disaster and Crisis Reduction

Mobilizing, Collecting and Sharing Information

Springer

Valerie November
CNRS
Laboratoire Techniques Territoires
et Société (LATTS)
Paris, France

Yvan Leanza
Laboratoire Psychologie et Cultures
Université Laval
Quebec City, QC, Canada

ISBN 978-3-319-08541-8 ISBN 978-3-319-08542-5 (eBook)
DOI 10.1007/978-3-319-08542-5
Springer Cham Heidelberg New York Dordrecht London

Library of Congress Control Number: 2014952304

Printed on acid-free paper

Springer is part of Springer Science+Business Media (www.springer.com)

Preface

The fact that information is available does not necessarily mean that those who receive it are well informed. Nor does the fact that information is being circulated mean that it will be taken up by those who could make good use of it. This has become apparent during the various crises and disasters that have shaken our planet in recent years. For this reason, any reflection focussing solely on the receipt of the information, the production of the information or the means of communication is bound to be fragmented. The book you are now holding is the final element of a project that started in 2006 with the formation of a special research team and the submission of a request for funding to the Geneva International Academic Network (GIAN) – called SNIS (Swiss Network for International Studies) since 2008. This request, and the project that was then funded, put forward an innovative approach intended to highlight the conditions required to achieve a satisfactory information flow in areas related to risk, through close observation of the way this information is collected, indexed, processed, distributed and used. One of the principles on which the project was based was Bateson's definition of information as "a difference that makes a difference" (1972). Given that such a difference only makes sense in a universe of meaning, or in a specific context, achieving the objective of the project required an interdisciplinary team and multiple research sites. Only with such a wide range of perspectives, methods and contexts related to the "risks" would it be possible to take a fresh look at the circulation of information in a way which goes beyond the limits of a given discipline or individual local characteristics. Thus, at the instigation of Professor Valérie November, a research team was formed combining geographers specialising in risk, sociologists working in the field of science and techniques, and psychologists specialising in intercultural research methods. As expected, the project is founded on a sound theoretical basis and a thorough methodological procedure; these will also be presented in this book.

A project of this nature would have been impossible without the necessary contacts in various regions of the world, and in the governmental and non-governmental organisations involved in risk management. The GIAN's mission is precisely to promote interaction between university institutions and international organisations. The research team could be assured of the cooperation of various bodies:

- The World Health Organisation (WHO), in the person of David L. Heymann M.D., Assistant Director-General – Health Security and Environment
- The Secretariat of the United Nations International Strategy for Disaster Reduction (UN/ISDR), in the persons of Silvano Briceño and Marie-Lou Darricau, at the time respectively the director and library manager of the Secretariat
- The *Bureau National de Gestion des Risques et des Catastrophes* of the government of Madagascar, in the person of Claire Rahasinirina
- The non-governmental organisations Medair (Nicolas Crettenand; Antananarivo, Madagascar), the WESDE Association (Léopold Kemkeng; Maroua, Cameroon) and PROSENAT (Jacques Unkap; Yaoundé, Cameroon)

This collaboration made it possible to include in a single research project three areas, each of which, in its own way, has to produce, process or distribute risk-related information: the SHOC Room of the WHO in Geneva; the field library project of the library of the UN/ISDR; and the activities of the two NGOs in Cameroon, WESDE and PROSENAT.

On the research institution side, the project was run by the University of Geneva (Yvan Leanza and André Wamba) and the ENAC faculty of the Ecole Polytechnique Fédérale de Lausanne (Valérie November, Charlotte Cabasse, Katia de Conto and Basile Barbey). During the course of the project, Yvan Leanza was appointed a professor at Laval University in Quebec. He continued to contribute to the project from Canada, with the help of a research assistant, Ekaterina Smali. Other participants were John Horekens, as consultant for international organisations, and Mireille Lador, as webmaster.

The results and reflections that emerged from the project have been published in a variety of ways. Firstly on a website – www.riskinsitu.info/home.html – and then later in a research report. A seminar held in Geneva on 5 November 2007, at which the content of this report was discussed by the members of the research team and representatives of the organisations involved. Following the seminar, a good practices guide was prepared and distributed. The final stage in the process is the publication of this book. Chapter 1 offers a new vision of the circulation of information in risk situations, and sets out the methodological framework used in the study of the three areas. Each of these areas is covered in detail in a separate chapter, starting with the WHO SHOC Room (Chap. 2), then crisis management in Madagascar (Chap. 3), and finally an analysis of the way information circulates during the activities carried out by the NGOs WESDE and PROSENAT in Yaoundé and Maroua (Chap. 4). We conclude in Chap. 5 with a synthesis of the discussions that took place at the seminar at which the results were presented and some theoretical considerations outlined in Chap. 1. It includes also the guidelines offered to risk management practitioners. While responsibility for the publication of this book lies with Valérie November and Yvan Leanza, other members of the research team were involved in the drafting of certain chapters. Katia de Conto contributed to Chap. 2; Charlotte Cabasse and Basile Barbey to Chap. 3; Ekaterina Smali and André Wamba to Chap. 4; and John Horekens to the conclusion. In addition, Estelle Lépine, of the EPFL, kindly assisted with the rewriting and updating of Chaps. 2 and 3. Valérie November would like to thank Christophe Buffet for his attentive rereading of the chapter on Madagascar.

We would like to express our sincere thanks to all those mentioned above, without whom this complex and ambitious project would not have been possible. Special mention is due to the GIAN for their financial contribution, as well as to the School of Architecture, Civil and Environmental Engineering of the EFPL for their translation support during the research project. We would also like to thank Joanna MacDaniel for her translation of this book, Boris Calame for his help for the figures, François René de Cotret and Rhéa J. Rocque for their editorial help and the publishing team at Springer for their support and their patience.

Paris, France — Valerie November
Quebec City, QC, Canada — Yvan Leanza

Contents

Chapter 1
Risk and Information: For a New Conceptual Framework

In the field of risks and crises, both the circulation of information and access to relevant information are seen as crucial factors. These two facets are well documented and everyone has agreed that they are essential (Maisonneuve et al. 1999; Maisonneuve 2005; Kasperson and Kasperson 2001, 2005; Pidgeon et al. 2003; Brodhag 2000; Bakis 1995; Rodriguez et al. 2007; Papy 2008). However, certain aspects remain unclear, most notably: the fact that the information is available is not enough to ensure that those for whom it is intended are informed. In other words, simply circulating the information does not mean that it will be picked up by those who could benefit from it. This has been amply demonstrated by the various crises and catastrophes that have shaken the planet in recent years. When the tsunami struck Southeast Asia in December 2004, not all those who could have been informed were aware of the approaching wave. Furthermore, this information was not available to all coastal dwellers to the same extent, leading to the evacuation of some hotels, but not of some villages. In many places, it was not possible to raise the alert in time, given the speed of events or the prescribed circuits for circulating such information (Bird and Lubkowski 2005). There are also many examples of information being retained or deliberately not being passed on. Consider, for example, the number of people who fell ill or died following the catastrophic events of 11 September 2001 in New York: having answered their president's plea to help the victims, for several months they breathed in air containing highly toxic dust particles. The Environmental Protection Agency (EPA) was aware that the air contained significant amounts of asbestos and unprecedented levels of dioxins, but no information about this was made public. Although the EPA has explained its conduct (Environmental Protection Agency 2003), the subject remains highly controversial. A number of associations (residents and NGOs) are fighting for compensation for the victims (for instance, Sierra Club 2006).

In order to be able to deal with risk situations and crises, it must be possible for information – when it circulates – to be understood and interpreted by a wide

V. November, Y. Leanza, *Risk, Disaster and Crisis Reduction*,
DOI 10.1007/978-3-319-08542-5_1

range of actors, working in fields such as health and natural or environmental risks. The key works relating to communication advocate the following: the information circulating should target specific destinations, and the roles played by each level of the organisation should be clear to all the actors involved. This is the familiar model of the transmitter and the receiver (the Shannon and Weaver model of 1949) which, although it has since been criticised and refined by a number of researchers, remains the predominant model.

However, in practice, the situations involving the circulation of information are more complex, less linear and far more heterogeneous. For example, in some cases the large amount of information available fails to reach the correct destination, while in others, the information is found and used, allowing the level of risk to be reduced. Surprisingly, literature on risks, in particular on the area of the communication of risks, has paid relatively little attention to these complex situations. *By observing closely, in three very different situations, the way in which information is gathered, processed, distributed and used, this book examines the countless reformulations, redefinitions and even reorientations to which all information is subjected. This multiple reformatting, at least according to the hypothesis put forward in this book, is an important element in ensuring that the information produced circulates and reaches those for whom it is intended.*

This hypothesis has a number of implications: it requires an original approach and a theoretical framework, which allows the successive formatting of the information to be charted. It also requires the means to follow – literally – how risk information is generated and how it is used and transmitted. Moreover, this hypothesis means having to exclude preconceived definitions of risks and adopting an intentionally open framework. The aim is not to examine the dialogue that ensues when a risk situation or crisis occurs, since this has been amply dealt with by previous publications (cf. among many others, Jasanoff 1994 on Bhopal or Suraud 2007 on the AZF disaster, Suraud et al. 2008, and also Chilvers 2008), nor to consider the role of the public (cf. Pearce 2005; Davidson et al. 2007, to name but a few), nor to propose a guide for the communication of risks (which has already been done very well by others, in particular Lundgren and McMain 2009; Maisonneuve 2005; Heath and O'Hair 2008). The intention is rather to analyse the way in which information circulates in situations of risk and crisis. To highlight the actual process, it is necessary to establish the stages of a progression and to present four successive theoretical milestones (statements). The first statement relates to crises and risk situations and the need to integrate temporality and spatiality into the understanding of risks. The second concerns the importance of taking account of the contextualised facts and varied levels of knowledge inherent in all risk and crisis situations. The third shows how information should be seen as a process and a succession of interpretations. Finally, the fourth stage sets out the milestones for a new conceptual framework for the circulation of information.

1.1 A Contemporary Look at Risks: Risks Are Plural and Transcalar

Over the last 15 years, there has been a change in the way risks are understood. This began with the realisation that the boundaries between natural risks and other types of risks (social, environmental, political or technological) were becoming increasingly difficult to define, since the various categories of risk seem to be intrinsically linked. As Pelling puts it (2003: 5), 'The difficulty of disentangling natural hazards from other sources of threat to life and livelihood – especially from technological hazards and social hazards of violence and war – is frequently commented upon by disaster researchers'. This vision of risks was first put forward in the United States, in the field of 'disaster studies' by researchers such as Burton, Kates and White (1978); Blaikie et al. (1994)[1]; Hewitt (1997); Mitchell (1999); Cutter (2003); and Wisner et al. (2004). This stance implies examining the phenomenon of risk in all its diversity. Hurricane Katrina could be considered from the point of view of natural hazards, but this would be to ignore other types of risk that also contributed to the disastrous consequences of the hurricane: 'The hurricane itself may have been natural, but the disaster is attributed more to the human contribution made by neglect of the levees, over-reliance on large-scale flood control projects, the destruction of wetlands and barrier islands that could have buffered impacts of the hurricane, and decisions that put evacuees at risk of death and injury' (Tierney 2007, quoting Cutter 2005).

This idea is gaining ground, and the first edition of the United Nations' report entitled 'Global Assessment Report on Disaster Risk Reduction' (UNISDR 2009) for the first time refers explicitly to the need to consider different risks – natural, environmental, social or even political – as a whole, rather than divided into sectors. What was initially a simple statement has now become widely accepted.[2] This has important implications for the analysis of risks, as it is now possible to use the same theoretical framework to study all risks, whether they be natural, technological, social or environmental. The 'Big Split', separating nature and society, is no longer needed (Latour 1993), as it forms an obstacle to a relevant analysis of the dynamics of the risks observed.

Following on from the plural dimension of risks, another idea has gained ground, driven by its inclusion in Beck's book (1992 [1986 for the German original]). We are now facing risks that are no longer isolated, easily identified geographically and within the responsibility of a single actor; rather, these risks have moved from local to global (e.g. climate change, which is a worldwide preoccupation while remaining

---

[1]It should be noted that this book is the second edition by Blaikie et al. (1994), which has been considerably reworked and expanded, in particular with regard to the subject of vulnerability.

[2]Nevertheless, the old categories do still reappear, particularly during conferences, which offer separate sessions dealing with natural risks, major technological risks or social risks; in addition, some books deal with these risks in separate chapters.

a local risk with regard to the submersion of certain islands and the first climate refugees) and now involve a multitude of different actors.

Risks associated with technology, health or natural phenomena tend to be identified and addressed by a whole range of actors, each with their own (formal and/or informal, collective and/or individual) procedures for taking the necessary steps required to prevent serious events or disasters. As a result, each risk situation generates its own process of arguments, strategies, calculations, alliances and procedures, which may lead to the subsequent adoption of preventive measures, with their respective spatial effects. Risk assessments must incorporate an analysis of their spatial dimensions, allowing for the fact that space is never neutral: space influences the implications of risk just as risks affect and alter spaces themselves. The spatiality of risk is always multifaceted (November 2008). Unlike disasters, risks are virtual threats, even though manifestations of risks have very real consequences. Consequently, the main challenge is to understand the concept of risk as it is defined and used by practitioners and then to recognise the role risks play in transforming the collective (Latour 2005). Only then will it become possible to grasp all the complexities of the relationship between risk and territory, and only then will the spatiality of risk help to improve our understanding of how to manage the risks that are so characteristic of contemporary societies.

The geographical scales affected by the risks are increasingly interlinked. Risk situations concern local territories and actors as well as meso- or macro geographic levels (Healy 2004; November 2002). The methods of monitoring and managing risks can be implemented simultaneously at different levels. A range of uncertainties – economic, scientific and ecological – remains, leading to a proliferation of views regarding the risks. Today, the risk analysis must include a transcalar approach – in parallel with an interdisciplinary analysis – setting out an explicit link between the local dimensions of risks and their development at national and international level.

These two ideas are emblematic of contemporary risks. However, while they are largely accepted and promoted by both researchers and risk professionals, they are by no means always taken together at the theoretical or methodological level. Let us now turn to information and examine the current issues in this field.

1.2 Information as a Process

It is said that never has so much information been in circulation and at such speed. Access to information has increased considerably thanks to new information technologies. Frequently, in the event of a disaster, information is first passed on via Twitter, Facebook or the web. However, being informed and aware of the risks is not enough; it is important to know how to use this information at the right time, in the right place and with the right people. Indeed, it has been demonstrated that in most risk situations and crises, the problem was not the lack of information but rather the fact that the information available did not lead to action. This applies to all levels in the chain. When discussing information provided to the public, Holmes observes that, 'While communicating with the public about an emerging infectious disease outbreak will be vital, it would be a mistake to assume it is simply a matter of informing the public about what steps to take to protect themselves' (Holmes 2008: 354). Communicating, and Ensuring that information circulates, is immensely complex. The first issue is to recognise that there is clearly a dynamic to information that requires further study.

According to Bateson (2000 [1972]: 459), information is 'a difference which makes a difference'. He tells us that information is not energy, nor does it contain any. It is simply this item of 'news' (in the journalistic sense) which derives from a relationship between at least two things. It is qualitative and only arises within meanings or context. Among the infinite number of possible differences between these two things, only those which have a relationship with other existing parts of the context are effective differences, in other words, bits of information. The following questions need to be asked: What are these 'differences' which become relevant in a crisis situation? How can these differences, which has arisen in a particular sociocultural and professional context, that is to say, anchored in a specific symbolic universe, be extended and then used by people in a different sociocultural and professional context? The research carried out by Fessenden-Raden et al. (1987) shows that, 'risk communication should be looked at not only in terms of how accurate, detailed, or intelligible the information is, but also in terms of how the information will be interpreted. Receivers of risk information are not just empty receptacles to be filled with simplified technical information about health risks but rather play a critical, interactive role in the process of risk communication' (p. 101). Paton's research (2008) also demonstrates that it is not the information as such that determines the action but how people interpret it and give it meaning in the context of their experience, beliefs and expectations. The second issue recognised today is that of the different interpretations through which all information passes.

These questions are among those covered by the field of risk communication. Starting in 1986, this area of study has become very fashionable (Plough and Krimsky 1987; Renn 1998; McComas 2006) and since then has been the subject of a considerable amount of literature (in particular Covello et al. 1986; Covello et al. 1989; Kasperson and Stallen 1991; Pidgeon et al. 2003; Gutteling and Wiegman 1996). According to a commonly used definition, 'Risk communication is the act of conveying or transmitting information between parties about (a) levels of health or environmental risks; (b) the significance or meaning of health or environmental risks; or (c) decisions, actions or policies aimed at managing or controlling health or environmental risks. Interested parties include government, agencies, corporations, and industry groups, unions, the media, scientists, professional organizations, public interest groups, and individual citizens' (Covello et al. 1986: 172). However, despite this issue having been identified from the outset, as can be seen in the inset below taken from Renn and Levine (1991), several elements have prevented the interpretation inherent in the existence of all information from being taken into account.

The literature offers different sets of objectives for risk communication, usually centred on a risk management agency as the communicator and groups of the public as target audiences. The list of objectives for entering a risk communication programme includes the following items:

1. Enlightenment function (to improve risk understanding among target groups)
2. Right-to-know function (to disclose information about hazards to potential victims)
3. Attitude to change function (to legitimate risk-related decisions, to improve the acceptance of a specific risk source, or to challenge such decisions and reject specific risk sources)
4. Legitimation function (to explain and justify risk management routines and to enhance the trust in the competence and fairness of the management process)
5. Risk reduction function (to enhance public protection through information about individual risk reduction measures)
6. Behavioural change function (to encourage protective behaviour or supportive actions towards the communicating agency)
7. Emergency preparedness function (to provide guidelines for emergencies or behavioural advice during emergencies)
8. Public involvement function (to educate decision makers about public concerns and perceptions)
9. Participation function (to assist in reconciling conflicts about risk-related controversies)

(with kind permission from Springer Science+Business Media: Communicating Risks to the Public, Credibility and trust in risk communication, 1991, 177–178, Renn, O., & Levine, D).

The following key points were discussed: firstly, the lack of attention paid to the context was highlighted. For Otway and Wynne (1989), this is explained by the fact that the paradigm of risk perception, together with that of risk communication, has remained deaf to the differences in the contexts in which the information is produced and transmitted. In their opinion, there are several reasons for this weakness, 'First, the risk perception tradition evolved from attempts to understand and overcome controversy about the social acceptability of hazardous technologies - although wrongly framed in terms of context-free risk acceptance. This early focus on acceptance subtly shaped our thinking as attention shifted from perception to communication of technological risks. Second, psychometric approaches to risk perception are quite limited, partly because they reflect a discipline that assumes that cognitions can be defined by what goes on in the head of an individual, excluding the social context in which cognitions are created and used. While appearing to benefit from the context-free universalism of the natural sciences, much risk perception work actually imposes a rigid and unrealistic set of assumptions about the relationship between experts and publics in the management of technology.' (Otway and Wynne 1989: 141–142)

These authors believe that each organisation should reflect its own information culture. 'For example, emergency information may be disseminated either via the police and prefecture systems, which have authoritarian and secretive relationships with the public, or via environmental authorities, which usually reflect more decentralized and liberal social relationships. Even when agencies are collaborating in response to the same communication requirements, the source of information can shape its meaning' (Otway and Wynne 1989: 142). It is also possible to pay greater attention to the context (in a spatial sense this time), as stated by Castenfors and Svedin (2001), referring to a quasi-accident in Stockholm, which occurred in an urban environment, since 'urban context provides very different types of information receivers, all of whom do not seek information in the same way, using the same language or the same cultural reference frames'.

It should also be noted that trust is at the heart of the response to an item of information, as described by Paton (2007, 2008), Poortinga and Pidgeon (2004) and Renn and Levine (1991). The familiarity of risk and crisis situations has a very marked effect on the level of trust accorded to the information circulating. 'When dealing with low familiarity hazards, people are more reliant on expert sources and [...] it is how they evaluate the information and its sources that determines their actions, not the presence of information *per se*' (Paton 2008: 8).

In the field of health care, for example, patients see doctors as being the ones with access to knowledge; they are expected to keep up to date with their subject through 'guidelines', scientific articles or training (Chapple et al. 2002). Such management and access to information represent one of the key aspects of the quality of health care. The information circulation systems must be particularly efficient in risk or crisis situations, be this in the face of a potential epidemic or when managing the medical consequences of a natural disaster. This health-care information calls upon a specific type of knowledge, drawn largely from Western medical science. Like any knowledge, this medical knowledge has its basis in society, and its boundaries are constantly changing. Certain anthropologists have no hesitation in considering this particular medical world – biomedicine – as a culture in its own right (Good 1998; Helman 1994; Lupton 1994). It produces its own representations of health and illness, as well as its own values and attitudes towards the health of individuals (such as what it is 'morally' acceptable or not to do with one's own body). Despite its universal vocation, this symbolic universe is not shared by the whole of humanity, especially with regard to the rationality of thought and behaviour (Young 1981, 1982; Kirmayer 1992). The information produced by this culture cannot be understood immediately by all the actors for whom it is intended. Conversely, information produced by sources not initiated into the biomedical culture may be ignored by the medical experts and not be included. When it comes to exchanges relating to health risks or crises on a global scale, the parties involved must not only establish a dialogue based on multiple national, linguistic and cultural foundations, they must also establish an intercultural dialogue about health matters. In other words, they need to create links between systems of meaning in relation to existential topics such as illness, suffering and death.

It is necessary to select a theoretical framework which can take account of the issues discussed above, in terms of both risks and information. The following point sets out the elements that form the basis of such a framework.

1.3 Definitions, Classifications and Models

The constructivist approach is particularly well suited to the analysis of contemporary risks (Tierney 2007), since it makes it possible to remain consistent with the theoretical issues outlined above. Therefore, we will opt for a deliberately broad definition that allows for the different ways in which actors define 'their' risks. In the definition to be used throughout this book, *a risk can be defined as a potential phenomenon, which has not yet occurred, but which we predict may develop into a harmful event (a crisis) affecting individuals or communities in one or more areas* (November 2008). Such description takes account of the definition used in the field of natural and economic sciences where, the risk indicates the economic consequences (including the loss of human life) that could be caused if an event were to occur, the event in question being an unstable situation or a process that is recognised in spatial terms and qualified by a level of danger. It also takes account of the definition adopted by the United Nations Office for Disaster Risk Reduction (UNISDR)[3]: 'A risk is the probability of harmful consequences, or expected losses (deaths, injuries, property, livelihoods, economic activity disrupted or environment damaged) resulting from interactions between natural or human-induced hazards and vulnerable conditions' (UNISDR 2009). It also includes the notion of vulnerability,[4] which has been examined in great depth by a number of authors (Wisner et al. 2004; Bankoff et al. 2004; Pelling 2003; Cutter 2003; Thomalla et al. 2006; Birkmann 2006; Turner et al. 2003; Kasperson and Kasperson 2005; Cardona 2004; Oliver-Smith 2004; Adger 2006; Cutter et al. 2008), and is similar to what some refer to as systemic risks (OECD 2003; Klinke and Renn 2006). According to Klinke and Renn, 'this term denotes the embeddedness of any risk to human health and the environment in a larger context of social, financial and economic risks and opportunities. Systemic risks are at the crossroads between natural events (partially altered and amplified by human action such as the emission of greenhouse gases), economic, social and technological developments and policy driven actions, both at the domestic and the international level. These new interrelated risk fields also require a new form of risk analysis, in which data from different risk sources

[3]The UNISDR was previously called ISDR (International Strategy of Disaster Reduction).

[4]According to Pelling, "Vulnerability denotes exposure to risk and an inability to avoid or absorb potential harm" (2003: 5).

are either geographically or functionally integrated into one analytical perspective. Systemic risk analysis requires a holistic approach to hazard identification, risk assessment and risk management. Investigating systemic risks goes beyond the usual agent-consequence analysis and focuses on interdependencies and spillovers between risk clusters.'

1.3.1 Reviewing Risk Categories

Risks are frequently looked upon as a function of their *sources*. For example, for a long time, urban space was viewed in terms of sectors. It was quite common to speak of natural risks in urban environments, or of the consequences of major technological risks on urban spaces, or even of social risks in an urban theatre. While several risk studies have been devoted to urban spaces, the approach taken in these studies focussed on the notion of vulnerability as applied to the urban context[5]; vulnerability was included either in terms of probability or of social representations.

These studies, which related primarily to natural risks, included little by way of a general reflection on the relationship between the concept of risk and urban transformation. The same applies to technological and industrial risks, where interest is concentrated on the social, political and cultural dimensions of risks; research in the field of social sciences has seen this principally as a sociocultural process (Lupton 1999), with no particular significance being given to the spaces involved.

The classification of the *spatial dynamics* of risks is interesting. Some authors distinguish between risk 'location' and risk 'transport', particularly in the field of major technological risks, and analyse the storage facilities and the transit routes of dangerous materials (Glatron 1996). Others refer to 'diffuse risks' and 'localised risks', based chiefly on the idea that risk situations can have either a widespread effect or, in contrast, may be extremely localised (Galland 1998; November 1994). However, it is also possible to classify risks on the basis of the diversity of their appearance over time. Some risks are transformed very rapidly into an accident or a disaster, while others evolve over a much longer period. Those with effects that are not felt immediately – they make take several generations – can be described as 'delayed', 'slow time' or 'cumulative' risks.

Economic and socio-technical dynamics also play a key role in understanding the deployment of risks. The work carried out by the American geographer Donald J. Zeigler et al. (1983), which uses a methodology based on cost-benefit analysis, distinguishes between the territories where risks occur and the territories which derive benefits based on these risks. In addition, depending on the technical systems, it is possible to identify 'territory-based risks', 'diffuse risks' and 'network risks',

[5] See for instance the Journal of Alpine Research/Revue de géographie alpine on this topic: "Natural risks and urban growth" (no. 4, 1994).

whereby each type of risk interacts differently with the territory; for a given space, in the case of territory-based risks, the link with the environment affected is greater than in the case of network risks (Galland 2003). Finally, it is possible to distinguish between the risks linked to the very nature of a technology and those arising from a combination of factors, such as the application of a technology and urban or economic development.

As mentioned earlier, over the last 10 years, the trend in research has been towards a wider understanding of risks and their territorial and social consequences. This is reflected in both the English- and French-speaking worlds by the publication of a thick volume on environmental risks (Kasperson and Kasperson 2001) and another on urban risks (Dubois-Maury and Chaline 2002). These ideas, together with those of the researchers of the Centre de Recherche Economie et Humanisme [Economy and Humanism Research Centre], who argued in favour of a more general vision of risks in an urban environment, questioning the approach to risk which focuses primarily on technical aspects and probability (Lavigne et al. 1988), have gradually gained ground. Further, also in other areas, the classic approach to risks, broken down into specialist disciplines, has been challenged. Since the Rio Summit in 1992, and its Agenda 21, this requirement has become increasingly acute, reflecting the challenges and difficulties involved in achieving sustainable urban development.

However, the principal distinction between risks comes from the objective approach and separates the ‘known’ risks from the ‘unknown’ risks. According to the strict definition, risks imply a calculation of probability, a capital, which is why they can, in principle, be covered by a contractual system of insurance (Ewald 1996). The ‘known’ risks relate to the history of insurance for people and property, social insurances and the classic ‘risk management’ model. In contrast, a number of ‘new’ risks, or new threats, are characterised by various levels of uncertainty, which are often the subject of lively public debate. These uncertain risks defy technocratic modes of management and of decision-making, moving further and further towards a governance model (Renn and Walker 2008).

There are also other new approaches to risk that focus on the *actors involved in the debates*. The work carried out by Callon et al. (2009) showed in particular that the course of these debates makes it possible to explore the possible issues and scenarios and that in many cases they represent a shortcut to reducing uncertainty. The proliferation of social groups concerned by the uncertainties linked to the emergence of new technology makes it possible, by assumption, to identify the territories of the risks and of the various issues involved.

Our definition of risks is in line with the approach adopted by social sciences (Taylor-Goody and Zinn 2006; Renn 1992; Covello and Johnson 1987) and is close to that used by Callon et al. (2009) in their study of environmental risks where risk is ‘[. . .] a clearly identified danger associated with the occurrence of an event or series of events, which are perfectly describable, events that we do not know will take place but that we know are capable of taking place’. It is important to bear in mind that risks evolve in time and space. At the same time, it is not possible to separate an idea relating to individual risks from an analysis of collective risks. This is possibly one of the greatest difficulties encountered by researchers. It is also important to note that the idea of risks being describable is essential. Why? On one hand, it is because this is what distinguishes risks from situations of uncertainty. In these, it is impossible to give a complete description of the situation as the knowledge has not yet been validated. On the other hand, the ability to describe a situation is an essential part of identifying risks, making it possible to respond to them. As will be shown later: 'Risk has always been associated with decision-making, from the most trivial to that of utmost important. The notion of risk has a performative character. In all cases, an action must be chosen. Discussions regarding risk touch the roots of society, knowledge, values, emotions and even its very existence. These include reflections on the nature of scientific knowledge, an understanding of the visions that substantiate different arguments, and rationalization as to what we fear and as to the ways we should act.' (Cardona 2004: 47)

1.3.2 Integrated Risk Management

Another change has gradually become apparent in recent research into risks: the need for an integrated vision of risks. 'Research and operational experience with disasters has conceptualized risk and emergency management in terms of four relatively distinct but clearly interrelated phases: mitigation, preparedness, response and recovery' (Lindell and Perry 2004).

There is another model widely used by experts at international level, known as 'integrated risk management'. The first version was put together in 2001 by the Federal Office for Civil Protection and the Federal Office for the Environment in Switzerland. Since then it has formed one of the foundations for risk prevention in Switzerland (Fig. 1.1). It comprises five major phases.

In the event of a disaster, the first phase involves intervention, which consists of a number of different actions (alert, help, intervention in situ, information). The second phase is reconditioning: in the hours and days following the disaster, a start is made on actions such as repair, emergency construction, clearing the terrain, re-establishing communication infrastructure and intervention with the help of insurance and relief organisations. The following phase, the reconstruction, can take many months. The fourth phase relates to prevention by technical, biological or land use planning measures. Finally, preparation brings together all the organisational measures put in place to deal with a disaster. The first two phases are intended to limit the amount of damage, while the last two are concerned more with reducing vulnerability.

This model has the advantage of breaking down and categorising the actions aimed at reducing vulnerability and managing the risk and presenting them in an easily accessible form. Although strongly oriented towards implementation, it is

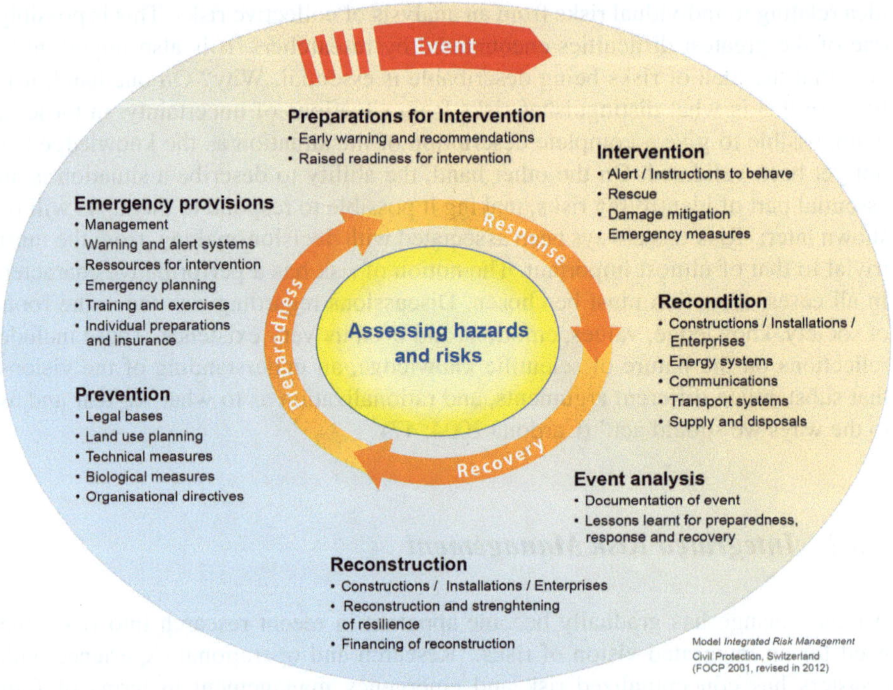

Fig. 1.1 The integrated risk management model (With the kind permission from the Swiss Federal Office for Civil Protection: Hazards and Risk, 2013, [Online] http://www.bevoelkerungsschutz.admin.ch/internet/bs/en/home/themen/gefaehrdungen-risiken.html)

nevertheless rather simplistic. It would be useful to add a number of elements which we feel are central to any attempt at overall risk management. In particular:

- This model appears somewhat 'disembodied'; it splits the problem up into a number of actions to be undertaken by experts at dealing risks but does not show clearly the wide range of actors concerned by the risk, the relations between them, their relative importance in risk management, the various types of information they produce;
- The circular and very uniform presentation of the model, seen as a succession of events over time, hides the temporal complexity of the events and actions; it does not make sufficiently clear the great variation in the chronology of the elements of the model (the alert sometimes lasts only a few minutes, while preparation is a constant component of risk management). Furthermore, for the same action, the timing may vary greatly between actors (the duration of the alert for a fireman is a matter of minutes, while for the meteorologist who has to decide on the content of the alert message, it may be several days, depending on the meteorological development of the disturbance);
- The model offers no means of understanding the spatial implications of the various actions included, in particular with regard to the different scales involved.

- The model takes insufficient account of the importance of the considerable variation in the institutional frameworks that constitute the reference base for the actions of the risk managers.

Taking this model as a starting point, our analysis is intended to take it further, with a view to including the differentiated roles of actors and their varied levels of knowledge of risk and risk management, together with spatial, temporal and institutional variations of their modes of action (cf. Fig. 1.2).

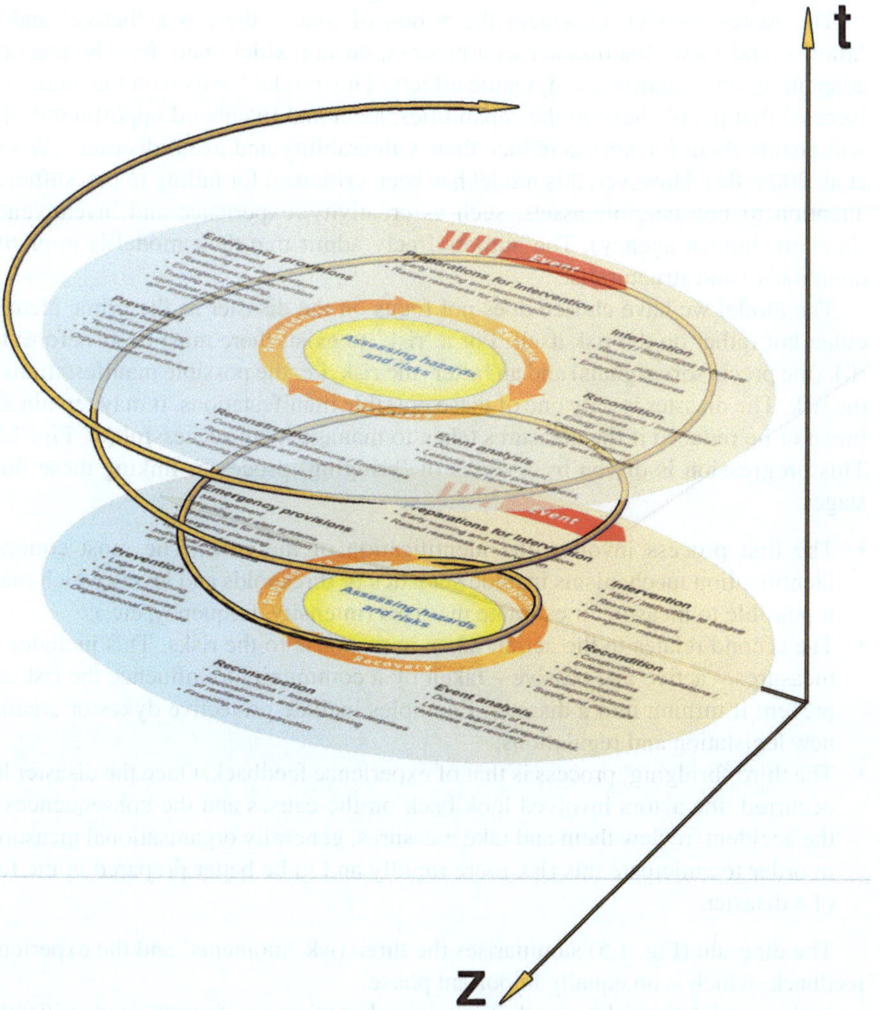

Fig. 1.2 Integrated risk management including temporal development (Illustration: Marion Penelas)

1.3.3 Temporal Risk Models

As we have indicated, the aim of this book is to highlight the transformation processes to which the risks are subject and the situations they will generate. The theoretical framework must be able to demonstrate the temporality of risks.

There are a number of models which incorporate the temporal dimension, the best known being the Access Model, which was devised as a complement to the Pressure and Release (PAR) model (cf. Figs. 1.3 and 1.4). In these two models the disaster is placed at the centre of the reasoning.

The Access Model introduces the notion of time – there is a 'before' and an 'after' – and views the disaster as a process, during which there may be reaction, adaptation, intervention and dynamic effects. This model 'deals with the amount of 'access' that people have to the capabilities, asset and livelihood opportunities that will enable them (or not) to reduce their vulnerability and avoid disaster' (Wisner et al. 2004: 88). However, this model has been criticised for failing to pay sufficient attention to non-tangible assets, such as creativity, experience and inventiveness (in short, human agency). The authors freely admit that their model is implicitly quantitative and structuralist.

The model we have chosen does not focus on the disaster as the prime element either but rather on the risk itself. For a 'risk' to exist, there must be a 'before' the risk (the precursory signals) and an 'after' the risk, i.e. the possible manifestations of the risk. The disaster is only one of these possible manifestations. It may remain as a threat or be reduced if the measures taken to manage it are successful (cf. Fig. 1.5). This progression is driven by a series of 'bridging' processes linking these three stages:

- The first process involves the identification of the risks. The most common identification mechanisms include statistics or thresholds and levels which make it possible to measure or estimate the risks (intensity, frequency, etc.);
- The second relates to the action taken in response to the risks. This includes all measures – active and passive – taken by a community to influence the risk and prevent it turning into a disaster. Examples include protective dykes or creating new legislation and regulations;
- The third 'bridging' process is that of experience feedback. Once the disaster has occurred, the actors involved look back on the causes and the consequences of the accident, review them and take measures, generally organisational measures, in order to anticipate this risk more rapidly and to be better prepared in the face of a disaster.

The diagram (Fig. 1.5) summarises the three risk 'moments' and the experience feedback, which is an equally important phase.

In this model, the risks pass through a number of stages, from their identification (which implies picking up the warning signs and establishing diagnostic measures, criteria and indicators), to their management (implementing measures to minimise the risks) and, finally, to their potential manifestation (disaster or resolution,

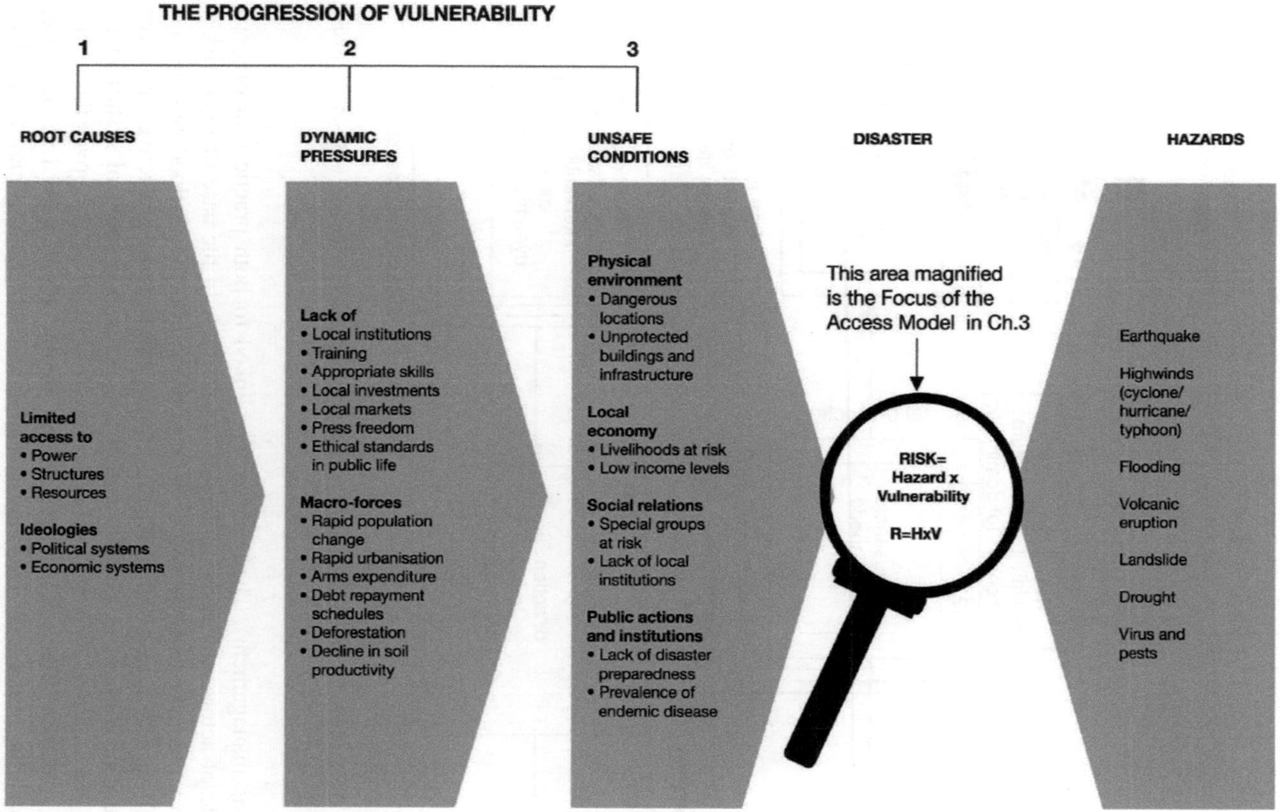

Fig. 1.3 Pressure and Release (PAR) model: the progression of vulnerability towards disaster (With kind permission from Springer Science + Business Media: Wisner et al. (2004: 51, Figure 2.1))

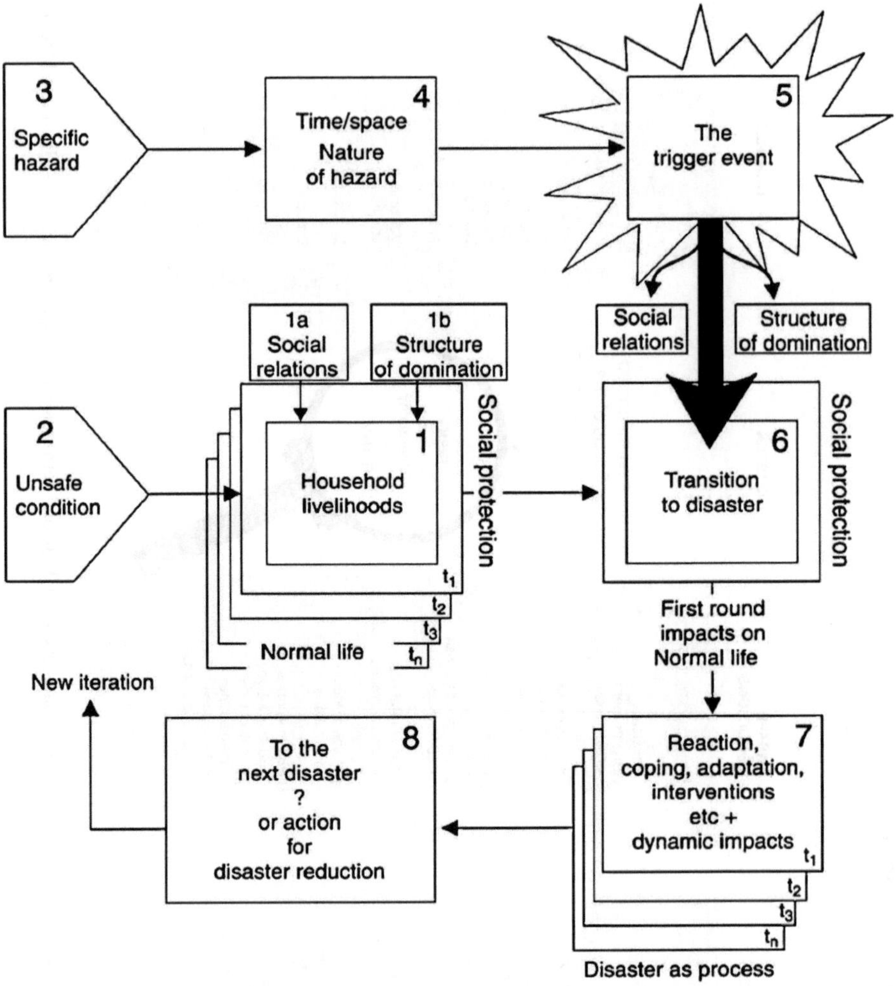

Fig. 1.4 The Access Model (With kind permission from Springer Science + Business Media: Wisner et al. (2004, 89, Figure 2.1))

post-crisis management). These phases are linked to both practices involving a multitude of actors and to the dynamics of the risks. In the case of flood risk, a situation previously analysed and deemed to present no risk of flooding may later find itself at risk because of a deterioration in the state of protective structures, or because of changes in climatic conditions, or even because of a shift in the level of risks caused by construction projects elsewhere which, over the course of time, produce effects which eventually become problematic (e.g. increased impermeability of the soil). This may also apply to health risks or industrial risks.

In order for a risk to pass from one stage to the next, and for the processes to take place, something must be transported, transmitted or circulated between the phases.

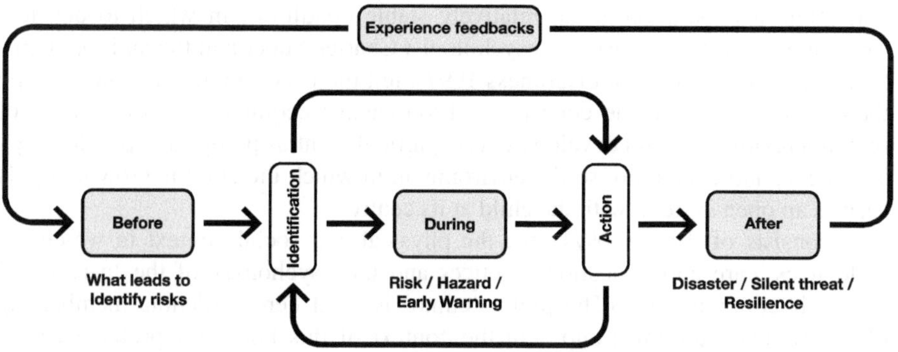

Fig. 1.5 The three phases of risk (Redrawn from November 2002)

This 'thing' is first and foremost information of various types. The information is collected before or after the risk becomes apparent; it is processed and interpreted by the actors involved, experts or computer systems; it is then recorded, archived or disseminated. In some cases, the information becomes knowledge once it has been validated according to academic or other criteria, epistemologies and sociocultural and institutional bases. This information and its circulation form the core of decision-making during all the stages of risk; they govern practices/interventions and modulate the contexts.

While this model highlights the different types of knowledge produced by different actors during the identification and management processes, it does not indicate how they are transmitted, nor how they are transformed as the risk situations develop. In other words, it offers no help in understanding how knowledge is absorbed and appropriated by the actors and how it is passed on from one actor to another. We therefore need to take a closer look at how the information and knowledge are produced. Furthermore, although it focuses on the qualitative aspects of the identification and management processes, this model does not consider the contexts in which the knowledge that allows the identification and management of risks is produced. It needs to be complemented by a model that concentrates on various types of expertise.

1.3.4 Contextualising the Stages of Risk and the Various Types of Expertise

The theoretical framework known as the Professional Activities Niche is drawn from the work of Leanza (2011), who was, in turn, inspired by a theoretical framework used in comparative developmental intercultural psychology (the area of psychology that deals with child development in different contexts): the developmental niche. The term 'niche' is borrowed from ecology and refers to a specific environment that offers a population group relatively stable conditions in which to develop. The initiators of this theory, the psychologist Charles Super and the anthropologist Sarah Harkness (Super and Harkness 1997), felt the need to integrate into a single theoretical framework the concepts and knowledge acquired in various areas of research relating to child development (in particular anthropology and psychology). The niche, and even more so the environment in which the child is growing up, is seen as an open system, with the child at its centre.

It consists of three subsystems: the physical and social context in which the child lives, care and education practices and the psychology of the 'caretakers' and their ethnotheories. (The prefix 'ethno' is used here to denote membership of a particular cultural group – in the context of this book, we prefer the term 'representations'.) These three subsystems interact and are, of course, connected to the wider community. This approach is marked by a complementarist view of epistemology, that is to say, the ability to integrate data from various disciplines.

Leanza has taken this framework and used it, not with the child at the centre but rather the professionals working with children. He named it Professional Activities Niche (cf. Fig. 1.6).

In the context of this project dealing with the circulation of information, the centre of a niche contains not only people but also objects or institutions that 'hold' information. These objects are part of networks and are activated by multiple actors. We have decided to study a group of actors and to observe closely their practices (and their representations), in order to be able to reconstruct the networks of which they are a part. In focussing on these people and objects which contain information, our aim is to retrace the paths followed by this information and to identify where it passes smoothly and where it encounters obstacles. Having chosen three very

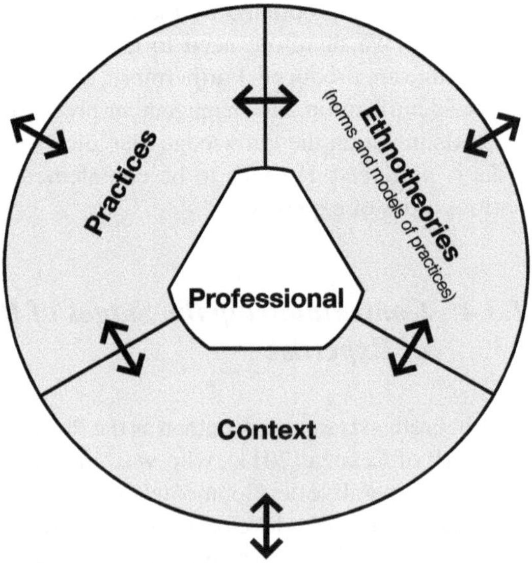

Fig. 1.6 The Professional Activities Niche, inspired by Leanza (2011)

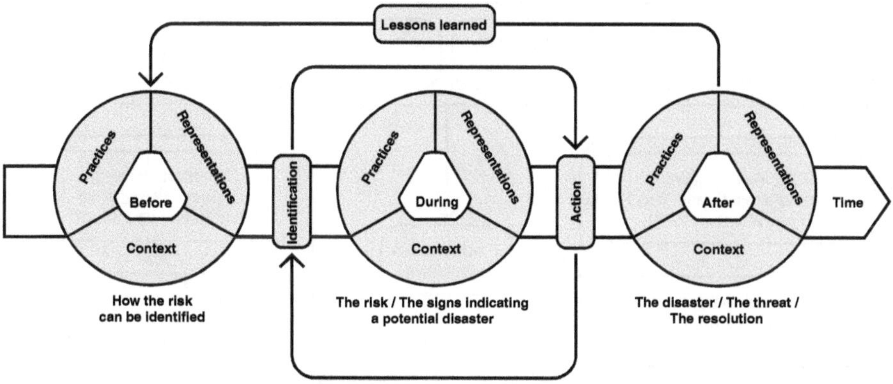

Fig. 1.7 The three phases of risk put into context

different areas, the context varies greatly, but not so our questions regarding practices and representations. A further constant is the north-south circulation of information specific to the question of reducing health and environmental risks. To this end we have reworked the figure showing the three phases of risk to include elements relating to context, practices and representations, which are inherent in any risk situation, whether it be before or after the risks have been identified (cf. Fig. 1.7).

Using this theoretical framework, it is possible to consider each phase of risk in detail. The transition from one to the next implies not only a change of physical and social context (the risk may have become apparent between during and after, or have been formally identified between before and during, or conditions may be such that the risk reappears between after and before) but also that the practices (prevention, intervention, information distribution, etc.) and the representations of the various actors may or may not change.

1.3.5 The Information Flow

Following on from the ideas set out above, giving weight to the contexts in which the actors operate and the practices and representations they embody, there are models which offer a different view of risk communication, such as that proposed by Lindell and Perry (2004). In their view, 'Risk communication should be a process by which stakeholders *share* information about hazards affecting a community'. Figure 1.8 shows the circulation of information associated with their model, which is known as the Protective Action Decision Model (PADM). The decision-making process is represented by arrows indicating the flow of information and the associated actions.

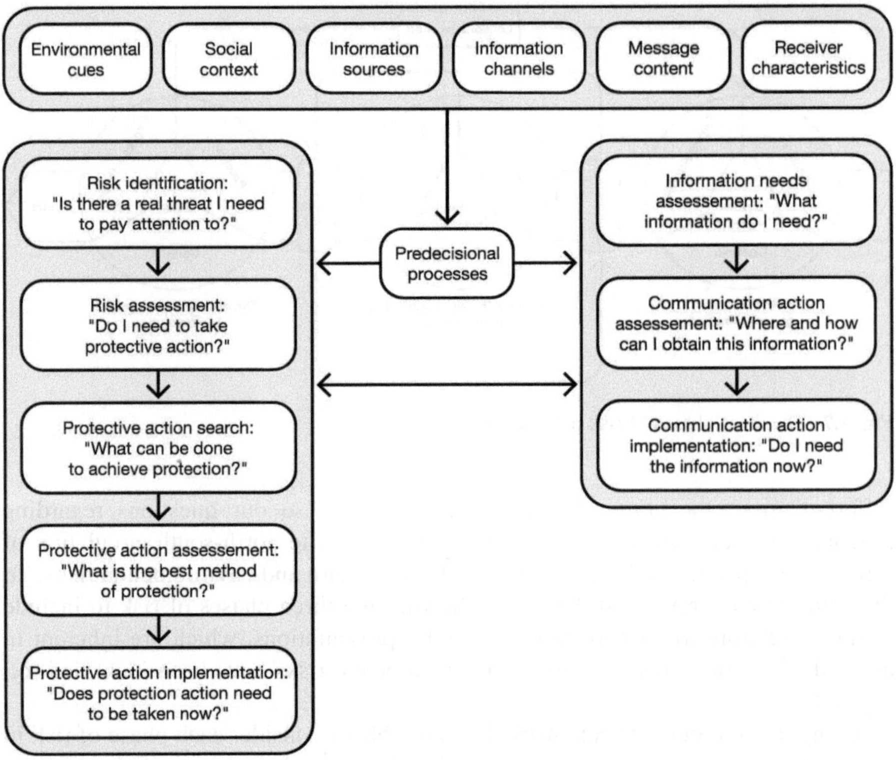

Fig. 1.8 Information flow in the Protective Action Decision Model (According to Lindell and Perry 2004: 47)

This is an important model as it highlights the fact that any decision is preceded by a pre-decision process influenced by the characteristics of the information receiver, the content of the message, the channels through which the information passes, the social context and the environmental situation.

This pre-decision process links the area of the risks with that of the information. The model sets out for each stage of the process the questions raised by the risks and the way in which they are translated into information requirements (which, when, etc.). The question 'Is there a real threat that I should monitor?' is followed by the question 'Do I need to take protective action?'. If the answer is yes, the questions 'What information do I need?', 'Where and how can I obtain this information?', etc. will follow.

While the relationship between risk and information is well indicated, and the decision-making process clearly set out, there is no information about the nature of the arrows. These arrows, shown in most diagrams as lines, are much more than that. Each represents a constantly evolving process. Strangely, the authors give very little importance to these processes. For this reason, we intend to supplement the models studied thus far by an approach allowing the arrows/processes to be qualified and to make the lines more prominent.

1.4 Proposing a New Conceptual Framework

The contemporary characteristics of risk were set out at the start of this chapter: risks are heterogeneous, plural and transcalar. We can speak of being in the presence of an entity – the risk – consisting of heterogeneous elements which undergo a series of *translations*. The risk is part of 'long chains of interactions between technical artefacts, natural substances, organised or disorganised human beings', in the words of Callon and Rip (1992: 154). With regard to information, we have seen that its mere existence is not sufficient for it to influence action. Information also undergoes a series of *translations* – major or minor transformations – so that it is accessible to those to whom it is addressed. If we combine these two aspects, we need a theory of action which can hold together the risks and the information.

1.4.1 The Translation Process

There is a theory of action in which this notion of translation is crucial. It is used in the sociology of science and technology, most notably in the actor-network theory. This theory, developed by Latour and Callon, has been written about at length since the 1980s (see in particular Latour and Woolgar 1986; Latour 1996, 1999a, b; Callon 1986; Callon and Law 1997).

The definition of the entity as a network bringing together heterogeneous elements – both human and non-human – leads Callon and Law to emphasise the dual dimension of the action: it constantly extends and transmits itself. 'Every entity has a variable geometry as it transforms itself as the same time as the configuration of actions that it extends and transmits is changed' (Callon and Law 1997: 115).

This way of considering the action requires the chains of interaction that make up the entity to be monitored. To do this, Callon and Law (1997: 109–110) suggest, 'it is enough to follow the process of their configuration and (possible) stabilisation. Rather than seeing the entities as discrete realities, which may be coordinated by rules and conventions, they should be seen as representing networks of heterogeneous elements, where each element is itself a network'.

In order to report on the 'circulation' of these entities, the concept of translation allows a more detailed understanding of this process. As Vinck explains, translation 'is a general process through which the social and natural world is gradually shaped and stabilised. Elements of these socio-natural components are moved and these movements offer a relative permanence. Translation comprises four stages, which may overlap: problematisation, interessement, enrolment and the mobilisation of allies' (Vinck 1995: 201).

What holds the elements of the network together is the *interessement*, one of the stages of the translation process. It consists of 'setting out and stabilising the identity of the other entities and positioning oneself among them. The aim is to implement the network of alliances established in the previous phase. (...) In addition, the actors are seeking not only to propose forms of problematisation, but to impose them and to give them greater reality. They put in place interessement mechanisms in order to divert the other entities from their aims and to interrupt the concurrent associations.' (Vinck 1995: 204–205)

As Callon and Rip emphasise, 'the strategies thus fluctuate between attachment (attaching to other actors, holding positions in networks that have become irreversible) and detachment (being able to leave a network to construct another, etc.). Attachment involves all the following concepts: irreversibility, trajectories, skills, procedural rationality, limited yet correct information, predictability, incremental innovation, hierarchical coordination ... Detachment is associated with concepts such as flexibility, uncertainty, unpredictability, risk (...) strategic invention, market ... ' (Callon and Rip 1992: 62)

In qualifying these attachments and detachments, Latour refers to 'bald objects' and 'hairy objects'. The former are those to which no attachment has been attributed. The latter are those caught up in a sequence of elements from which they cannot be dissociated. In *Politics of Nature*, Latour takes the example of asbestos to demonstrate the passage from the first notion to the second: 'In the case of this perfect – inert, efficient and useful - material (also called the magic material), it took decades for the effects of its widespread use on health to rebound and call it into question, together with its inventors, manufacturers, apologists and inspectors. It took dozens of alerts and affairs before the industrial illnesses, cancers and the problems of its removal eventually identified the cause and exposed the properties of asbestos, which transformed slowly from an ideal, inert material to a nightmarish tangled mess of law, health and risk.' (Latour 2004) From this perspective, understanding the attachments constituting the objects makes it possible to demonstrate their heterogeneousness.

In Callon's view, translating also means expressing in one's own words that which others say and want. It means setting oneself up as a *spokesman*: 'Translation is the mechanism by which the social and natural worlds progressively take form and stabilise. (...) The repertoire of translation is not only designed to give a symmetrical and tolerant description of a complex process which constantly mixes together a variety of social and natural entities. It also permits an explanation of how a few obtain the right to express and to represent the many silent actors', as Callon (1986: 205) puts it, referring to the political economy of power proposed by Foucault. The notion of the translation chain describes the series of movements and transfers needed to produce a wording or an object (Vinck 1995). In an article dealing with the design of architecture, Callon explains that, 'for the translations to become apparent (...) one simply has to follow the actors themselves as they consider exactly the same question as the analyst: how is it possible to keep together (is there a better definition of architecture?) economic interests, social action and the shape of buildings, without falling victim to the engineers' cuts?' (Callon 1996: 34). Translation implies movement and all movement implies a certain cost.

It is only recently that this theory has been used in connection with risks. In the field of risks, the actor-network theory has been used to understand specific risks, such as biosecurity (Donaldson 2008; Bingham et al. 2008); genetic testing (Williams-Jones and Graham 2003); health risks, such as SARS (Schillmeier and Pohler 2006; Ali and Keil 2006), foot-and-mouth disease (Law 2004; Bickerstaff and Simmons 2004) and BSE (Hinchliffe 2001); or even nuclear risks (Wynne 1996) or the heating plant (Akerman and Peltola 2006).

In all these studies, the risk is shaped through the different translations made by the actors and helps to stimulate action in new directions. As explained by November (2002: 310): 'The risk appears when an assemblage becomes endangered (...) when the combinations able to maintain the unity of the system are difficult to anticipate and when an element – human or non-human – of the collective does not fulfil the role expected by the network in the configuration process, thereby extending or expanding the ongoing action in an unexpected direction, in another place and in a different way'. A similar proposition is put forward by Healy (2004), defining risk as 'a dynamic entity resulting from the interactions of the elements of complex ensembles of humans and non-humans (that currently are of all scales including planetary). The sense of risk intended is the familiar one of the product of the occurrence and consequences of undesirable events. In this perspective then, risk is neither a property of the human or non-human world but arises from the interactions between them and is performed by the complex ensembles they constitute. A condition of risk exists when the performance of an ensemble varies or deviates from that intended so as to result in unwanted, deleterious consequences. A key concern here is to provide an account of these dynamics and to explain how conditions of risk arise and might be ameliorated.'

As Healy emphasises with regard to risk: 'Translation describes successful ensemble building in which both human and non-human agents are enrolled or delegated into a common endeavour. It can be characterized by the drift or shift in meaning that occurs when agents, human and non-human, integrate their interests with those of others in order to develop and satisfy common goals' (Healy 2004: 286).

1.4.2 Grasping the Risks

In order for the translation to take place and the problematisation, interressement, enrolment and mobilisation of allies stages to become effective, the knowledge and information must be grasped and held onto. This is an interesting notion: when faced with a risk-laden universe, it is possible to create different strategies, but those which succeed will always be the result of a sorting process, and the selection of relevant characteristics and anchor points; in other words, as a function of what can be grasped. According to Bessy and Chateaureynaud, such a hold is never a foregone conclusion, it is 'the outcome of a meeting between a strategy, pursued by the relevant stakeholder(s), and a network of bodies, characterized by their peaks, folds and cracks' (Bessy and Chateauraynaud 1995: 39). It emerges from the interaction between bodies and strategies, 'like a climber's holds emerging from a series of confrontations between the mountaineer and the rock face. Holds can describe the relationship between people and objects in two ways: as having a hold on something, an expression often used to describe humans (active, interactive and inquiring) gaining the upper hand over objects and their environment (inert, passive and subject to human endeavour); or as suggesting the irreducible nature of objects and the difficulty of even getting a hold'. (1995: 239)

Berque also uses the same concept: 'These are the holds that the environment affords to perception and, at the same time, of the capacity this perception affords to gain a hold over or to be in tune with these holds. Thus they are relative. They are the very incarnation of the relationship of an animal or a human being with the environment' (Berque 2000: 151). The concept of holding, or grasping, is based on the concept of affordance developed by the psychologist James Gibson. He developed the term in his book *The Ecological Approach to Visual Perception*, published in 1979. Gibson defines affordances as 'all 'action possibilities' latent in the environment, objectively measurable and independent of the individual's ability to recognize them, but always in relation to the actor and therefore dependent on their capabilities'. It should also be noted that Jakob von Uexküll (1980 [1929]) had already discussed the concept in the early twentieth century, calling it the 'functional colouring' (funktionale Tönung) of objects.

To be able to grasp, or hold, there must be affordances, latent possibilities of action, which can be activated by the translation process.

1.4.3 The Trajectories

This understanding of entities means that, first, the information, and then the knowledge – information that has been validated and stabilised within a community sharing the same epistemology – becomes a trajectory, 'a *vector* that projects 'retroactively' its 'validating power'. In other words, we don't know *yet*, but we *will* know, or rather, we will know better whether we *had known* earlier or not. (. . .) Knowledge becomes (. . .) plainly accessible if you allow it to become a continuous vector where time is of essence' (Latour 1999a).

It is for this reason that we are proposing a model that includes the three elements: the four stages of translation (problematisation, interessement, enrolment and the mobilisation of allies), information as a trajectory and the concept of hold (Fig. 1.9).

In the first stage of this trajectory, the risk (or its appearance as an actual event) will be described by various actors. This is the initial outline of what later becomes information about the risk. A difference emerges between a known state and what could happen to this state (in the health, technological, social or other areas, or even in several areas at the same time). This difference is put into words, situated in relation to other phenomena or issues, and connected to or dissociated from these on different scales. This is the problematisation. Once the community

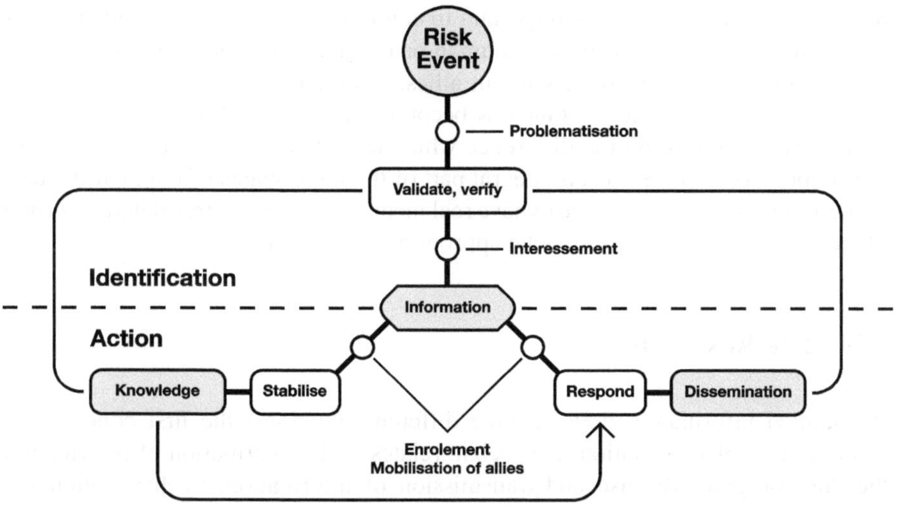

Fig. 1.9 The flow of information and knowledge integrating the three stages of risk put into context and the actor-network theory approach

(urban, scientific, institutional, international or other) supports this difference, after verification and/or validation, the aim is to increase awareness beyond those directly affected. The form must therefore be adapted in order to interest, recruit and present the risk to a network of actors able to respond to it. Once this difference has been introduced to one or more networks, it becomes an item of information, as it has been placed in a context which gives it meaning, but prior to that, it is simply the identification of the risk and the potential resources to counter it that mobilises efforts. This information may be used to respond immediately to the risk, for example, by deciding to implement preventive measures or urgent action. To do this, it will be necessary to disseminate the information more widely and most probably also to render it understandable and useful. This involves a further round of verification and interessement which will produce a new item of information, with the same content as the previous one, but expressed in a manner relevant to the new context. It may also be stabilised (the response mode and the stabilisation mode are not mutually exclusive; both may occur) and become knowledge. This may be through research and validation by the researcher's scientific community; however, other epistemologies for stabilising information also exist. For example, the construction of a narrative which presents the information/knowledge and allows it to be passed on from generation to generation. This knowledge makes it possible to respond to the risk when needed and when conditions are appropriate, as we have shown. (Simply having the information or knowledge does not always make it possible to respond to the risk.) Knowledge may also be questioned and verified in the light of new events if a difference becomes apparent between this state of knowledge and the reality of a specific context. Whatever mode of action the information may lead to, it is important to continue to enrol allies, in other words, to continue to mobilise resources (human or non-human) to sustain the trajectory of the difference/information. Without allies, information will be lost or will lose meaning, and the likelihood of the risk becoming a reality will increase.

The path followed by the difference which imparts meaning is on a continuous repeat loop. This process is an integral part of the three stages of risk. During each of these stages, for a difference to have real meaning, it must be translated according to the Professional Activities Niche appropriate to that stage.

1.5 The Research

We studied information flow in three different situations: the first concerns the centralisation of information; the second relates to the distribution of information; the third observes the use and transmission of information. Each situation was observed in a different location. They are described in Chaps. 2, 3 and 4. In order to be able to reproduce the information circuits, we gave greater emphasis to the types of information than to the types of crises, epidemics or disease, on the hypothesis that the way information flows and is understood encounters the same obstacles and resistance whatever the nature of the information and the situation involved. Indeed, we saw at the beginning of this chapter that nowadays there is general acceptance of analysing different types of risk simultaneously for the same problem, since they are often intrinsically linked.

1.5.1 Case Studies

We chose three areas in which to research these problems. We see them as inextricably linked. In fact, the relevance of the research lies in the confrontation of three situations, where the risk information is produced, transmitted and disseminated in different contexts.

1.5.1.1 Centralisation of Information

In the first information flow situation selected, the information is centralised. An increasing amount of information is concentrated in risk monitoring centres, which may be dedicated to monitoring traffic, epidemics or the risk of terrorism. Following November's studies of risk monitoring centres (e.g. November 2004 on road-related risks), we have opted for a case study on the risks of epidemics. This study focuses on the centralisation of information as practised within a monitoring room dedicated to epidemiological and health risks: the World Health Organisation's SHOC Room (Strategic Health Operations Center) in Geneva. During the time we spent at the headquarters in 2007, we were able to observe how the information networks were set up and operated, how the crisis cells are connected, the technical systems and instruments through which the information passes (remote conferencing, satellite imagery, etc.), and, finally, the conditions leading to the globalisation of information. The analysis of this first situation figures in Chap. 2.

1.5.1.2 Dissemination of Information

The second case study relates to the dissemination of information. We have established a partnership with the International Strategy for Disaster Reduction (ISDR, now known as the United Nations Office for Disaster Risk Reduction) in order to develop a prototype for a French-language mobile field library to form part of a multi-agency (IGOs and NGOs) pilot project. This project was launched by the ISDR secretariat in October 2005 in Indonesia and is expected to continue.

This case study consisted of participating for 6 months in setting up a mobile field library (Inter-agency Field Library for Disaster Reduction), comprising around a hundred books on the prevention of environmental and health risks in Africa. This case study consisted of two stages: we first examined how the academic, scientific and technical books were selected, collected and put together in a 'trunk' to be sent into the field in Madagascar. Madagascar was chosen because the island contains most of the risks found on the African continent: desertification, drought, cyclones, epidemics, HIV, malaria, etc. During the second stage, we observed in situ how the information distributed was assimilated and mobilised in the field. On this occasion we studied the organisation of risk and crisis management in Madagascar. (We arrived just as the last cyclones of the season reached the island in April 2007.) Thus, our analysis is part of an information flow continuum, based on an information dissemination tool. This analysis of how information is used in the field was also intended to validate and, where necessary, modify the way the 'trunks' are put together. At that time, these trunks were seen as an important support for UN agencies and local actors in areas at risk. This analysis will be covered in Chap. 3.

1.5.1.3 Use and Transmission of Information

The third case concerns the use and communication of information. It was carried out in partnership with two information dissemination structures in Cameroon: PROSENAT (Common Initiative Group Progrès Santé par Espèce Naturelle [Progress in Healthcare through Natural Means]) and the NGO WESDE (Water, Energy and Sanitation for Development). These two organisations are involved in health care and prevention among high-risk populations (vulnerable and/or isolated). PROSENAT is an association of therapists who use plants from the traditional pharmacopeia to treat a range of diseases. It has branches in the main cities in Cameroon (Yaoundé, Douala and Bafoussam). WESDE is an NGO offering mediation services in the event of a crisis, such as between a company causing pollution and the local population or between the authorities and a population group hit by an epidemic (e.g. WESDE collaborates with CARE in HIV/AIDS prevention work). We evaluated these two organisations' access to information, as well as how the information on prevention disseminated by government institutions (Ministry of Public Health) and/or international bodies (WHO, UNICEF) in relation to endemic diseases (polio, HIV/AIDS, malaria, etc.) is taken up and used as part of their activities. This third case is discussed in Chap. 4.

The analysis of the conditions and impact of these three information flow situations has led to recommendations which may help both organisations (non-governmental and international organisations) operating in situations of risk or health crisis and academic institutions interested in research action. These recommendations are set out in the summary chapter. The final chapter focuses very much on a pragmatic approach: it offers a guide to best practices entitled 'Information sharing in situations of risk: Guidelines for Practitioners'. This guide is based on the primary recommendations derived from the research and is aimed at practitioners active in the information chain, at international, national or local level.

1.5.2 Methodology

Following the model of the contextualised stages of risk, in the first phase we established the niche of each of the objects: how an information centre functions (Fig. 1.10), the production of a field library for the ISDR (Fig. 1.11a) and its reception in the target area (Fig. 1.11b), and the information communication practices in two NGOs in Cameroon) (Figs. 1.12 and 1.13), while the remaining focused on the need to find the same data in relation to practices (use, transformation, communication of the information) and to representations (what are the risks for each actor, what are the available sources of information, etc.).

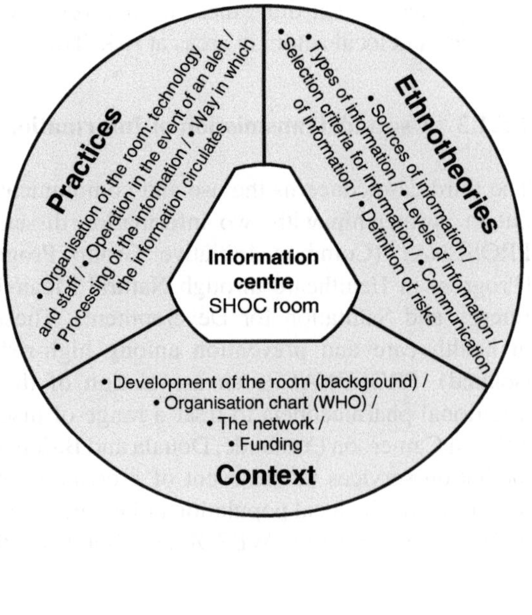

Fig. 1.10 Questions to investigate in the case of the centralisation of the information, the Strategic Health Operation Room, WHO (Illustration: Boris Calame)

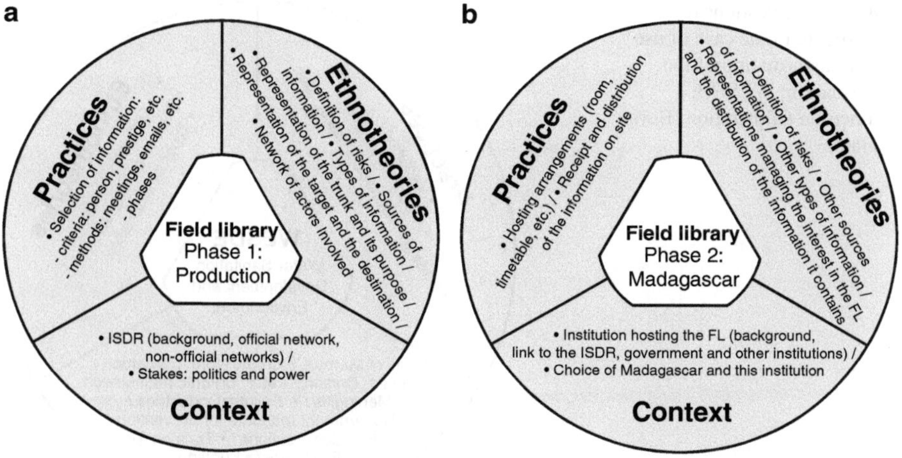

Fig. 1.11 (**a**) Questions to investigate in the case of the production of the field library, UNISDR (Illustration: Boris Calame). (**b**) Questions to investigate in the case of the dissemination of the field library, Madagascar, UNISDR (Illustration: Boris Calame)

Fig. 1.12 Questions to investigate in the case of use and transformation of the information, PROSENAT, Cameroon (Illustration: Boris Calame)

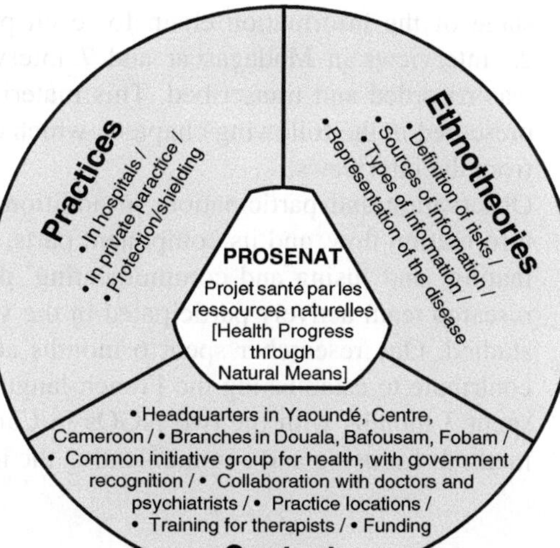

1.5.3 *Field Research*

Our wish to ensure that we remain consistent is also reflected in our use of the same research methods for the three cases. For each location, we followed the basic principles of the sociology of science and technology:

1. Giving great importance to the actors: in most instances, we questioned them for several hours, sometimes returning to see them on a number of occasions

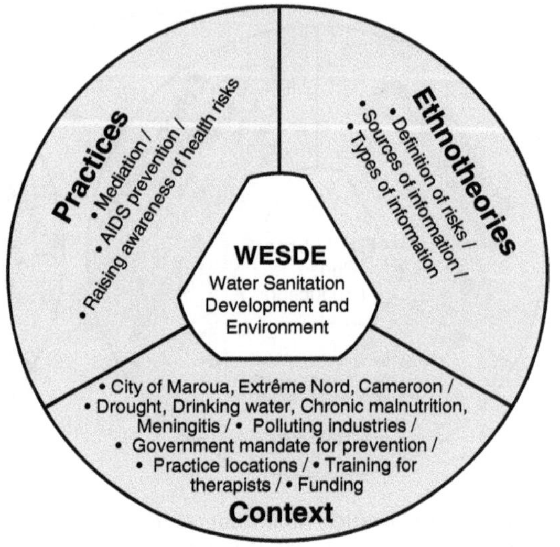

Fig. 1.13 Questions to investigate in the case of use and transformation of the information, WESDE, Cameroon (Illustration: Boris Calame)

(Cameroon). We carried out several interviews with the key actors from each stage of the information chain for each project: 19 interviews in Cameroon, 25 interviews in Madagascar and 7 interviews at the WHO. Each interview was recorded and transcribed. This material formed the basis for the analysis presented in the following chapters, which contain a large number of quotations from the interviews.

2. Observation and participation: in addition to the interviews, we observed the information flow, and its component parts, in situ. In the situations of 'disseminating' and 'using and communicating' the information, the members of the research team actively participated in the various stages of the situations being studied. One researcher spent 6 months at the ISDR in order to monitor and contribute to establishing the French-language field library. Another researcher spent 3 months with the two NGOs in Cameroon in order to learn about their methods for using and communicating the information on health risks.

References

Adger, N. (2006). Vulnerability. *Global Environmental Change, 16*, 268–281.

Akerman, M., & Peltola, T. (2006). Constituting the space for decision making – Conflicting calculations in a dispute over fuel choice at a local heating plant. *Geoforum, 37*(5), 779–789.

Ali, H. S., & Keil, R. (2006). Global cities and the spread of infectious disease: the case of Severe Acute Respiratory Syndrome (SARS) in Toronto, Canada. *Urban Studies, 43*(3), 491–509.

Bakis, H. (1995). Communication et changement global: un defi politique et culturel. *International Political Science Review / Revue internationale de science politique, 16*(3), 225–235.

Bankoff, G., Frerks, G., & Hilhorst, D. (Eds.). (2004). *Mapping vulnerability: Disasters, development and people*. London: Earthscan Publishers.

Bateson, G. (2000 [1972]). Steps to an ecology of mind. Chicago: The University of Chicago Press.
Beck, U. (1992). *Risk society: Towards a new modernity*. London: Sage.
Berque, A. (2000). *L'écoumène: introduction à l'étude des milieux humains*. Paris: Belin.
Bessy, C., & Chateauraynaud, F. (1995). *Experts et faussaires: pour une sociologie de la perception*. Paris: Métailié.
Bickerstaff, K., & Simmons, P. (2004). The right tool for the job? Modeling, spatial relationships, and styles of scientific practice in the UK foot and mouth crisis. *Environment and Planning D: Society and Space, 22*, 393–412.
Bingham, N., Enticott, G., & Hinchliffe, S. (2008). Biosecurity: Spaces, practices, and boundaries. *Environment and Planning A, 40*(7), 1528–1533.
Bird, J., & Lubkowski, Z. (2005). Managing tsunami risk. *The Lancet, 365* (January 22), 271–273.
Birkmann, J. (Ed.). (2006). *Measuring vulnerability to natural hazards presents a broad range of current approaches to measuring vulnerability*. New Delhi: TERI Press.
Blaikie, P., Cannon, T., & Davis, I. et al. (1994). *At risk: Natural hazards, people's vulnerability, and disasters*. London: Routledge.
Brodhag, C. (2000). Information, gouvernance et developpement durable. *International Political Science Review / Revue internationale de science politique, 21*(3), 311–327.
Burton, I., Kates, R. W., & White, G. F. (1978). *The environment as hazard*. New York: Oxford University Press Inc.
Callon, M. (1986). Some elements of a sociology of translation: Domestication of the scallops and the fishermen of St Brieuc Bay. In J. Law (Ed.), *Power, action and belief: A new sociology of knowledge?* (pp. 196–223). London: Routledge.
Callon, M. (1996). Le travail de la conception en architecture. In D. Valabrègue (Ed.), *Situations* (Vol. 37, pp. 25–35). Les Cahiers de la Recherche Architecturale. Marseille: Editions Parenthèses.
Callon, M., & Law, J. (1997). L'irruption des non-humains dans les sciences humaines. In B. Raynaud (Ed.), *Les limites de la rationalité, Les figures du collectif, Colloque de Cerisy* (Vol. 2, pp. 99–118). Paris: La Découverte.
Callon, M., & Rip, A. (1992). Humains, non-humains: morale d'une coexistence. In J. Theys & B. Kalaora (Eds.), *La Terre Outragée, les experts sont formels* (Vol. 1, pp. 140–156). Paris: Ed. Autrement.
Callon, M., Lascoumes, P., & Barthe, Y. (2009). *Acting in an uncertain world an essay on technical democracy*. Cambridge, MA: MIT Press.
Cardona, O.-D. (2004). The need for rethinking the concepts of vulnerability and risk from a holistic perspective: A necessary review and criticism for effective risk management. In G. Bankoff, G. Frerks, & D. Hilhorst (Eds.), *Mapping vulnerability: Disasters, development and people* (pp. 37–51). London: Earthscan Publishers.
Castenfors, K., & Svedin, L. (2001). Crisis communication: Learning from the 1998 LPG near miss in Stockholm. *Journal of Hazardous Materials, 88*, 235–254.
Chapple, A., Campbell, S., Rogers, A., & Roland, M. (2002). Users' understanding of medical knowledge in general practice. *Social Science & Medicine, 54*(8), 1215–1224.
Chilvers, J. (2008). Environmental risk, uncertainty, and participation: Mapping an emergent epistemic community. *Environment and Planning A, 40*(12), 2990–3008.
Covello, V., & Johnson, B. (1987). The social and cultural construction of risk: Issues, methods and case studies. In B. Johnson & V. Covello (Eds.), *The social and cultural construction of risk: Essays on risk selection and perception* (pp. vii–xiii). Boston: D. Reidel Publishing Company.
Covello, V. T., von Winterfeldt, D., & Slovic, P. (1986). Risk communication: A review of literature. *Risk Abstracts, 3*(4), 171–182.
Covello, V. T., McCallum, D. B., & Pavlova, M. T. (Eds.). (1989). *Effective risk communication. The role and responsibility of government and nongovernment organizations*. New York: Plenum Press.
Cutter, S. L. (2003). The vulnerability of science and the science of vulnerability. *Annals of the Association of American Geographers, 93*(1), 1–12.

Cutter, S. L. (2005). *The geography of social vulnerability: Race, class, and catastrophe. Understanding Katrina: Perspectives from the Social Sciences*. Available via Social Science Research Council. http://understandingkatrina.ssrc.org/Cutter/. Accessed 5 Dec 2013.

Cutter, S. L., Barnes, L., Berry, M., Burton, C., Evans, E., Tate, E., et al. (2008). A place-based model for understanding community resilience to natural disasters. *Global Environmental Change, 18*, 598–606.

Davidson, C. H., Johnson, C., Lizarralde, G., Dikmen, N., & Sliwinski, A. (2007). Truths and myths about community participation in post-disaster housing projects. *Habitat International, 31*(1), 100–115.

Donaldson, A. (2008). Biosecurity after the event: Risk politics and animal disease. *Environment and planning A, 40*(7), 1552–1567.

Dubois-Maury, J., & Chaline, C. (2002). *Les risques urbains*. Paris: Armand Colin.

Environmental Protection Agency, Office of Inspector General. (2003, August 31). *Evaluation report: Epa's response to the world trade center collapse: Challenges, successes, and areas for improvement* (Report No. 2003-P-00012).

Ewald, F. (1996). *Histoire de l'Etat-Providence: les origines de la solidarité*. Paris: Grasset.

Fessenden-Raden, J., Fitchen, J., & Heath, J. (1987). Providing risk information in communities: Factors influencing what is heard and accepted. *Science, Technology, & Human Values, 12*(3/4), 94–101.

Galland, J.-P. (1998). *Les risques du Ministère de l'Équipement, des Transports et du Logement. Notes du Centre de Prospective et de Veille Scientifique*. Paris: Ministère de l'Équipement, des Transports et du Logement, Direction de la Recherche et des Affaires Scientifiques et Techniques.

Galland, J.-P. (2003). Calculer, gérer, réduire les risques: des actions disjointes? *Annales des Ponts et Chaussées, 106*, 37–44.

Gibson, J. J. (1979). *The ecological approach to visual perception*. Boston: Houghton Mifflin.

Glatron, S. (1996). Evaluer les risques liés au stockage et au transport des hydrocarbures en milieu urbain: l'exemple du dépôt d'Ivry-sur-Seine. *Revue de Géographie de Lyon, 71*(1), 17–22.

Good, B. (1998). *Comment faire de l'anthropologie médicale? Médecine, rationalité et vécu* (S. Gleize, Trans., Les empêcheurs de penser en rond). Le Plessis-Robinson: Synthélabo.

Gutteling, J. M., & Wiegman, O. (1996). *Exploring risk communication* (Advances in natural and technological hazards research, Vol. 8). Dordrecht: Kluwer Academic.

Healy, S. (2004). A 'post-foundational' interpretation of risk: Risk as 'performance'. *Journal of Risk Research, 7*(3), 277–296.

Heath, R. L., & O'Hair, D. H. (2008). *Handbook of risk and crisis and crisis communication*. New York: Routledge.

Helman, C. (1994). *Culture, health and illness*. Londres: Butterworth & Heinemann.

Hewitt, K. (1997). *Regions of risk: A geographical introduction to disasters*. Singapore: Addison Wesley Longman Limited.

Hinchliffe, S. (2001). Indeterminacy in-decisions – Science, policy and politics in the BSE (Bovine Spongiform Encephalopathy) crisis. *Transactions of the Institute of British Geographers, 26*(2), 182–204.

Holmes, B. J. (2008). Communicating about emerging infectious disease: The importance of research. *Health, Risk & Society, 10*(4), 349–360.

Jasanoff, S. (Ed.). (1994). *Learning from disaster. Risk management after Bhopal*. Philadelphia: University of Pennsylvania Press.

Kasperson, J. X., & Kasperson, R. E. (2001). *Global environmental risk*. London: Earthscan/The United Nations University Press.

Kasperson, J. X., & Kasperson, R. E. (2005). *The social contours of risk*. London: Earthscan.

Kasperson, R. E., & Stallen, P. J. M. (Eds.). (1991). *Communicating risks to the public: International perspectives*. Dordrecht: Kluwer Academic Publishers.

Kirmayer, L. J. (1992). The body's insistence on meaning: Metaphor as presentation and representation in illness experience. *Medical Anthropology Quarterly, 6*(4), 323–346.

Klinke, A., & Renn, O. (2006). Systemic risks as challenge for policy making in risk governance. *Forum Qualitative Sozialforschung/ Forum: Qualitative Social Research [on-line Journal], 7*(1), 33.
Latour, B. (1993). *We have never been modern*. Cambridge, MA: Harvard University Press.
Latour, B. (1996). On actor-network theory. A fey clarifications. *Soziale Welt, 47*(4), 369–381.
Latour, B. (1999a). *Pandora's hope. Essays on the reality of science studies*. Cambridge: Harvard University Press.
Latour, B. (1999b). On recalling ANT. In J. Law & J. Hassard (Eds.), *Actor network and after* (pp. 15–25). Oxford: Blackwell Publishers.
Latour, B. (2004). *Politics of nature: How to bring the sciences into democracy*. Cambridge, MA: Harvard University Press.
Latour, B. (2005). *Reassembling the social*. Oxford: Oxford University Press.
Latour, B., & Woolgar, S. (1986). *Laboratory life: The construction of scientific facts*. Guildford: Princeton University Press.
Lavigne, J.-C., et al. (1988). *Dynamique urbaine et gestion des risques: les processus en jeu dans la COURLY*. Paris: Plan Urbain.
Law, J. (2004). Disaster in agriculture: Or foot and mouth mobilities. *Environment and Planning A, 38*(2), 227–239.
Leanza, Y. (2011). *Exercer la pédiatrie en contexte multiculturel. Une approche complémentariste du rapport institutionnalisé à l'Autre* (Collection Médecine Société). Genève: Georg.
Lindell, M., & Perry, R. (2004). *Communicating environmental risk in multiethnic communities*. London: Sage.
Lundgren, R., & McMain, A. (2009). *Risk communication: A handbook for communicating environmental, safety, and health risks* (4th ed.). Hoboken: Wiley.
Lupton, D. (1994). *Medicine as culture. Illness, disease and the body in Western societies*. Londres: Sage.
Lupton, D. (Ed.). (1999). *Risk and sociocultural theory: New directions and perspectives*. Cambridge: Cambridge University Press.
Maisonneuve, D. (Ed.). (2005). *La communication des risques: un nouveau défi*. Montréal: Presses de l'Université du Québec.
Maisonneuve, D., Saouter, C., & Char, A. (Eds.). (1999). *Communications en temps de crise*. Québec: Presses de l'Université du Québec.
McComas, K. A. (2006). Defining moments in risk communication research: 1996. *Journal of Health Communication, 11*(1), 75–91.
Mitchell, J. K. (1999). Megacities and natural disasters: A comparative analysis. *GeoJournal, 49*, 137–142.
November, V. (1994). Risques naturels et croissance urbaine: réflexion théorique sur la nature et le rôle du risque dans l'espace urbain. *Revue de Géographie Alpine, 4*, 113–123.
November, V. (2002). *Les territoires du risque: le risque comme objet de réflexion géographique*. Bern: Peter Lang.
November, V. (2008). Spatiality of risk. *Environment and Planning A, 40*, 1523–1527.
OECD. (2003). *Emerging risks in the 21st century: An agenda for action*. Paris: OECD Editions.
Oliver-Smith, A. (2004). Theorizing vulnerability in a globalized world: A political ecological perspective. In G. Bankoff, G. Ferks, & D. Hilhorst (Eds.), *Mapping vulnerability: Disasters, development and people* (pp. 10–24). London: Earthscan Publishers.
Otway, H., & Wynne, B. (1989). Risk communication: Paradigm and paradox. *Risk Analysis, 9*(2), 141–145.
Papy, F. (Ed.). (2008). *Problématiques émergentes dans les sciences de l'information*. Paris: Hermès Lavoisier.
Paton, D. (2007). Preparing for natural hazards: The role of community trust. *Disaster Prevention Management, 16*(3), 370–379.
Paton, D. (2008). Risk communication and natural hazard mitigation: How trust influences its effectiveness. *International Journal of Global Environmental Issues, 8*(1/2), 2–16.

Pearce, L. (2005). The value of public participation during a hazard, impact, risk and vulnerability (HIRV) Analysis. *Mitigation and Adaptation Strategies for Global Change, 10*, 411–441.
Pelling, M. (2003). *The vulnerability of cities: Natural disasters and social resilience*. London: Earthscan.
Pidgeon, N., Kasperson, R. E., & Slovic, P. (Eds.). (2003). *The social amplification of risk*. Cambridge, UK: Cambridge University Press.
Plough, A., & Krimsky, S. (1987). The emergence of risk communication studies: Social and political context. *Science, Technology, & Human Values, 12*(3/4), 4–10.
Poortinga, W., & Pidgeon, N. (2004). Trust, the asymmetry principle, and the role of prior beliefs. *Risk Analysis, 24*(6), 1475–1486.
Renn, O. (1992). Concepts of risk: A classification. In S. Krimsky & D. Golding (Eds.), *Social theories of risk* (pp. 53–79). London: Praeger Publishers.
Renn, O. (1998). Three decades of risk research: Accomplishments and new challenges. *Journal of Risk Research, 1*(1), 49–71.
Renn, O., & Levine, D. (1991). Credibility and trust in risk communication. In R. E. Kasperson & P. J. M. Stallen (Eds.), *Communicating risks to the public* (pp. 175–218). Dordrecht: Kluwer Academic Publishers.
Renn, O., & Walker, K. D. (Eds.). (2008). *Global risk governance: Concept and practice using the IRGC framework* (Vol. 1). Dordrecht: Springer.
Rodriguez, H., Quarantelli, E. L., & Dynes, R. R. (Eds.). (2007). *Handbook of disaster research*. New York: Springer.
Schillmeier, M., & Pohler, W. (2006). Cosmo-political events. Towards the Topology of SARS. *Soziale Welt, 57*(4), 331–349.
Shannon, C. E., & Weaver, W. (1949). *The mathematical theory of communication*. Urbana: University of Illinois Press.
Sierra Club. (2006). *Harmful legacy of pollution and deception at ground zero: How post 9/11 disaster policy endangers America*. New York: Sierra Club.
Super, C. M., & Harkness, S. (1997). The cultural structuring of child development. In J. W. Berry, P. R. Dasen, & T. Saraswathi (Eds.), *Handbook of cross-cultural psychology* (Vol. 2, pp. 2–39). Boston: Allyn & Bacon.
Suraud, M.-G. (2007). *La catastrophe d'AZF. De la concertation à la contestatio*. Paris: La Documentation française.
Suraud, M.-G., Blin, M. P., & De Terssac, G. (Eds.). (2008). *Information, Communication, sur les Risques Industriels*. Toulouse: Maison des Sciences de l'Homme et de la Société de Toulouse – Octarès.
Taylor-Goody, P., & Zinn, J. (2006). Current directions in risk research: New developments in psychology and sociology. *Risk Analysis, 26*, 397–411.
Thomalla, F., Downing, T., Spanger-Siegfried, E., Han, G. Y., & Rockstrom, J. (2006). Reducing hazard vulnerability: Towards a common approach between disaster risk reduction and climate adaptation. *Disasters, 30*(1), 39–48.
Tierney, K. J. (2007). From the margins to the mainstream? Disaster research at the crossroads. *Annual Review of Sociology, 33*, 503–552.
Turner, B. L., Kasperson, R. E., Matson, P. A., McCarthy, J. J., Corell, R. W., Christensen, L., et al. (2003). A framework for vulnerability analysis in sustainability science. [Article]. *Proceedings of the National Academy of Sciences of the United States of America, 100*(14), 8074–8079.
Uexküll, Jakob von. 1980 [1920]. *Kompositionslehre der Natur*. Frankfurt am Main: Thure von Uexküll.
UNISDR (United Nations International Strategy for Disaster Reduction Secretariat). (2009). Global assessment on disaster risk reduction. Geneva: United Nations International Strategy for Disaster Reduction.
UNISDR. (2009). *UNISDR terminology on disaster risk reduction*. Geneva: United Nations International Strategy for Disaster Reduction.
Vinck, D. (1995). *Sociologie des sciences*. Paris: Armand Colin.

Williams-Jones, B., & Graham, J. E. (2003). Actor-network theory: A tool to support ethical analysis of commercial genetic testing. *New Genetics and Society, 22*(3), 271–296.

Wisner, B., Blaikie, P., Cannon, T., & Davis, I. (2004). *At risk. Natural hazards, people's vulnerability and disasters* (2nd ed.). London: Routledge.

Wynne, B. (1996). May the sheep safely graze? In S. Lash et al. (Eds.), *Risk, environment & modernity. towards a new ecology* (pp. 44–83). London: Sage.

Young, A. (1981). When rational men fall sick: An inquiry into some assumptions made by medical anthropologists. *Culture, Medicine & Psychiatry, 5*, 317–335.

Young, A. (1982). Rational men and the explanatory model approach. *Culture, Medicine & Psychiatry, 6*, 57–71.

Zeigler, D. J., Johnson, J. H. J., & Brunn, S. D. (1983). *Technological hazards*. Washington, DC: Association of American Geographers.

Chapter 2
Centralising Information: Predicting and Managing the Risk of Pandemics at the WHO

2.1 Introduction

At last we are here, in The Room; the room to which so many researchers, journalists and external experts can only dream of gaining access. It has taken us almost 9 months to get permission to enter, and finally we are able to attend one of the daily morning meetings.[1] Caught between the emotion of actually being there and the requirement for confidentiality that has been made quite clear to us ('nothing that is said in this room may leave the room'), we settle down unobtrusively and listen. No recordings may be made, no notes taken.

Dr A. is in charge of the session. A qualified veterinarian, she is part of the Epidemic Intelligence and Risk Assessment unit. We are in the Upper SHOC Room (Strategic Health Operations Centre) of the World Health Organization (WHO). Opened in May 2004, this room is where any events that might have dramatic epidemic repercussions on a global scale are discussed. With the help of a large screen, Dr A. presented a list (prepared by her team), which was then discussed by the experts assembled round the table. This list contains the situations requiring careful monitoring; some have already been through the verification process and others still need to be verified with the member countries concerned. At the same time, other screens display the geographical location of the countries concerned

Part of this chapter has been written in collaboration with Katia De Conto and has been published in French under the title '*Politiques des pandémies: de la détection des risques à l'action*' in Houdart S. et Thiery O. (dir). 2011, *Humains, Non-Humains: comment repeupler les sciences sociales*, Paris, La Découverte, pp. 101–110.

[1]We are extremely grateful to David L. Heymann for having made it possible for us to visit and to meet the key figures involved.

V. November, Y. Leanza, *Risk, Disaster and Crisis Reduction*,
DOI 10.1007/978-3-319-08542-5_2

by the threat and the number of cases declared that day (as well as figures from the preceding days). The discussion determines the cases on which the experts will focus their attention.

Over the following days we continue to follow the observations and discussions. On leaving the building at the end of our few days of research, we are feeling distinctly shaky: the WHO, this international organisation with such a serious reputation and which puts so much effort into disseminating credible information, is essentially following . . . rumours[2]!

We have entered into the highly regulated world of the circulation of information in the WHO, in particular into their system for monitoring pandemic diseases. We are able to observe at first hand how the various socio-technical intermediaries are deployed to capture, translate and transform the rumours to produce information, that is to say, identified risks or perhaps even alerts.

2.2 Institutional Framework and Investigation

2.2.1 The Risk of Epidemic and the Role of the WHO

Societies have always been subjected to epidemics of infectious diseases, the spread of which has often caused high mortality. The WHO defines an epidemic as 'a disease contracted by a relatively high number of people in a given region in a relatively short period of time'. The risk of an epidemic is the probability of a disease arising in a given time and place and spreading at different scales. During the course of history, populations, ignorant of how to protect themselves, opted to separate those affected from those in good health. The notion of quarantine goes back to at least the fourteenth century (WHO 2007). The idea was to guard themselves against evils of 'foreign' origin, such as the plague. Over time, scientific progress and, most notably, the introduction of sanitation to towns (in the nineteenth century) allowed some infectious diseases to be contained, such as cholera. Then, during the twentieth century, the advent of better hygiene, vaccinations and medicines enabled certain diseases to be brought under control. Smallpox, for example, has been totally eradicated, following a widespread vaccination campaign organised by the WHO.

The World Health Organization is an agency of the United Nations that specialises in public health. It was founded on 7 April 1948, shortly after the end of the Second World War, and currently has 194 member states. However, the origins of the WHO go back to the nineteenth century (Poulain 2003). The major European cholera epidemics which raged between 1830 and 1847 led to the first International Sanitary Conference, held in Paris in 1851. Following this conference, two conventions were signed: the first in 1892 on cholera and the second in 1897 on the plague. In 1907, a number of the states that had signed these conventions met

[2]Our findings are in keeping with the work of Elisabeth Remy (1993), who proposes that rumours be taken seriously and endorses the definitions given by the actors.

in Rome, where they established the International Office of Public Hygiene. After the First World War and the epidemic of Spanish influenza that was responsible for the death of over 20 million people in 1918–1919, the League of Nations set up a Health Committee, which was the 'embryo' of the WHO.

The various functions of the WHO[3] are defined as follows:

- Providing leadership on matters critical to health and engaging in partnerships where joint action is needed;
- Shaping the research agenda and stimulating the generation, translation and dissemination of valuable knowledge;
- Setting norms and standards and promoting and monitoring their implementation;
- Articulating ethical and evidence-based policy options;
- Providing technical support, catalysing change and building sustainable institutional capacity;
- Monitoring the health situation and assessing health trends.

Despite the considerable efforts made by the WHO, as well as by the Member States and other bodies, such as NGOs, there are still infectious diseases that develop as a result of the ability of microorganisms to adapt to their environment or their host. For this reason, the possibility of an outbreak of a new epidemic remains a reality and an unpredictable reality at that. Over the course of the last 30 years, epidemiologists have noted both the emergence of new diseases (such as legionellosis and AIDS) and an increase in the number of old diseases. There are various reasons for this: 'demographic and behavioural changes, economic development, land use, the internationalisation of travel and trade, changes in the climate and in ecosystems, poverty, conflicts, hunger and even the deliberate release of infectious or chemical agents' (WHO 2007).

The risk of an epidemic still exists, despite the considerable scientific progress that has been made. Diseases are not confined within borders, but cross them rapidly as a result of increased international traffic of all types: 'By altering viral traffic patterns, the introduction of modern agricultural or industrial technologies in one location – 'local' causes – might produce an international epidemic or pandemic – 'global' effects' (King 2004: 66). The aim of the strategies and methods deployed by the WHO is to counter such risk of an epidemic at the earliest possible stage, in conjunction with the Member States, who are also becoming increasingly active in this area. It is for this reason that a permanent monitoring system was set in place. This system covers all geographical scales (from local to global).

A pandemic – an epidemic that affects a vast region, possibly even covering all continents – is part of a phenomenon even greater than a simple epidemic. The WHO activities are intended to coordinate the actions of the various countries affected, or likely to be affected, by a problem that has been identified.

As we have seen, the WHO is an interstate organisation, which plays a central role in global public health. It works together with its Member States and through

[3]These are the functions as set out on the WHO website: http://www.who.int/about/role/en/.

treaties and inclusions in national legislation to ensure that its decisions are implemented on a wide scale. If a case arises that poses a threat to public health, no matter where in the world this may occur, a number of experts are ready to respond. WHO staff are in a constant state of watchfulness, and the role of the organisation in the management of epidemic risks is crucial.

The work of the key actors takes place in various locations: the Headquarters, regional offices, national laboratories and also with the help of intermediate bodies, such as NGOs.

2.2.2 Investigation

We chose to focus our study on the WHO SHOC Room in Geneva in order to provide the best possible illustration of our analysis of the *centralisation of information*. Our starting point is that it is this room that receives and collects all the information acquired by the Headquarters, verifies it and then decides whether an alert should be issued.

The field work was divided into two parts: individual interviews and time spent observing the operation of the room and the participants. Our core research questions were as follows: How does the information circulate? What are the technical resources available? What are the risks targeted? What sort of data does the central organisation receive? What are the most commonly used geographical scales? How is the information processed, then redistributed and disseminated to a wider audience? And, finally, how was this system set up?

During the 2 days spent on site, we were able to observe the operation of the SHOC Room and the tasks of the various experts who work and meet there. We took note of the technical resources and the various technological tools available in the room (screens, computers, etc.). We were also able to form an understanding of the 'life' of the central organisation; the monitoring and alert phases, as well as the working rhythms of the teams. This allowed us to visualise how information is communicated among the various public health professionals. Lastly, we were interested in the content of the resources, such as maps and charts, that were visible in the SHOC Room itself.

Significantly, the day of our study coincided with the entry into force of the International Health Regulations (IHR), on 15 June 2007. There was a degree of palpable excitement regarding the implementation of this tool. As explained later, it had taken a long time to get to this stage. The quotations and the information we gathered make it possible to understand the hopes invested in the new IHR; hopes which have since been confirmed as the IHR has been instrumental in transforming a certain number of practices, which we will also report on later.

The WHO, like any major organisation, regularly implements reforms and changes to its organisational chart. Since our visit the names of units have changed and new departments have been created. At that time the 'Epidemic and Pandemic Alert and Response Unit' was the unit in which we were interested for our study. It is now known as the 'Alert and Response Operations Unit (ARO)'. The primary objective of this department is to set up efficient risk management systems in order to safeguard international public health. To a great extent, the reduction of risks is achieved through collaboration with Member States, which must have the capacity to detect and verify diseases rapidly in order to tackle an event more effectively.

In 2007, the organisational chart consisted of two major groups: Director's Office and IHR Coordination Programme. The former comprised four subgroups: Alert and Response Operations, Global Influenza Programme, Epidemic Readiness and Interventions and Bio-risk Reduction and Bio-terrorism Dangerous Pathogens.[4] These subgroups also have their own working areas. The second major group was also divided into four subgroups: Lyon Office for National Epidemic Preparedness and Response, including Training Support Programmes; National Systems Strengthening; IHR Secretariat; and SIG Public Health Map.

In 2011, the Health, Security and Environment Division (HSE) merged the teams responsible for epidemic and pandemic alert and response operations with those in the WHO department responsible for coordinating the IHR, to create a new department entitled Global Capacities, Alert and Response (GCR). This is divided into a number of units, including the ARO, that cover global alert and response operations in the event of an epidemic. This unit consists of four teams:

1. Risk Assessment and Decision Support, which processes the information on epidemics received and carries out a rapid evaluation of the risks;
2. Global Outbreak Alert and Response Network (GOARN), which brings together institutions and networks to pool human and technical resources in order to identify, confirm rapidly and respond to global outbreaks;
3. Logistics, which provides a comprehensive logistic capability to support the operations responding to outbreaks and maintains and distributes stocks worldwide;
4. Strategic Health Operations (SHO), which acts as the organisational hub for the WHO Headquarters and manages the JW Lee Strategic Health Operations Centre.

During our investigation we were able to talk to the following individuals:

- The Director of the IRH Coordination Programme. This interview was helpful as it gave us a better understanding of the functioning of the department in general and, more particularly, it provided an explanation of the revised IRH, in which he was greatly involved. The Director also explained the global implications of the changes and the perspectives of these new regulations, the new assessment criteria and the responsibilities of both the WHO and the Member States;
- A veterinarian working in the Epidemic Intelligence and Risk Assessment team, which is part of the Alert and Response Operations subgroup.[5] She first

[4]This also included Programme Management and Communications.

[5]The present-day equivalent of the Risk Assessment and Decision Support (ADS) team, in the Alert and Response Operations (ARO) group.

described the general context of the actions carried out by this department. This was followed by more detailed information on the work of her team, which is primarily concerned with assessing the risk and verifying the information available to the WHO through its various networks;
- A SHOC Room technician. His role is primarily to maintain the equipment in the room and to develop high-performance software;
- The coordinator of the Alert and Response Operations team. In this interview, he described the work of the group he leads. He emphasised the verification of the information and also the quality of the information required in order to respond rapidly to an outbreak;
- The manager of the Global Outbreak Alert and Response Network. He described an emergency response. He also set out the roles of the various institutions in ensuring a better response to epidemics in the field;
- A doctor from the Global Influenza Programme team. This discussion gave us a good overview of the measures and actions related to influenza. He also talked about avian influenza, which is being monitored permanently;
- The Assistant Director-General for Communicable Diseases and the Epidemic and Pandemic Alert and Response department. He explained the role of the WHO. The organisation is backed up by the revised International Health Regulations. He also described the way various teams operate within the department and their role on a global level.

2.3 Managing Epidemic-Type Risks

For many years, the WHO has attempted to contain those diseases liable to constitute an epidemic. The initial WHO International Sanitary Regulations of 1951 were revised and renamed the International Health Regulations in 1969. The aim of these regulations was to provide protection against the spread of infectious diseases on a global scale, with the least possible disturbance to trade or tourism. Initially, Member States were required to notify six diseases to the WHO: cholera, plague, yellow fever, smallpox, typhus and relapsing fever. Following a number of amendments, the number of notifiable diseases was reduced to three: yellow fever, plague and cholera. However, the rise in both the number of international exchanges, and the forms these take, favours the propagation of microbes and also increases the likelihood of new or re-emerging infectious diseases. Between 2002 and 2007, the WHO confirmed 1,100 epidemiological health events across the world (WHO 2007). Five years later, in 2012, 291 events were recorded for evaluation or response in the Event Management System (Department of Global Capacities, Alert and Response 2013). According to the organisation, no country is able to resolve or overcome the consequences of such events alone and to curb an epidemic. This is an event – a 'focusing event' as Birkland calls it (2007) – which has made a major contribution to transforming the categories of risk used within the WHO and to the contents of the new IHR: the Severe Acute Respiratory Syndrome (SARS) epidemic, generally considered to be the first major epidemic of the twenty-first century, was able to spread very rapidly using international air travel routes, with no country being spared from this risk (Heymann and Rodier 2004).

This vulnerability led to the revision of the IHR, which had been decided upon at the WHO General Assembly in 1995, being brought forward, with a view to making it more appropriate and able to cope with widespread risks,

This re-evaluation of both the regulations and the links between the organisation and the Member States is based on a change in the approach to the risk of a pandemic, the management of the risk and the recommended action. In the context of the study of the centralisation of information within the WHO, we have applied the three phases of risk (Chap. 1: Fig. 1.7, p. 19) in order to understand the processes of managing the pandemic crisis and the reorganisation following an event within the WHO.

We identified key moments and intermediaries who play a vital role in the circulation of information. The thread of our investigation is based on the lessons learned from the SARS experience; this experience had a profound effect on the mindset of the organisation and has contributed to major changes on the management of epidemic risk within the WHO.

Indeed, SARS was mentioned as a turning point by all those we interviewed. It offers the most complete image of the transformation from rumour to risk, capable of triggering and relaunching action (Callon and Law 1997) in a variety of different directions. In other words, the pandemics detected at a very early stage through rumours, such as SARS, avian influenza and Ebola virus in particular, are nothing more than the result of a multitude of translations of a risk to public health. Our study will demonstrate that this is a continuum, bringing together simultaneously a number of temporal or spatial scales, in which a non-human element, linked to a range of repercussions – or a 'hairy' element, to use the term favoured by Latour (2004) – goes beyond the expected framework of the action.

2.3.1 *What Did SARS Change?*

When SARS arrived on the scene in 2003, it illustrated how quickly a new disease can travel around the world. SARS presented a serious threat to global public health: 'It spreads from person to person, requires no vector, displays no particular geographical affinity, incubates silently for more than a week, mimics the symptoms of many other diseases, takes its heaviest toll on hospital staff and kills around 10 % of those infected. These features enable it to spread easily along the routes of international travel, placing every city with an international airport at risk of imported cases' (WHO 2007: 37).

On 7 August 2003, the WHO noted 8,422 cases and 916 deaths (WHO 2003). The economic repercussions were also catastrophic, particularly for Asia. The economic impact on Hong Kong is estimated to have amounted to losses of over 3.8 billion euros, according to an edition of the electronic newsletter of the French Embassy that looked back at the situation 10 years later (Ambassade de France en Chine 2013).

The spread of SARS was halted 4 months after it was identified, thanks to the emergency systems already put in place and the collaboration between Member States. However, this epidemic highlighted shortcomings with regard to both management and coordination, particularly in relation to the speed of implementation of emergency measures. In addition, it brought about a change in the position of public and political opinion in the face of a potential pandemic.

SARS can be seen as a 'focusing event' (Birkland 2007). Indeed, this event drove the WHO and the Member States to rethink the way in which the risk of an epidemic is managed on a global scale. In addition, following this crisis, the World Health Assembly[6] urgently recommended the drafting of a revised version of the International Health Regulations (IHR) by May 2005.

The new version of the IHR, the 'backbone' of the directives to be followed by both the WHO and the Member States, entered into force on 15 June 2007. This was the result of a revision process that had taken 10 years and which contributed to a change in the understanding of health risks. The worldwide community now has a new legal framework. The primary aim of the changes was to allow better management of risks and emergency situations. However, the innovative feature of the approach adopted is the expansion of the notion of risk. The authorities and the WHO no longer await the arrival of an event before responding; rather they go to the source of any information linked to an 'extraordinary' event in order to verify the information for themselves. As one of our interviewees emphasizes it,

> Today every event is subject to analysis, a risk evaluation and proposed measures. Today we work on a tailor-made basis.

The notion of risk is therefore no longer limited to three diseases, but now includes events of chemical, radioactive, environmental and animal origin, meaning that the spectrum of risks has widened considerably. The Member States are equipped with criteria to be used as the basis for assessing the likelihood of a future pandemic. If two criteria are met, the event must be notified to the WHO. Furthermore, notification is mandatory in the case of the following diseases: 'smallpox, poliomyelitis caused by a wild-type poliovirus, human influenza caused by a new virus subtype and SARS' (WHO 2007: 12).

A Member State can also notify the case of a pathogen agent emerging in a different Member State. The WHO also has the right to request verification from all Member States. The information and the notifications are communicated to the WHO through the 'focal point' established in each Member State. The focal point receives information on a round-the-clock basis, allowing it to establish an efficient network between the WHO and its Member States. In addition, countries are responsible for developing their own national monitoring and health emergency systems. They are able to request advice from the WHO if they are unfamiliar with the pathogen agents involved. In the case of a very serious event, the

[6] Supreme governing body of the WHO, responsible for policy matters. http://www.who.int/mediacentre/events/governance/wha/en/

Director-General of the WHO, after consulting with the Emergency Committee, which consists of external experts, is authorised to take a decision in order to prevent the spread of disease on an international scale. The revised IHR has therefore improved communication between Member States. The effectiveness of the international response to a health emergency has been improved and information can be communicated more rapidly.

In order to detect the information at source, the WHO must monitor all events and verify them as soon as possible. As one of our interviewees put it,

> The information we receive here is the information we collect ourselves proactively.

The slightest bit of information (the rumours) that may announce the risk of a pandemic is immediately intercepted by the server located in Canada, according to a predefined classification established with the help of a WHO expert group. This information, whether official or non-official, comes from a wide range of sources: international and national newspapers, blogs and the Internet. The prototype, which was developed primarily thanks to the determination of an official in the Public Health Agency of Canada, detected the information in English and in French (Mawudeku and Blench 2006). The system is somewhat reminiscent of whistle-blowers, who provide an advance warning, or perhaps of the 'sombre precursors' referred to by Chateauraynaud and Torny (1999).

To achieve this, the WHO worked together with the Public Health Agency of Canada (in 1997) and they set up the Global Public Health Intelligence Network (GPHIN) (Michelson 2005: 382). The idea was to develop a system capable of detecting information by recognising key words in English and in French. The information came from all forms of telecommunications: television, radio, press, Internet, etc. In 2002, a new version appeared: GPHIN II (Mykhalovskiy and Weir 2006: 43). This search engine covers nine languages: all the official languages of the United Nations (Arabic, Chinese – traditional and simplified – Russian, Spanish, French and English), plus Farsi and Portuguese. What is interesting about this approach is that a 'rumour',[7] in other words non-official information, is taken into account at a very early stage in the chain. It is emailed to the WHO. This information has no official status, but as it is a 'rumour', it is important to check it out. This system for detecting events highlights the fact that information is traced right back to its source. Thanks to the range of key words selected by the WHO, the slightest bit of information pointing to risk of a potential pandemic is immediately intercepted by the server, then analysed in order to short circuit any problems. There is constant monitoring, making it possible to identify all the indications of the risk of a pandemic.

The first cases of SARS (when the epidemiologists discovered the symptoms) appeared in November 2002 in the province of Guangdong, in China. The GPHIN flagged up this information in Chinese in November 2002 and then flagged it up again in English in January 2003 (without however using the term 'SARS', as the

[7] This is the term used by the WHO.

name was only invented later). On 12 March 2003, the WHO published the first official report mentioning an outbreak of atypical pneumonia. On 2 April, a WHO team confirmed that the reported cases did indeed match the definition of SARS, and the first recommendations issued to travellers also designated the areas where there was a risk of infection. In the meantime, a doctor, who had himself been infected by one of his patients, 'exported' the virus to a hotel in Hong Kong. Within a few days, residents and travellers had carried the disease to hospitals in Hong Kong, Vietnam and Singapore. Cases were also recorded in Toronto.

The GPHIN should be seen as an assembly of human and non-human actors. Every day analysts examine the strength of the information received and verify the automatic processes incorporated in the system. As an indication of what these automatic processes entail, one might say that the articles are first filtered according to their classification (e.g. animal diseases, human diseases, plant diseases and natural disasters). Then each article is scanned and awarded a percentage figure according to the number of predefined key words it contains. If the level is high, the information is immediately entered into the GPHIN database and emailed to the WHO, as an alert. Conversely, articles scoring below the agreed threshold are discarded. In the case of articles with a median score, it is up to the analyst to decide whether the article should be published or rejected. In addition the analyst checks whether the articles discarded by the automatic system have been translated correctly, ensuring that no suspect case is missed. The human element is therefore essential as it offers a more discerning look at the elements collected by the machine. With the GPHIN there is a shift: rather than considering it as a system, it should be seen as a heterogeneous 'calculation centre' (Latour 1987), where risk situations are identified and considered to be a possibility. It is an intermediary that plays a role in transforming the qualities of the information, providing new translations on the subject.

2.3.2 Verifying the Information

The revised IHR is in keeping with what the WHO developed in 1996 a system for managing events. At the Headquarters and in the regional offices, there are 'strategic operations centres' capable of intervening in an emergency. The verification of information will, of course, give rise to measures that must be implemented in order to alleviate risks and crises.

The Headquarters receives the information and then decides on the appropriate measures that should be taken, in the knowledge that the regional and national offices (the focal points) are also involved in verification. One of the principal difficulties of the WHO is not so much processing the amount of information it receives, but rather guaranteeing the quality of that information. Within the Headquarters the department responsible for this task is the Epidemic and Pandemic Alert and Response department, which includes the Alert and Response Operations section. As the name implies, the objective is to respond as rapidly and as effectively as possible to any alert of a potential epidemic. Within this structure is the Epidemic Intelligence and Risk Assessment team which is 'focussed on the information; on receiving it, digesting it, and assessing it in order to take the decisions needed, in collaboration with other teams'.

This team assesses the risks by analysing the sources of the information it receives as part of a 'generic box'. The source of the information is described as official or non-official.

The information from official sources, such as Ministries of Health, the WHO regional and national centres or national laboratories and institutes, is official, or formal, information. These sources represent 39 % of the total. Despite not being numerous, there has been a growing trend in recent years. More and more Member States communicate their information to the WHO. According to our interviewees, this increase is the result of a greater sense of mutual trust that has developed among the parties.

The information from non-official, or informal, sources (61 % of the information), is primarily based on rumour and is transmitted by the GPHIN, other websites or by the media. For example, data may be received from ProMED.[8] ProMED-mail was the first prototype of web-based data sources for the monitoring of infectious diseases (created in 1994). It is an electronic discussion group which raises public awareness of public health issues. It mainly sends articles to the WHO. NGOs also sometimes pass on information about potentially suspicious events occurring in their area.

Since then, other types of software based on informal information have been developed, such as Healthmap or EpiSPIDER. (For a detailed comparison of these two types of software and the GPHIN, cf Keller et al. 2009.) This trend continues to grow, thanks to digital detection and detection using automated web-crawling programmes, as well as increasingly sophisticated display tools (Brownstein et al. 2009).

According to Pollack (2013), both types of source have their strengths and weaknesses. As illustrated in Table 2.1, the informal, or nontraditional, sources allow information to be diffused more quickly and earlier, whereas formal sources transmit information more slowly and are not as good at early detection. In contrast, information obtained from formal sources is more credible and requires less verification. However, information from unofficial sources is disseminated through official circuits, although it is publicly available from informal sources, which Pollack considers to be a good point.

On receiving this type of informal information, the WHO instigates a procedure to verify the quality of the information. The aim is to have established information,

[8] ProMed (Program for Monitoring Emerging Diseases) is an 'Internet-based reporting system dedicated to rapid global dissemination of information on outbreaks of infectious diseases and acute exposures to toxins that affect human health, including those in animals and in plants grown for food or animal feed. Electronic communications enable ProMED-mail to provide up-to-date and reliable news about threats to human, animal, and food plant health around the world, seven days a week', in www.promedmail.org.

Table 2.1 Strengths and weaknesses of formal versus nontraditional information sources

Issues	Formal source	Nontraditional source
Quick, early dissemination of information	Often a weakness	Strength
Early detection	Often a weakness	Strength
Reliability of information	Strength	Variable
Accessibility to information	Often private	Publicly available
Forms of information dissemination	Official channels	Multiple sources, freely available
Language used for communication	Language of country	More in English

Adapted from Pollack (2013: 61)

verified by the structures of the WHO, where the list (cf point 4.2.) is an intermediary that enables the status of the information to be negotiated.

The team contacts the regional offices in order to obtain more information on the disease concerned. Clearly, the regional office closest to the location will deal with this rumour, using the same criteria as the Headquarters. It then asks the Ministry of the Member State, through the intermediary of the WHO national office, to carry out its own examination. If the government of the country affected submits a request to the WHO, the Headquarters will also contact the reference laboratories to carry out the required analyses. However, at this stage of the proceedings, the WHO is willing to provide any assistance requested.

Once the information has been verified and confirmed, it returns to the Headquarters. There a re-evaluation takes place and, on the basis of the same criteria, a decision will be made regarding the importance of the event:

> We carry out a re-evaluation with the information, which has now become official, and decide whether we were right or whether it was a false alarm. At that point we decide whether to reject the event or to generate a response if the need is felt.

The Headquarters usually receives a reply within 24 h.

The following principal criteria are used to determine whether an event has an international nature (according to the new criteria of the revised IHR):

- The severity of repercussions on public health;
- Unusual or unexpected nature of the event;
- Significant risk of international disease spread;
- Significant risk of restrictions being imposed on trade;
- Significant risk of restrictions being imposed on international travel.

If two of these five criteria are met, notification is obligatory.

Following the adoption of the new IHR, risk has gradually been expanded to include new situations and new objects (travellers, trade and unexpected events), and the definition of risk has also been extended.

Information is then shared, as one of our interviewees explained, adding that 'informing those who have a need to know in order to act is a key step'.

The information is then delivered 'to the heart of the WHO and the key people who play an important role in the response – of whatever nature – to a given event. The information may also be published on the IRH secure website, to which the focal points in all Member States have access'.

Within the Headquarters, the information is also shared among the various experts (cholera, plague, smallpox, influenza, viral haemorrhagic fevers, SARS, etc.). In the evening, the Epidemic Intelligence and Risk Assessment team prepares a list containing the new elements likely to spread at an international level. This list includes information from both official and non-official sources. The next morning this list is passed on to the various experts for discussion and risk evaluation. At this stage decisions are taken; these are then communicated within the Headquarters and to the regional offices.

The Epidemic Alert and Response department is responsible for detecting risks at the earliest possible stage. It is part of a global network and thus is able to receive information, verify it and, where required, transmit an alert to key personnel. The aim of this coordinated action is to detect any indications of an infectious disease that could have disastrous consequences if it were to spread. As viruses propagate so rapidly, it is important to receive information in 'real time' in order to be able to respond as promptly as possible. The diagram (Fig. 2.1) gives an overview of how information is verified.

2.3.3 *Setting Up Emergency Responses*

In 2000, the WHO decided to set up a collaboration mechanism: the Global Outbreak and Response Network (GOARN) (Heymann 2006: 351). This network incorporates 140 institutions in 60 countries that guarantee a rapid response to Member States in the event of a global epidemic. It facilitates the coordination of operations, by following a number of basic principles, and provides an operational framework which enables countries to be supplied rapidly with resources (such as vaccines and medication) and expert assistance. GOARN's primary aims[9] are to:

- Assist countries with disease control efforts by ensuring rapid and appropriate technical support to affected populations;
- Investigate and characterise events and assess risks of rapidly emerging epidemic disease threats;
- Support national outbreak preparedness by ensuring that responses contribute to sustained containment of epidemic threats.

This network is a system intended to aid emergency response when faced with the risk of an epidemic. The aim is to reduce as far as possible the scale of the

[9] http://www.who.int/csr/outbreaknetwork/goarnenglish.pdf

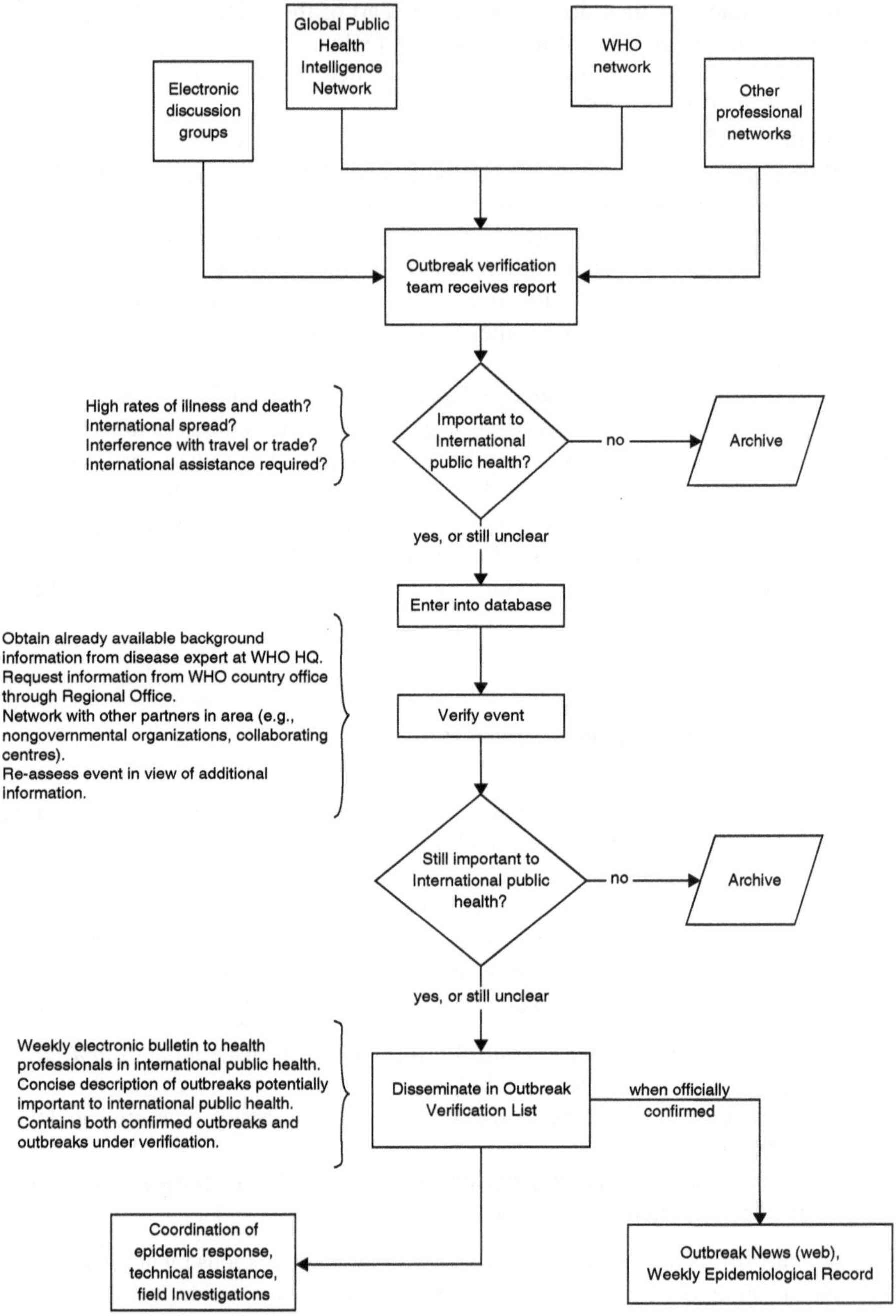

Fig. 2.1 Outbreak verification at the World Health Organization (With kind permission from Grein et al. (2000: 98, Figure 1))

disaster through rapid and effective action in the field, thanks to the information received being communicated in a timely manner.

One of the doctors working in the Epidemic Intelligence and Risk Assessment department explained that once an epidemic starts to spread and the situation gets out of control (and thus has the potential to become an international public health emergency), the WHO experts carry out an assessment of the situation, which they then pass on to the GOARN institutions in the form of a request. GOARN then compiles a list of experts appropriate to the emergency. This response is provided within 24–28 h of the WHO request, depending on circumstances (visas, tickets, logistics, etc.). Then, provided the WHO and the country affected agree, the experts and the logisticians are sent to the area to provide help and support.

Between 2000 and 2007, the WHO and GOARN responded to over 97 events across the world, deploying over 500 experts in the field, in 63 countries. Michelson (2005) highlighted how effectively GOARN performed during the SARS episode. It linked 13 laboratories, located in 9 different countries, with over 50 doctors from 14 different countries in an attempt to identify the causes, means of transmission and possible responses to SARS.

GOARN has a heterogeneous range of partners. The network makes it possible to bring together the technical and operational resources of diverse scientific establishments[10]: Member States, medical surveillance initiatives, regional technical networks (e.g. laboratories), universities, United Nations organisations (e.g. UNICEF, UNHCR), the Red Cross and non-governmental organisations (e.g. Médecins sans Frontières Doctors Without Borders).

In the case of an urgent and serious event, the Director-General (DG) of the WHO is entitled to decide on the measures to be adopted, in accordance with the revised IHR. However, as one of our interviewees explained, before making such a decision, the DG must consult with an emergency experts committee and his own experts.

This information communication phase is a final resort as this is an extremely rare international health emergency. This is the final link in the internal decision-making chain that governs emergency intervention in the event of an international epidemic.

The WHO keeps the public informed through its website 'Disease Outbreak News (DONs)'. The information on this site is official; that is to say, it has been subject to prior verification, and the Member State concerned has agreed to the publication of this event. The WHO publishes the 'Weekly Epidemiological Record (WER)', which is a means of disseminating rapidly epidemiological information that may have consequences for public health, including on emerging or re-emerging infectious diseases. This newsletter includes all the latest information on the Member States and is automatically archived. Following an epidemic, the WHO also writes an article giving a summary of the information relating to the crisis. The WHO also publishes annual reports. These various publications keep the public abreast of the different events that occur. They provide background information for

[10]http://www.who.int/csr/outbreaknetwork/en/

any re-examination of an event and assist in improving the procedures and resources deployed in managing a crisis, as discussed previously.

2.4 The Intermediaries in the Circulation of Information

2.4.1 The SHOC Room: A Modular Space

The SHOC Room (Strategic Health Operations Centre) was opened in May 2004, at the WHO Headquarters in Geneva. Following the death of the Director-General, Dr Lee Jong-wook, in May 2006, the room was renamed in his memory and is now known as the JW LEE Centre for Strategic Health Operations (WHO 2006). It is in this room that events that could have dramatic epidemic repercussion on a global scale are discussed. Here the experts analyse the various situations: both those that have already been confirmed and those still awaiting confirmation from the countries affected.

In short, the SHOC Room is where rumours are examined and transformed into information. It has a range of 'high-tech' infrastructure and security is high in order to be able to withstand any form of attack, either deliberate or unintentional, such as attacks, earthquakes, computer viruses, etc. To this end it has a bunker-like construction, with an airlock entrance, autonomous generators and a stock of food.

This room actually consists of three separate areas, with complementary roles. Firstly, there is the SHOC Room itself, which is the main room in the event of a crisis. It is only activated when a problem situation arises. Next to this room is the technical room, where the technicians work on the development of the IT system and the maintenance of technical equipment. There is round-the-clock monitoring. Finally, on a mezzanine level above the technical room, there is the Upper SHOC Room, the location of the daily meetings at which discussions take place and decisions are made. It has an oval table, a wall screen and two telephones.

The SHOC Room is the largest of the rooms. It has seating for 16 people and there are 8 desks, each of which has a computer. (If necessary, two people can share a desk.) Each station is equipped with a telephone and microphones in order to allow a telephone conference with over thirty participants simultaneously. The meetings are recorded by a suite of cameras. On the wall opposite the work stations is a large screen, which is used during video conferences. On the side wall there are four screens, each of which has a separate function. The first displays a table giving the data for a particular disease at a specific location at a specific time. It lists the number of deaths, the number of people who have contracted the disease and the potential or actual risk that it will spread. The second screen shows the list of events currently under investigation and those that have been confirmed. These events are dealt with and discussed, and the information is displayed at the morning meetings.

The third screen displays maps of the places affected by the events defined in the lists. They are shown at different geographical scales in order to give a better idea of the territorial implications of the crises. The fourth screen displays a photo of Dr LEE, as homage to his work.

The Upper SHOC Room is considerably smaller. It has a central table, with six seats and six microphones. It is used primarily when it is considered preferable to reduce the number of participants when important decisions have to be taken. There are telephones, and two screens on the wall facing the table. The first displays the list of events to be discussed. The second displays maps related to the subject of discussion.

The SHOC Room is only activated in the event of an international public health emergency. The room can be used for activities related to different types of emergency, including pandemics (such as avian influenza), natural disasters (such as earthquakes or tsunamis), bio-terrorism and chemical accidents. It is a modular space that can be arranged to suit the needs of the unit using it. The room was set up in order to improve coordination between the Headquarters, the regional offices and focal points. Experts spend a lot of time in this room and are kept abreast of the situation in 'real time' through video conferences.

In contrast, the Upper Room is used every day to provide easy communication between the Headquarters and the regional offices.

> We always work in close collaboration. Every day we have a video conference with the regions; there is a constant dialogue with the regions.

In this way the Headquarters can keep a regional offices informed on a daily basis. Together they reassess the risks related to a particular disease and exchange new data.

The Upper SHOC Room is in use most of the year. Every morning, at the same time, there is an internal meeting to assess the information received on a specific case:

> The information is shared systematically at 09:00. The key element in managing the information is the risk assessment.

This is the moment at which the key decisions are taken. Every evening the Epidemic Intelligence and Risk Assessment team prepares a list for discussion in the meeting the following morning.

The SHOC Room and the Upper SHOC Room offer a place to meet and to exchange information, forming a 'node' where all the networks come together. The Upper SHOC Room is the place where the key decisions are taken by the experts with the aim of ensuring optimum management of the risks associated with an epidemic. It is the principal site for communication between the different actors involved: within the Headquarters, with the regional offices (via a video conference) and with the focal points (which can also be contacted via a video conference if necessary).

2.4.2 The List

As has been shown, one of the main problems for the WHO is not the processing of the quantity of information it receives, but rather the ability to guarantee the quality of this information. All this information, whether from formal or informal sources, is recorded and put on a list drawn up by the Epidemic Intelligence and Risk Assessment team.[11] This is the list presented by Dr A. at the daily meeting held in the Upper SHOC Room.

This list is a crucial element in the health monitoring system established by the WHO in 1997 (Martinez 2000: 223). Its use makes the process of identifying and confirming cases that are out of the ordinary more transparent. The aim of this system, known as the 'Outbreak Verification System', is to verify, on the one hand, that the unofficial information is indeed current and, on the other hand, that the epidemic has an international dimension (Heymann and Rodier 2001: 349). The Outbreak Verification System makes use of rumours – the actual term used by the WHO – which are defined as non-official information relating to the risk of an epidemic on an international scale (Grein et al. 2000: 97). However, this list may also contain information received from official sources. It is this list that determines the expertise required and thus who will attend the meetings. If, for example, a cholera epidemic has been identified, cholera experts will come and bring their analyses and assessments of the subject. They will also be responsible for any monitoring required. The length of the meeting depends on the list and the ongoing events.

2.4.3 Databases for the Monitoring Process: From Rumour to Event

The mission of the Epidemic Intelligence and Risk Assessment team is to populate the databases used for decision making and so to create an archive of events. All events, whether confirmed or not, are entered into the database. Rumours are included alongside other validated sources or information. This creates the history of each event: when it took place, whether it was verified, how serious it was and so on.

The most important, and most commonly used, database is the Event Management System (EMS). It is an Access database. Information on events likely to present a risk to international public health is stored in this database. All stages – from receiving the information to making the decisions, via the verification phase – are recorded here, as well as resources and the records of communications (emails).

[11] As mentioned earlier, this team belongs to the Alert and Response Operations group, which is part of the Epidemic and Pandemic Alert and Response unit.

This database will record all the stages, from the opening of the event to its closure. It will record all the decisions taken, all the actions, all the updates and all the documents linked to them. So, everything will be there.

The information is primarily entered into the database by the Alert and Response Operations team. This database is particularly important as it forms the basis for the lists discussed during the daily morning meetings.

Another database used in this context is the Field Information Management System (FIMS). Using the FIMS it is possible to follow the development of a disease. The initial case is registered as case no. 1. This is followed by the contacts, such as father, mother, brother, etc. The team will then attempt to find out whether there have been any new cases or deaths. It is a very useful tool in the field. 'It is a system that travels with our teams' was how one of our interviewees described it.

There is also the Early Warning Alert and Response System (EWARN). According to this same interviewee, this is a system allowing countries 'to set up their own monitoring system'.

It is quite clear that these databases are indispensable tools in identifying a risk as rapidly as possible. They follow the various cases – from rumour to event – in order to have a clear overview of the situation. They also allow the 'memory' of an event to be carefully preserved, thereby making it possible to reassess the decisions taken.

2.4.4 Collaboration and Expanding the Sources of the Alert

The revised International Health Regulations, together with the new methods for managing epidemic risk, have contributed to changing the contours of the notion of risk. Nowadays, the WHO no longer waits for the notification of an event before taking any action. Rather, it makes great effort to anticipate as far as possible the arrival of an international health crisis. In order to pick up on very first indications of such an event, the very notion of risk needs to be redefined and expanded. The event can then be examined from its source; the investigation of the first signs of a probable epidemic begins immediately. There is an announcement of an irregularity identified using GPHIN, or one of the databases or a formal or informal source. The aim is constantly to make further progress. Scientists have become aware that human and animal diseases are closely linked. For this reason, the investigation of indications is no longer limited to humans but also includes animals. The management of a pandemic risk is expanding its circle of interest to ensure that any risk will be detected and treated. It has therefore become essential to monitor the animal world: 'We have realised that over the last 10 years, 75 % of emerging diseases were zoonoses'.

There is a certain degree of porosity in the border between animals and humans. This means that as well as detecting any risk of an epidemic, it is essential to take account of the risk of an epizootic, both of which also need to be considered in connection with food. As a result of this expansion of the area of risk, the WHO is faced with an even more complicated risk management task, as its field of action is also expanding. For this reason, the WHO is opening up its range of collaborative partners and approaching other organisations, such as the World Organisation for Animal Health (OIE) and the Food and Agriculture Organization (FAO). This expands the field of monitoring. Any rumours relating to animal cases are also included in risk reduction management operations. This was explained to us by a member of the Alert and Response team:

> In fact, this is an agreement reached between the three organisations – the OIE, the FAO and the WHO – to ensure that within each organisation there is a 'focal point' designated by the organisation and that, through this network [. . .] information is circulated and any rumour of animal origin is verified.

The case of avian influenza is a good example. The WHO set up a group of experts specialising in this field: the Global Influenza Programme. These experts study the pathogenic agents of the disease, but their primary focus in on avian influenza because

> it's a virus playing hide-and-seek between the world of birds and that of humans. We are interested in the H5N1 because that is the one that may cause a pandemic.

This is why they are studying every event:

> For avian influenza, and for probably no other disease, we are interested in every single case. The theory is that each case (. . .) could be the initial source of the pandemic. Thus we cannot afford to miss any of them (. . .).

To this end they work together with laboratories throughout the world in an attempt to pre-empt the risk and to avoid the uncontrolled and uncontrollable spread of avian influenza.

> What we say at the moment is that what we would like is, if not to be able to stop the start of a pandemic, at least to be able to put a brake on it in order to minimise its effect on the human populations. (. . .) Broadly speaking, what we have at the moment is a virus that is solely animal, but there have been some cases in humans. (. . .) This disease could be transmitted from person to person very quickly, and the whole planet could be affected. That could be tomorrow or in a month or in ten years. It's something that is very difficult to manage. In my opinion, it's the time factor that is the problem. (. . .) We would like to see signs as soon as possible that something is happening (. . .) then we could put measures in place to stop it spilling over into a pandemic.

The experts have available to them an evaluation scale which allows them to measure the risk. Depending on how it develops, they alert the authorities who can then put in place the emergency measures required. This scale consists of six levels:

> Roughly speaking, it goes from phase 1 – low risk – to phase 6 – pandemic (. . .). We go through the various stages. Currently [June 2007] we are in phase 3 – increased risk.

The risk of an epizootic is fully integrated into the human pandemic risk. There is no longer any barrier between human and animal pathology. The WHO has expanded and developed its fields of investigation and verification of the sources of alerts. It considers and verifies every case, both human and animal, with the aid and support of the OIE in particular, as well as of Member States. The notion of epidemic risk has been expanded and is investigated right back to its source. The human and the animal factors are essentially two sides of the same coin.

2.5 Analysis: From Centralisation to Globalisation

When this research project began, observing the SHOC Room was intended to provide an example of the centralisation of information. Our aim, at that time, was to understand how information was processed in a monitoring centre. We had assumed that the SHOC Room was a place where information would be centralised as part of crisis management. However, after completing the field study, we had to reconsider this idea.

2.5.1 Nuances in the Centralisation of Information

During the interviews, and also during the time we spent observing in the Headquarters, we realised that this idea of general centralisation did not apply to the way the SHOC Room operated when dealing with a pandemic crisis and that we needed to modify our ideas. We were frequently told that the WHO is a fully decentralised organisation. Indeed, the coordination system is not highly centralised, as the Headquarters prefers to delegate the actions required.

> Starting about a year ago [2006], we have been regionalising our teams. So we have the same teams at regional level. It's more logical because they are closer to the real situation. They can get information much more quickly. But we still work in close collaboration.

The Headquarters is made aware of the most important information and is involved in its verification. However, it is not the only place where decisions are made. The regional offices also play a key role in both communicating and verifying information. There is no exclusive centralisation of all information at the Headquarters, as was explained by one of our interviewees: 'Not all the decisions are taken in any one place'.

One of the actors we spoke to told us that

> The SHOC Room is the centre of our activities, but with a decentralised organisation. Many initiatives are taken by our regions. And sometimes they respond even before notifying us. There is no rigid system. We want to keep bureaucracy to a minimum, so that we can act when we need to.

The SHOC Room should be seen as a "hub" (November and De Conto 2010). It does play a key role in risk management as it enables the various experts from around the world to connect easily and allows authorities to obtain information in real time and to act, or even react, to events, thanks to the technical resources available to them.

WHO staff responsible for coordinating the actions of the various actors involved in risk management have access to sophisticated technological equipment. The SHOC Room has a range of technical instruments, enabling staff to process and disseminate the information obtained: computers, Internet, telephones and video conferences. These are part of the information and communication technology (ICT) equipment. The use of these instruments plays a major part in allowing decentralised coordination. Indeed, the various locations where decisions are made are not confined to the Headquarters in Geneva, as we had previously supposed. Thanks to modern technology, the actors spread across the world can communicate in real time, in collaboration with the other key experts. For example if the Headquarters has some information that needs verifying, the experts in that field meet in the SHOC Room, where they can communicate with the regional office closest to that case. They communicate by telephone or video conferencing, thereby enabling the intelligence to be transmitted directly to the appropriate person. It also works the other way round if the regional office has crucial information to pass on:

> The work is facilitated by being closer together, by having quicker access to telephones, by having too many video conferences to constantly run to and fro, by sitting face-to-face rather than being lined up like ducks in a row. It's purely for practical considerations; there is nothing else beyond that. We have telephone conferencing capabilities on every telephone, but if we want to link in 17 parties instead of two, if we have two or three video conferences, or if the Director-General is there, then we activate the SHOC. It's completely needs-driven and depends on whether it makes our life easier or not.

The same is true of the focal points that use the technical resources available. However, thanks to the new IHR, Member States are more actively involved in identifying cases and notifying the WHO. The network has thus taken on a global dimension and is no longer central. All Member States participate actively in transmitting information through their focal point.

As was mentioned earlier, the WHO makes use of an IT tool that is intended to group together and store all the information received: the database of the Event Management System (EMS). As part of its quest to decentralise the Headquarters activities in order to give the regions greater responsibility, the WHO has set up a 'global EMS'.

> I told you that we have regionalised our monitoring team across the six regions. Instead of waiting for information to arrive and to be entered into our database, we are constructing a 'global EMS'. This will be a 'web-based' database, making it accessible to all six regions and to the Headquarters. Thus, if the African region has an event involving Uganda or Kenya, they will enter the information and, in the Headquarters I will be able to see the information in the database. I will also be able to amend it or to add information. So, instead of relying on getting emails from the African region, I will know that something has been added. The plan is to have it up and running on 15 June 2008.[12] It will be introduced at regional level. It will save us a lot of time. It will also improve the flow of information, and the quality (. . .).

[12]In the meantime this system has been successfully brought into use.

In this way, the notion of centralising information has changed. The organisation of risk management within the WHO is no longer physically located in one place in the Headquarters, more exactly in the SHOC Room. Information will now be centralised within the 'global EMS', which will also mean that it can be more easily accessed and amended by the people concerned, at any time and from any location:

> It is not correct to say that it is centralised in the SHOC Room. It is centralised in the EMS. This is a global system. (. . .) It is not centralised in the SHOC Room; it is centralised using a platform known as the Event Management System.

In contrast, one of the roles of the WHO is to gather together the key experts required to deal with the new cases of a disease that have been identified. Using modern technology it is possible to put experts from around the world in contact with each other, in a manner appropriate to the urgency of the situation. Thus, there is a global coordination of events at one main point, which means that there are different geographical scales:

> The project talks to the regions electronically every day to exchange views through the event management system. They also have telephone conferences at least once a week when they go through all the events in the region. It's important to understand that the world has moved on and that expertise no longer resides in one place. Everyone has something to contribute: the regional aspect, the country aspect and the truly global aspect. Everybody needs to be heard and our job is to bring together the right people.

2.5.2 *'Living' Information*

Currently, an item of information can follow a variety of paths. It can be picked up by a number of protagonists and be transmitted in different ways. In a crisis, the speed at which it is picked up and then transmitted to the relevant actors is the determining factor. Following the development of new communication technologies, and thanks to the Internet and the increasing use made of it, information can be disseminated on a very 'small' scale. This makes it impossible to keep control of everything:

> You can't hide or control information, and you can't force it to go one way or another. We are constantly adapting to this ever-changing environment.
>
> Information just gets disseminated everywhere and some of it comes up to us here.

The WHO therefore has to adapt constantly to this new way in which information is communicated, which can no longer be centralised at one specific location:

> It's all becoming interconnected. The notion that you can centralise and control, information is screwed.

The WHO is paradoxically also very wary when it comes to rapid dissemination on a large scale. It is concerned about the possible onset of a sense of panic within the population, leading to panic-driven movements, which could have disastrous repercussions within a country or even at international level. For this reason, it is important to verify and confirm information with official institutions before taking decisions and communicating the status of a crisis situation to a wider audience. The WHO needs to monitor all the information it possesses, in a proactive manner:

> (...) in today's world you can't control information. It is going to leak out in some place or another or in many places all at once. And rather than waiting for that to happen, it requires a much more proactive approach to managing the media and the risk communication aspects.

While it is impossible to control the quantity of information on a global level, the WHO goes to great lengths to analyse the quality of the information. Risk management at the WHO includes verification and an examination of the truth of the information. These are the criteria which Member States and the experts then use to analyse and study the risks inherent in the situation under consideration and then act accordingly. In the words of the head of the Alert and Response Operations team:

> Obviously, information is available and nobody can control it, but it's the quality of information that counts. Even if there is tons of information about the same event, our role is to bring quality to the information that exists. Many others disseminate information on our behalf.

The dissemination of information is something that cannot necessarily be controlled, as the information can be picked up and sent around the world as widely as technology will permit. This information 'lives' or exists if it is received by an active receptor and subsequently confirmed to be true. In order for it to be useful, and to be used as long as it is still useful, it must be picked up by key actors, who will then transmit it to the appropriate people, who will act upon it if required. For the WHO it is the quality of the information that determines whether it will be kept. This is the goal of this risk management system, which uses these networks linking together different scales, people and decision levels.

2.5.3 Transcalar Circulation of Information

As a result of the decentralisation of the structure of the WHO, every scale has to be taken into consideration, both in the information circulation process and in decision-making. Communication does not only flow upwards or downwards, passing through a central point. The flow may circulate between the focal point and one of the regional offices, or between the focal point and the Headquarters, or even between a regional office and the Headquarters. If the information proves to be important, it will automatically pass through these three decision-making levels. Each of these stages forms an important node in the WHO risk management system. Each transmits information aimed at one of the other receptors or even both simultaneously. It is worth pointing out that the Headquarters represents one node, the regions 6 and the focal points 193 nodes (reflecting the number of Member States). However, they are mutually interdependent. When a crisis occurs, the information must reach all these levels in order to allow a response as fast as possible, as well as to respect the revised IHR. Also there are subnodes that interact with the principal actors, most notable the laboratories, the NGOs, the IOs the GPHIN and the GOARN.

The key actors involved in risk management are located at different levels: national (focal point), regional (regional office) and international (Headquarters). Their role is to circulate and disseminate information across the various levels. This management system and its associated efficient logistic system allow rapid and effective coordination (according to the WHO) in the event of an increased risk or a crisis. Each level is composed of experts, notably doctors and veterinarians.

The decisions taken within the nodes have repercussions at different levels, depending on the severity of the event. If there are only a few suspect cases, any intervention required will be arranged at the location in question, so at local level. If, however, the isolated case or cases spread to national and then to international level, the intervention measures will be taken on a corresponding scale. The primary aim of risk management in this case is to 'contain' the disease at local level as far as possible and then to eradicate it. For this reason the WHO developed the Global Outbreak Alert and Response Network, which makes it possible to respond immediately, as soon as the first suspect cases are reported:

> In terms of a preference, we would prefer the event to stay local and, if it can't stay local, at least only regional . . . We really would prefer the event not to become global. That's why many of WHO's activities are focused on building national capacities, so that events can be identified and dealt with as quickly as possible, so that they remain local issues.

The circulation of information is relevant to all geographical scales, each of which is important in its own way. However, it would be wrong to classify and restrict each node to a single geographical level. If we take the Headquarters, we see that it is in Geneva, in other words, in a canton (regional level) and in a country (national level). However, its role is to coordinate actions on an international scale, for example, by organising conferences between Member States. At the same time, the Headquarters may also affect the local level, for example, by sending a team of experts to Nairobi. The scales are not fixed, but random, being determined as a function of the aims and intentions of the actions agreed:

> Here at headquarters we work at global level, and regional offices are also international for us, because they deal with many countries.

2.6 Conclusion

This excursion into the WHO system for monitoring epidemic diseases brought home to us that information only 'lives' if it is grasped, translated and eventually transmitted to the next level, which should then proceed in the same way, and so on, forming a succession of 'holds'. A rumour follows this route and is transformed. It is reconfigured at every stage of the analysis, thanks to the interweaving of human and non-human actors. These are the socio-technical intermediaries that make it possible to create links between the different levels, ensuring that information can move rapidly across the networks and facilitating an effective system of monitoring the risk of a pandemic. The list, the Global Public Health Intelligence Network and the IHR are examples of such intermediaries. As for the severe acute respiratory syndrome, as it passed through the successive phases and translations, it gradually became 'SARS', progressing from a rumour to an identified epidemic. During the identification process, and the many translations it underwent, SARS has played a role in improving practices in detecting and managing epidemic risks on a global scale.

The intermediaries would not have the same capacity for translation if it were not for the information and communication technology resources available. ICT is able to amplify the range of possible human interventions, using diverse spatial logic. As we have seen, SARS played an important role in bringing about a review of the monitoring system. Paradoxically, to a certain extent it was new technology that enabled this virus to emerge, as once it had been identified it started to exist. It moved from a state in which it did not exist, to acquiring an individuality, on which an identity was conferred. It was precisely the circulation of this information, with the help of ITC that brought it to everyone's notice. For this reason, these technologies must be considered as actants allowing, in this case at the WHO, the creation of both new objects and new knowledge, which can lead to new actions.

Finally, we can highlight the fact that the intermediaries have played a role in expanding the notion of risk and in demonstrating the emergence of a new spatiality. The IHR now demands collaboration with new international organisations. The WHO and the GPHIN work closely with the World Organisation for Animal Health (OIE) and the Food and Agriculture Organization (FAO). In this way, risk is forcing an interstate organisation to go beyond the spatial logic on which it was founded and to follow the spatiality demanded by the risks. Furthermore, the barriers between the human and the animal world have also undergone considerable change, becoming more 'porous' – scientists have noted that 'over the last 10 years, 75 % of emerging diseases were zoonoses'. In addition to this, consideration must be given to food and food production and the need to get to grips with risks at source. In other words, it is not only disease that has proved to be a vector of change but rather the new spatiality inherent in the risk.

Risk management within the WHO has been improved to allow better coordination between experts, Member States and institutions, as well as to increase the effectiveness of actions carried out on site. The SARS epidemic, which has been mentioned as a turning point in the management of pandemic risk, allowed lessons to be learned within this international organisation and led to a rapid revision of risk management measures. All the phases involved in this process, which we have assimilated to 'the three stages of risk' (November 2002), have been included by the WHO. First, the 'before' and the detection of early indications anywhere in the world and their verification by experts at the earliest possible stage; then the 'during', with the emergency measures introduced in the field, notably by the GOARN; and finally, the 'after', including training experts in national laboratories (especially in developing countries), so that all Member States are able to stem the risk of a pandemic.

Another new feature of the WHO's working method is the increased emphasis on seeking to discover the source of the event, no longer restricting the search to humans. The risk of an epizootic and the need to monitor the quality of food are now firmly included in the prevention of epidemic risk. The notion of 'rumour' referred to by our interviewees also demonstrates a desire to strengthen and improve pandemic risk management. All information received is verified and analysed by the experts, including that emanating from unofficial sources. Since it is not possible to manage and control information on a global scale, the emphasis is now on the quality of the information so that it is usable and also used wisely by the various decision-making levels (Headquarters, regional offices and focal points).

The Outbreak Verification System works on the basis of rumour – it is important to recall that this is the term used by the WHO staff themselves – which it defines as non-official information regarding the risk of an epidemic on an international scale (Grein et al. 2000). For this reason, rumours are subject to particular vigilance. This vigilance (Jacques Roux 2006), requires there to have monitoring, together with a cautious approach to unknown or little known risks. The conditions required to deal with unexpected danger are adjusted to allow a response where needed. This is the way the WHO sees rumour, remaining vigilant at a very early stage in the process that may lead to an actual alert. We understand that SARS, before becoming a risk, also started as a rumour and required vigilance, monitoring and warning.

Following the discussion of the agenda at the daily meeting, the Headquarters contacts regional and national offices (focal points), which then also proceed with the task of verification. (Generally speaking, the verification process takes 24–48 h.[13]) Once rumour becomes information, having passed through the stages of verification and becoming official according to the WHO, it is transformed into a fact. At this point the actual action mechanism (the response) is initiated, following a further round of discussions in the SHOC Room. Within the WHO, it seems to have been established that 'information lives', as one of our interviewees put it, and it is simply not possible to control the vast amount of information that is available across the globe. For this reason, the WHO has chosen to adopt a strategy of verifying the quality of the information. This is the construction of an item of information verified by the structures of the WHO, whereby the list acts an intermediary, allowing the status of information to be negotiated.

The circulation of information is no longer centralised, rather it has become a global process. Information and communication technologies make it possible to operate across the different geographic and institutional levels using a decentralised organisation. For this reason, we can state that information circulates on the basis of relations of connexity. This term 'describes the density of the links between the nodes of a network' (Brunet et al. 1992). As we have already seen, the transmission of information within the WHO takes place within the networks, where it transits through three major nodes: the Headquarters, the regional offices and the national focal points in the Member States. In addition, this same proximity can be found at

[13]This was the information given to us by Dr A during our interview.

all levels and is intensified by the regionalisation of activities within the WHO. The teleconferences between the experts (from these three nodes) are a good example of this connexity. The transmission of information does not depend on the physical distances between locations, but makes use of platforms and networks that negate the geographical distances. The transmission of the information and the communication between experts is possible thanks to technology (in this case the video conferences) and can be achieved in 'real time', with no physical or temporal obstacle preventing the information from reaching the desired target. This makes for greater precision regarding the decisions made, the choice of the most appropriate personnel and the action aimed at the location or locations affected.

Air travel has shortened distances. Travellers can go from one country to another, without having to suffer the inconveniences caused by the climate or the territory. The same is true of viruses. They are carried round the world by tourists and can easily adapt to their new environment. Microbes are transmitted in a similar way. National borders have been eliminated, both with regard to the spread of microorganisms and in the management of epidemic risk across the globe, thanks to the interconnecting networks that have been established. The borders, and the links to a particular territory, exist only in terms of identifying the source of the risk. As soon as an event has been detected, the networks take on the key role in ensuring the circulation of information and also the management of epidemic risks within the WHO.

References

Ambassade de France en Chine. (2013). Le SRAS, dix ans après. Available via *Bulletins électroniques Chine.*http://www.bulletins-electroniques.com/actualites/074/74290.htm. Accessed 5 Dec 2013.

Birkland, T. A. (2007). *After disaster: Agenda setting, public policy, and focusing events.* Washington, DC: Georgetown University Press.

Brownstein, J. S., Freifeld, C. C., & Madoff, L. C. (2009). Digital disease detection – Harnessing the web for Public Health Surveillance. *New England Journal of Medicine, 21*(360), 2153–2157.

Brunet, R., Ferras, R., & Thery, H. (1992). *Les mots de la géographie: dictionnaire critique.* Montpellier/Paris: GIP Reclus, La Documentation française.

Callon, M., & Law, J. (1997). L'irruption des non-humains dans les sciences humaines. In B. Reynaud (Ed.), *Les limites de la rationalité, Les figures du collectif, Colloque de Cerisy* (Vol. 2, pp. 99–118). Paris: La Découverte.

Chateauraynaud, F., & Torny, D. (1999). *Les sombres précurseurs: une sociologie pragmatique de l'alerte et du risque.* Paris: Éditions de l'École des Hautes Études en Sciences Sociales.

Department of Global Capacities, Alert and Response. (2013). *Activity report 2012.* Lyon/Geneva: WHO.

Grein, T. W., Kamara, K.-B. O., Rodier, G. R., Plant, A. J., Bovier, P., Ryan, M. J., et al. (2000). Rumors of disease in the global village: Outbreak verification. *Emerging Infectious Diseases, 6*(2), 97–102.

Heymann, D. L. (2006). SARS and emerging infectious diseases: A challenge to place global solidarity above national sovereignty. *Annals Academy of Medicine, 35*(5), 350–353.

Heymann, D. L., & Rodier, G. R. (2001). Hot spots in a wired world: WHO surveillance of emerging and re-emerging infectious diseases. *Lancet Infectious Diseases, 1*, 345–353.

Heymann, D. L., & Rodier, G. R. (2004). Global surveillance, national surveillance, and SARS. *Emerging Infectious Diseases, 10*(2), 173–175.

Keller, M., Blench, M., Tolentino, H., Freifeld, C. C., Mandl, K. D., Mawudeku, A., et al. (2009). Use of unstructured event-based reports for global infectious disease surveillance. *Emerging Infectious Diseases, 15*(5), 689–695.

King, N. B. (2004). The scale politics of emerging diseases. *Osiris, 19*, 62–76.

Latour, B. (1987). *Science in action*. Cambridge, MA: Harvard University Press.

Latour, B. (2004). *Politics of Nature: How to Bring the Sciences Into Democracy*. Cambridge, MA: Harvard University Press.

Martinez, L. (2000). Global infectious disease surveillance. *International Journal of Infectious Diseases, 4*(4), 222–228.

Mawudeku, A., & Blench, M. (2006, August 8–12). *Global Public Health Intelligence Network (GPHIN)*. Paper presented at the 7th conference of the Association for Machine Translation in the Americas, Cambridge, MA.

Michelson, E. (2005). Dodging a bullet: WHO, SARS, and the Successful Management of Infectious Disease. *Bulletin of Science Technology Society, 25*(5), 379–386.

Mykhalovskiy, E., & Weir, L. (2006). The global public health intelligence network and early warning outbreak detection – A Canadian contribution to global public health. *Canadian Journal of Public Health, 97*(1), 42–44.

November, V. (2002). *Les territoires du risque: le risque comme objet de réflexion géographique*. Bern: Peter Lang.

November, V., & De Conto, K. (2010). Politique des pandémies: De la détection des risques à l'action. In S. Houdart & O. Thiery (Eds.), *Humains, Non-Humains: comment repeupler les sciences sociales* (pp. 101–110). Paris: La Découverte.

Pollack, M. P. (2013). Digital disease detection. In E. Mordini & M. Green (Eds.), *Internet-based intelligence in public health emergencies* (pp. 41–64). Washington, DC: Ios Press.

Poulain, M. (2003). La gestion par l'OMS des situations d'urgence sanitaire de portée internationale: l'exemple du syndrome respiratoire aigu sévère (SRAS). Available via *Actualité et Droit International*.http://www.ridi.org/adi/articles/2003/200311pou.htm. Accessed 17 Mar 2005.

Rémy, E. (1993). Comment saisir la rumeur? *Ethnologie Française, 23*(4), 591–601.

Roux, J. (Ed.). (2006). *La vigilance active: une expérience partagée*. Saint-Etienne: Presses Universitaires de Saint-Etienne.

WHO. (2003). Chapter 5: SARS: Lessons from a new disease. In *The World Health Report 2003 – Shaping the future*. Geneva: World Health Organization.

WHO. (2006). Openness is key in fight disease outbreaks. Available via *Bulletin of the World Health Organization*. http://www.who.int/bulletin/volumes/84/10/06-011006/en/. Accessed 5 Dec 2013.

WHO. (2007). *The World Health Report 2007. A safer future. Global public health security in the 21st century*. Geneva: World Health Organisation.

Chapter 3
Communicating Information and Risk Management in Madagascar

The circulation of information is a crucial element in relation to risk. In the particular case of the island of Madagascar, it is capital. This territory is regularly hit by a series of recurrent risks, notably cyclones and other natural disasters. These have left the population weakened and villages devastated. The difficulties of getting around and of communication between strategic points, independently of the actual geographical distances involved, are significant obstacles to the understanding of crisis situations and, most importantly, to their management. This management takes place at different levels and is complicated by the fact that it combines several geographical levels (national, regional and local). This chapter examines these structures and the ways in which information is communicated in difficult situations.

One of the reports of the United Nations Secretary General on the International Strategy for Disaster Reduction (United Nations 2011) speaks of a significant increase for 2010 in the number of disasters, the scale of destruction of economic and social property caused, and the devastating effects on populations. According to the Annual Disaster Statistical Review 2009 (Vos et al. 2010), there has been an increase in the number of natural disasters over the past 20 years, particularly as a result of hydrometeorological disasters: on average 190 million people were affected annually during the 1990s, compared with an average of 243 million during the decade from 2000. Climatologists' forecasts indicate that this trend will continue: the most vulnerable populations will be increasingly affected by climate-related disasters (Buffet 2010). This highlights the fact that the risk of disaster is concentrated geographically and follows the growing exposure of people and property to natural hazards. In 2010, 394 disasters caused by natural hazards were recorded. They affected over 203 million people and caused more than 238,000 deaths and over 77.9 billion dollars' worth of economic damage (Guha-Sapir et al. 2011). 2013 was also a very difficult year, as Madagascar was hit by a series of cyclones, notably Haruna in February 2013.

V. November, Y. Leanza, *Risk, Disaster and Crisis Reduction*,
DOI 10.1007/978-3-319-08542-5_3

According to the ISDR, reducing vulnerability requires a greater knowledge of risks and the development of appropriate actions. This UN organisation has set about developing field libraries intended to combat the lack of information on these matters in the developing countries most at risk from disasters.[1]

It is within the framework of monitoring one of these field libraries, recently introduced into Madagascar, that this study was carried out in order *to analyse the information communication process in a crisis situation.*

The initial contacts in the field were established through the national platform for risk and crisis management. The main actors involved in crisis management were to be found within the BNGRC (Bureau National pour la Gestion des Risques et Catastrophes – National Office for Risk and Disaster Management) at various strategic locations: in the crisis centre in Antananarivo and also in the towns directly affected by the disaster, such as Maroantsetra, in order to see directly how effectively information was circulating during the emergency and thereafter.

Field study work generally encounters unforeseen events and difficulties. Institutional changes within the BNGRC, as well as an emergency situation created by climatic hazards, meant that the study in Madagascar was no exception to this rule.

The political situation in Madagascar proved to be unstable. As part of the preparation for the field trip, contacts were established in advance between the study team and the then Executive Secretary of the BNGRC, Mr Jacky Randimbiarison. He had been informed of the arrival of the team and had arranged to facilitate contact with other parties involved. In the event, Mr Randimbiarison was replaced by Colonel Jean Rakotomalala a week before the team arrived. In spite of his considerable workload, Colonel Rakotomalala welcomed the team on its arrival and facilitated contacts with the various partners of the BNGRC in both Antananarivo and Maroantsetra.[2]

Madagascar is located in the Intertropical Convergence Zone (ITCZ) and is regularly threatened by violent winds and lashing rain brought by the series of tropical depressions that form over the Indian Ocean and travel from east to west from December to April. These frequent hazards are generally moderate or limited in size, although major cyclones are also possible, such as Danaé in 1974 or Justine in 1982. In addition, widespread poverty, demographic growth, food insecurity and the decline of the natural environment have rendered the Madagascan population very vulnerable in the face of natural disasters. During the cyclone season of 2008, Madagascar was hit by two tropical cyclones, Ivan and Fame (category

[1]This programme was launched in 2004 following the tsunami in the Indian Ocean. The first field libraries supplied were in English. Madagascar opted to develop the first field libraries in French, using a similar model. For more information on the role played by the ISDR within the United Nations, see Revet (2009).

[2]Later, the political crisis of 2009 also occasioned the replacement of senior figures we had met, but the institutional structures were maintained. In the course of the text, any significant changes since our trip in 2007 will be indicated.

4 cyclones with winds reaching over 230 kph). 324,000 people were affected, of whom 191,000 lost their homes and 100 were killed. 10 % of infrastructure was destroyed (schools, basic health-care centres, bridges, etc.). Damage and loss were estimated at 333 million USD, equivalent to 4 % of GDP (Buffet 2010). According to the Maplecroft Institute, Madagascar is the world's third most vulnerable country to climate change, after Bangladesh and India (Maplecroft 2011).

The field trip took place towards the end of the cyclone season in Madagascar, which lasts roughly from November to April (summer in the southern hemisphere). We arrived right in the middle of an emergency: Cyclone Indlala, which hit the north of the island on 14 and 15 March 2007, caused significant damage, in the form of destruction and flooding. Although the various reports and figures do not always agree, Indlala is estimated to have been responsible for around 150 deaths and 200,000 other victims.

Then, on 3 April, another cyclone, Jaya, hit the north of the country. Although less violent than Indlala, Jaya nonetheless caused considerable flooding, creating many victims and requiring emergency measures (see Figs. 3.1 and 3.2). The attention of the BNGRC and its partners was fully concentrated on providing relief as rapidly as possible. Despite the emergency, the vast majority of the actors questioned responded favourably to our request for an interview. The tension also decreased during the course of our stay and the situation gradually calmed down.

In total, our research was focused on around 30 interviews and numerous informal meetings. It was decided to conduct an in-depth analysis of 25 of these interviews. In the interests of the research, it was important to vary the perspectives and the discourse. For this reason, we took care to ensure the diversity of the actors and the variation in the geographical scales of the levels of intervention. The participants were drawn from Madagascan institutions (the old and the new Executive Secretary of the BNGRC, a project leader from the BNGRC, a member of the Civil Protection Corps, a Member of Parliament, a fokontany (village) leader, a school principal, a representative of the Madagascan meteorological service, a representative of the early warning service and a university professor), from the population (inhabitants of the village of Ankofa), from the UN system (UNDP, World Bank), from international NGOs (Care International, Medair, and Doctors of the World), from Madagascan NGOs (Madagascan National Red Cross) and from the international system (International Federation of Red Cross and Red Crescent Societies, European Commission and French Civil Protection Cooperation Programme).

In order to understand the issue of the circulation of information in Madagascar, it is important to describe the Madagascan situation in terms of risks but also in terms of the existing organisation, institutional structures and all actors involved in crisis management. The description of this context will help us to understand the local mechanisms of the circulation of information and usual practices.

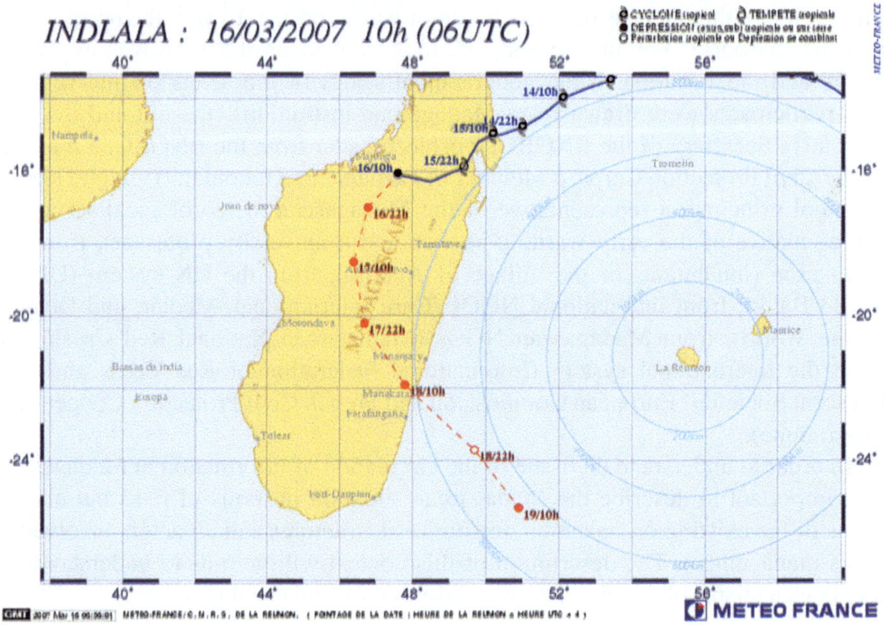

Figs. 3.1 and 3.2 Satellite view and trajectory of the approaching Cyclones Indlala and Jaya (With kind permission from Météo-France©)

3.1 Risk Management in Madagascar

3.1.1 The Institutional Structures of Crisis Management

For a clear understanding of risk management in Madagascar, it is important to give an overview, albeit a very brief summary, of the institutional structure surrounding it at the time the research was undertaken: it is based on the period from March to April 2007 and includes no detailed analysis of the changes that have taken place since. In fact, despite the political crisis of January 2009, the institutional structure has remained stable. Any significant changes will be mentioned.

The first element is the Madagascar Action Plan (MAP). This sets out the broad outline of the policy of the government of the former President Marc Ravalomanana during his 5-year term of office 2007–2012. This is a national strategic development framework, which was new at the time of our visit, together with a plan of action for the medium term, which more or less follows on from the Document Stratégique pour la Réduction de la Pauvreté (DSRP), which was established in 2003.

The MAP, designed to be 'a bold plan for rapid development', lists commitments in eight areas:

1. Responsible governance
2. Joined-up infrastructure
3. Transformation of education
4. Rural development
5. Health, family planning and the fight against HIV/AIDS
6. Strong economic growth
7. The environment
8. National solidarity

Although the area of risk management does not feature explicitly in this general policy document, it is nevertheless implicit in certain of these commitments. Our interviewees frequently mentioned the MAP during our discussions. It would seem that the MAP is a positive influence on risk management in Madagascar, as it is accepted by all and provides a structure for action.

With regard to risks, the National Strategy for the Management of Risks and Disasters (SNGRC – Stratégie nationale de gestion des risques et catastrophes) acts as a reference. This document, which originally appeared in 2003, and was revised in 2010 (Rodriguez 2010), first analyses the risks and vulnerability, as well as capacities, weaknesses, requirements and priorities, and then sets out the foundations of a Madagascan policy on risk and crisis management, together with the corresponding institutional and financial structures. Finally, the SNGRC identifies 6 major axes or strategic priorities:

- The implementation of institutional mechanisms for risk and crisis management
- Long-term capacity strengthening for risk and crisis management at national, provincial, local and municipality level

- The development of a comprehensive information system
- The development of long-term financial mechanisms
- General reduction of risk and vulnerability
- Regional and international cooperation

Like the MAP, the SNGRC is supported by international organisations. There are also numerous reference documents that guide the action in certain areas. In addition, there is a contingency plan, an action plan for rural development, etc.

In the first version, the document states that the National Council for the Management of Risks and Disasters (CNGRC) constitutes

> the principal institution for the coordination of the management of risks and disasters in Madagascar. (...) It is the highest advisory body. (...) It is not a rigid structure centred on its members, but rather a flexible institution centred on the specialised tasks and 'projects'. It is a functional representation rather than a figurative one. It has produced teams of key members organised into Crisis Cells to deal with specific emergencies (cholera, locusts, cyclones, etc.). The CNRGC and its temporary Crisis Cells are supported by the BNGRC.

In terms of its composition and its operation, the CNRGC constitutes an inter-ministerial council which is chaired by the prime minister and meets at least once a month. Decisions are implemented by its 'operational arm', the National Office for the Management of Risks and Disasters (BNGRC). The BNGRC is responsible for coordinating the various agencies and partners (Madagascan government and authorities, financial backers, international organisations, NGOs, etc.) with regard to prevention and relief and emergency response as well as restoration and construction. (See also the presentation of this organ at pt. 1.2.) The national system is mirrored at lower levels: the coordination role is replicated at provincial and regional level, in the form of provincial and regional councils for the management of risks and disasters (CPGRC and CRGRC) etc. The decree on national policy relating to the management of risks and disasters, adopted in 2005, created a fine mesh network of risk and disaster management committees covering all levels, with those at provincial level (CPGRC), regional level (CRGRC) and district level (CDGRC) still in existence. In addition, there are risk and disaster management councils at municipality level (CCGRC) and local level in the fokontany (CLGRC).[3] The BNGRC is also responsible for organising the meetings of the CRIC (National Humanitarian Platform), a body which coordinates the various parties involved: sponsors, NGOs and Madagascan government.

> In fact, the CRIC has no official status. No resources are specifically allocated to it. In current practice it acts primarily as a platform for discussion and exchange of information that brings together those in charge of the humanitarian organisations and NGOs. It makes no decisions but simply offers recommendations, advice and personal opinion on a particular situation. (Rodriguez 2010)

[3] A *fokontany is* a Madagascan administrative subdivision and is equivalent to a village.

3.1.2 The Focal Point in Madagascar: The BNGRC

Created in 1970 as the Conseil National de Secours (CNS) (National Assistance Council),[4] the BNGRC (National Office for the Management of Risks and Disasters) is attached to the Ministry of the Interior and is the operational arm of the CNGRC National Council for the Management of Risks and Disasters, an inter-ministerial organisation headed by the prime minister. Since 2006, the picture has been completed by the Cellule pour la prévention et la gestion des urgences (CPGU) (Cell for the prevention and management of emergencies) set up at the instigation of the World Bank (Morisset 2010).

The BNGRC is responsible for coordinating emergency measures at national level and, if the situation allows, also at local level. In a crisis situation, the members – representatives of national ministries, international organisations (IOs) and local and international non-government organisations (NGOs) – gather together in the premises in Antananarivo, within the CRIC (National Humanitarian Platform) to discuss what action should be taken. These meetings offer the opportunity to exchange information and to discuss the sectors in which the various participants are involved. Outside the cyclone season these meetings take place twice a month.

In the words of the then Executive Secretary, the BNGRC is there 'primarily to coordinate and steer'. It is 'an organ providing general coordination between the financial backers, the NGOs and the government'. More exactly, its terms of reference include the coordination between minsters and national and international partners with regard to:

1. The prevention and alleviation of risks
2. Emergency response
3. Restoration and construction

Its mission also includes the coordination of actions in the island's provinces, through the district and local disaster risk management committees. It organises training, develops and implements information programmes and acts as an operational headquarters during a crisis.

In addition to those already described, there are also, in parallel, specialised structures and agencies such as the National Anti-locust Centre (Centre National Anti-acridien (CNA)), the National Committee for Water and Sanitation (Comité National de l'Eau et Assainissement (CNEA)) and the Anti-Cholera Coordination and Support Group (Groupe de Coordination et Appui à la Lutte contre le Choléra (GCALC)).

[4] The principal role of the CNS is to define a specific policy for the prevention and relief of disasters and for emergency intervention to safeguard the lives and property of the population, with a view to sustainable development.

3.1.3 The Roles and Responsibilities of the Actors

Table 3.1. gives an overview of the interviewees, grouped as a function of their responsibilities in the risk chain set out in Chap. 1 and with reference to the three phases of risk: before, during and after. This table summarises the responsibilities of the actors with regard to risk management, be that prevention (before) or response (after), based on what the interviewees told us during our discussions.[5]

We elected to focus on four types of actors whose characteristics are typical of each of the 'phases' of risk.

3.1.3.1 'Before': The Early Warning System (SAP)

This Early Warning System covers two provinces in Madagascar: Fianarantsoa and Toliara (in the south), consisting of nine regions and twenty-two municipalities. The system produces monthly bulletins based on questionnaires completed by an observer in the municipality who has received training in areas relating to food security, such as livestock farming, pasture management, water distribution points, food consumption, state of the market and health indicators. The aim is to detect 'unusual behaviour patterns in the municipality or unusual population movements' at the earliest possible stage:

> Our intention is to provide our partners with a methodology which considers the impact of external factors on both the accessibility and the availability of food. To offer our partners early detection, an early warning for the population groups unable to meet all their needs for the year. This methodology takes account of risks such as insufficient rainfall, flooding, invasions of locusts, etc., as well as economic risks. For certain population groups, access to food is determined by their income level.

Once the forecast for food problems has been established, it is incorporated into a scale of risks:

> This forecast sets out how we expect the communities to get through the lean season, by making recommendations for certain municipalities. These might include suggestions relating to distribution, offering food as payment for work, or other similar ideas. This initial forecast is then refined later in the year to produce a definitive forecast. During the lean season we carry out a diagnosis to see whether our forecast was correct.

The agency then further anticipates the risk and produces fresh information, obtained through observation and measurement. This information is mainly destined for the BNGRC.

---

[5]This table reflects the approaches of the actors at the time the field study was carried out. In the meantime, the approaches of certain actors have changed. For example, since 2008, Doctors of the World has moved into disaster risk reduction (DRR) in the before phase. Since October 2008, ECHO, through its DIPECHO division, has also funded the before and during phases, and CARE is now very much engaged in restoration.

Table 3.1 Actors and responsibilities in Madagascar (in alphabetical order)

Actors		Before	During	After
BNGRC (National Office for Risk and Disaster Management)	1	Prevention, simulation exercises, procedure handbooks, evaluation sheets	Coordination of teams, warning system, humanitarian aid	Evaluation
	2	Awareness, training, "trunk", simulation exercises, contingency plan	Emergency plans, coordination of teams	–
	3	Prevention, training, books, handbooks (since 2005)	Responsibility for communication	–
	4	Prevention, procedure manuals, contingency plan, training the trainers (e.g. guides for teachers), training local communities, evaluation sheets, awareness, simulation exercises, "mobile" library	Tools for warnings (e.g. weather updates), alerts	Evaluation
CARE	1	Define vulnerability in Madagascan	Emergency operations	–
			E.g. famine: provide food supplies	
Civil Protection Corps (CPC)	1	–	Provide day-to-day assistance, interventions	–
	2	Preparation, training and instruction of military, prevention	In state of alert, interventions, provide food and medicines, build shelters	Set up disaster prevention projects to avoid repetition
	3	Training, preparation on military, awareness raising among population	Response to disasters, relief operations, supply of food and medicines to victims	Rehabilitation, damage assessment
Doctors Of The World	1	Monitoring programmes: HIV, malnutrition indicators	Emergency programmes	–
		Sets up specialist libraries		

(continued)

Table 3.1 (continued)

Actors		Before	During	After
ECHO	1	–	–	Funding of IOs and NGOs rebuilding projects, e.g. road infrastructure, water points.
FID	1	–	–	Rebuilding of infrastructure, evaluation reports of post-cyclone damage, funding of sub-projects
Local Representatives	1	Radio awareness raising programmes	Information transmitted by radio, "local aid committee"	Listening to population,
	2	Awareness raising among the population (radio)	Radio broadcasts	–
	3	Gives recommendations to school pupils	–	–
Malagasy Red Cross (CRM)	1	Prevention, identification of risks, simulation exercises, "strategic project" 2007–2010	Emergency aid, e.g. tents	Repair of roads, construction of dykes
	2	Simulation exercises, planning	Humanitarian aid, coordination (and evaluation of emergency operations)	Rehabilitation
MEDAIR	1	Aims to anticipate to reduce vulnerability	Re-establishing access to drinking water (in time of crisis), disinfection of wells, distribution of buckets	Restoration, evaluation
	2	Simulation exercises, prevention, brochures and posters, discussions	Relief action plan, emergency access to drinking water and disinfection of wells, distribution of buckets and jerry cans.	Evaluation (forms), restoration
Meteorology	1	Monitoring of cyclones, awareness raising in schools, warning 'ads'	Alerts the BNGRC in the event of cyclone risk, weather warning updates, distribution of information (television, radio, press)	–

SAP (Early Warning System)	1	Monthly warning bulletins, forecasts, recommendations	Diagnostics	–
UNISDR	1	Preparation of field library in Geneva	Distribution of field library within BNGRC	–
UNDP	1	Prevention in development plans, project: "Reinforcement of implementation of the national strategy for disaster management"	Emergency measures: "Inter-Agency Standing Committee"	–
			"Flash appeal"	
	2	Establishing contingency plans	Coordination between different UN agencies, facilitation of interface between NGOs and government partners	Disaster response
University	1	Simulation exercises among the population, education in schools, SSBs	Transmits earthquake warnings to BNGRC	–
World Bank	1	Funding prevention project with the BNGRC		Funding projects

3.1.3.2 'Before-During': Identification (Meteorology)

This actor is mainly concerned with monitoring tropical cyclones and has a dual role. Firstly, this service works to increase the awareness of the population to the risk of cyclones, operating primarily through the schools:

> We encourage schools to visit our headquarters. That's our thing. There are lots of schools that come and visit the meteorological service and we grab the opportunity to explain to them what happens. We also have a weather programme on television.

Secondly, in collaboration with the BNGRC, it keeps the partners involved in risk and disaster management in Madagascar informed of the development of risks and broadcasts a 'public service message that explains what people should do during a cyclone'.

Thanks to the satellite stations and the bulletins issued by the World Meteorological Organization (WMO), this service is able to anticipate and identify the arrival of a cyclone. It plays a crucial role in the immediate warning: 'the meteorological service is the only body putting out warnings', a manager explained to us. There are three phases of alert: a cautionary notice, notice of a threat and notice of imminent danger. This alert acts as the trigger for actions to reduce the effects of the disaster: communication of information to all geographical levels, coordination of the different actors involved, help for the population, etc.

The BNGRC and the meteorological service use the media to communicate information: television, national radio and the press. The message transmitted is intended to be clear and accurate, using 'appropriate language'. Once a cyclone has been announced, weather flash reports on the radio give instructions every three hours.

3.1.3.3 'During-After': Action (The Madagascar Civil Protection Corps)

This is a unit of the Madagascan Army, which belongs to the Ministry of Defence. The Civil Protection Corps was set up in November 2003 to provide disaster response, and the soldiers are trained to provide assistance in a crisis situation. The CPC 'participates in prevention, relief and restoration operations'. The CPC is based in Antananarivo, but in a crisis, a team is sent to the affected area. This operational section is on constant alert, in order to be able to respond and aid victims as rapidly as possible.

Over the last year, the CPC has strengthened its collaboration with non-governmental organisations:

> Our role is to support the NGOs' logistic needs, to ensure that medicines and food can be taken as close to the victims as possible, as quickly as possible. We also work with local operators who have small boats, for example to transport food. (...) We have a medical team that can be sent to isolated areas. We also have a disease vector control team.

The actions carried out by the CPC differ according to the state of the disaster but include providing aid to victims, clearing roads, supplying the population with food and other basic needs, carrying out an inventory of the communication system, educating the population, etc.

The CPC receives and implements instructions from the BNGRC and the CRIC. Once the immediate emergency has passed, it works with the BNGRC to assess the damage. Through the lessons learned, knowledge of the risk can grow and evolve:

> We adapt our education and training a lot to take account of our experiences in the field. That's why we always try to adapt our knowledge of the risk on the basis of what we know, and to adapt it as we go along. We try not to have too rigid a definition so that we can be flexible and deal with what we find.

3.1.3.4 'After': The Investment Fund for Development (FID)

The Investment Fund for Development is an agency funded by the state of Madagascar and the World Bank, with a view to implementing the community development programme. Its primary role is to rebuild infrastructure damaged as a result of natural disasters. Our interviewee was involved with assessing the damage and producing reports to be passed up through the organisation, which could then define the plan of action and how it should be funded:

> When an event occurs, the Investment Fund for Development repairs the anti-cyclone infrastructure, and the ability of those who benefit from it to maintain these facilities is improved so that they become more resistant to damage.

The Fund also finances community level subprojects in order to help reduce poverty and promote development. To this end the organisation trains the local actors to manage their own infrastructure themselves, both the technical and the financial aspects:

> We provide the members of the association of beneficiaries with simple technical and financial management training. For example, where infrastructure is intended for the local authority, such as a primary school, if this is carried out as a "classic community project", we set up an association of beneficiaries and a project cell. We then give them some training in how to award contracts, and how to monitor them when the work is taking place. That is all pretty technical. But we also teach them about financial management for paying their partners, such as the planning office and companies in general.

Risk management in Madagascar is structured round the BNGRC, and some of the information relating to the before, during and after circulates during the CRIC meetings. However, while decisions may be taken at national level, the information frequently originates at international level – for example, the WMO meteorological bulletins, cooperation with Réunion Island (seismic data), international conferences, etc. – or at local level, as demonstrated by the way the Early Warning System, local NGOs and the mayors, etc. operate. It should be noted, however, that the Madagascan meteorological service also performs its own trajectory calculations when a cyclone is approaching the island. There are a considerable number of actors involved in risk management, with various functions and at various levels.

Furthermore, a rhythm marked by two seasons – the prevention season and the emergency season – determines the different risk 'times'. 'The emergency season is the implementation of the prevention season' is how one interviewee explained it. According to the Executive Secretary of the BNGRC, the emergency period lasts 5 months and the prevention period 7 months, during which time his aim is to improve consultation and the circulation of information.

3.1.4 The Terminology and the Categories of Alert Used

The table setting out the roles of the actors (Table 3.1) illustrates clearly that most concentrate their activities in a prevention-intervention continuum, even if in some cases their activities are evidently restricted to one phase only. A quick overview of the terminology reveals that three series of terms are commonly used:

3.1.4.1 Prevention, Alleviation, Preparation, and Intervention

These terms are used by a lot of actors, from Civil Protection, the BNGRC, the Malagasy Red Cross and other NGOs. For example, we were told on several occasions:

> When I talk about the forms of intervention, it's mainly for the three phases of the development cycle of the natural disaster. These are prevention, alleviation and preparation, both in the emergency aid phase and the restoration and reconstruction phase.

For these actors, alleviation relates to the actions undertaken in order to prevent the risk impacting on the population. Prevention is a matter of making the population more aware of what they should be doing to avoid the effects of the disaster as far as possible. Vulnerability – another word commonly used here – refers to a situation where a weakened population struggles to cope with a negative event. Finally, as one interviewee put it, resilience is the ability of the population to withstand a disaster:

> When we've done the awareness raising we've passed on the message that to prepare themselves they need to stock up and to strengthen the roofing and so on. The women and children need to have the necessary means to hold out for a certain period of time when the cyclone comes through. So it's the ability of the population to withstand the disaster. So we tend to focus on education and awareness raising. In August 2005 we started up training in Madagascar.

This continuum also applies to others, as was explained by another key actor in intervention in Madagascar:

> There need to be coordinated actions around the highest stakes. And we divide these mitigation actions – we call them mitigation – into three categories: prevention, prediction and intervention.

3.1.4.2 Vulnerability

The stakes – the word has already been used. Everything revolves around this term which, when talking about disasters, is translated as 'vulnerability'. By way of illustration, we can offer the way in which a local representative living in Maroantsetra used the word:

> In this region the risk is constantly growing. The reason for that is, in spite of the NGOs who are working here to protect nature, we are witnessing the deterioration of the environment ... This is making vulnerability greater, flooding worse, for example. There shouldn't be flooding on this scale, but if there is no reforestation in the area upstream it's going to get worse and worse and that wouldn't happen if the environment hadn't been damaged.

We also heard the word used by several NGOs. This is what one representative told us:

> When we are defining vulnerability we analyse risk situations, looking for instance at climate-related hazards, the economic context and collective risks. In terms of the level of risk, we analyse the ability of the population to withstand these risks. In particular, the diversity of income-generating activities, the options for emigration and the various strategies that could be put in place to make it possible to adapt. Once we've had a look at these different components we can give each municipality, which is our analysis unit, a category of structural vulnerability. The assessment should consist of examining how these different factors are influenced by external events, taking account of the vulnerability context of the current year. So there might be a reduction of the potential rice crop because it will be affected by flooding, or livestock farming could be affected by disease, for example. In this way the picture changes according to the situation and the level of vulnerability.

3.1.4.3 The Warning

This term indicates the imminence of the danger. There are three levels of alert, explained briefly below. The categories that define them are extremely precise for the meteorological service, which works with three levels: a cautionary notice, notice of a threat and notice of imminent danger:

> We have three phases of alert. The instructions are different for each phase. So we put out that broadcast. When we announce a cyclone, we broadcast weather updates every three hours. And before each update we broadcast that public service message so that people remember what they should do. (...) Journalists ask us questions as well: what is a cautionary notice exactly? What should people do? What does notice of a threat mean?

Some NGOs have also established alert levels:

> We are on alert from November onwards, and we try to update everything. From December onwards, we are in the cyclone period so we go up a level. After that we have alert levels and, depending on the level, we have intervention procedures that set out what we need to do. It's always the same: the first priority is to restore access to drinking water, through the distribution of Sûr'Eau and buckets. Once that has been done, the next thing is to disinfect the wells, and after that we move into the restoration phase, then into the vulnerability phase and that's ... well. It's part of development.

In the field, the alert phases also correspond to distinct actions that have to be undertaken:

> We have five alert levels. The first is simply the cyclone seasons, so there's the action plan which is updated. It's updated every year. What do we do if a there's a cyclone that hits the island? Should we stock up again? Do we need to get more stuff? The first year we were here we wrote a specific plan of action for Maroantsetra: how to evacuate the office, where to put the vehicles, what to do with that, what to do with our base that's out in the bush. All that is sorted. When we move from level 1 to level 2 it's because there's a warning that things could turn nasty and then we have to check our emails twice a day. (...) When it gets to the final level, 5, we have evacuated the place, everything is put away. We also have contact via satellite phone, at least once a day, as well as the emails.

For the people living in the villages on the east coast, the categories are less clear-cut, as we were told, first by a member of an NGO and then by a local representative:

> There are people in the villages on the east coast and we talk to them and ask 'Didn't you get the weather forecasts, and didn't you get the national weather warnings that there was a cyclone on its way?' They answer 'Yes, well we heard it on the radio, but how can the guys in Tana[6] know what's going to happen here?' So you can see what the situation is there. That means that they don't believe it! They don't believe that it's possible for people who are in Tana to know what's going to happen in Maroantsetra or Antala. They don't believe it; they just don't understand how that can be possible!

> We always do what the guide says: we know we have to put up a red flag to warn that there's a cyclone coming, but usually people don't even know, and the municipalities don't even do that. It's better to listen to the radio because the information is more accurate, because if you put up the flag everyone knows there's a cyclone coming, but you don't know when it will get here. If you listen to the radio, and they give detailed information, everyone knows what's going on.

However, for some actors an alert signifies an early detection which means that the risks can be identified correctly. This is especially true of the SAP Early Warning System whose role is

> (...) to offer our partners early detection, an early warning for the population groups unable to meet all their needs throughout the year.

3.1.4.4 Permeable Categories

It appears that these terms frequently refer back to each other. We were told that prevention can be seen as an 'umbrella', covering all the other activities:

> (...) prevention should be active throughout the period. For me the warning is prevention; the responses are prevention; recovery is prevention. And so, in a country like Madagascar, it's something that needs to be done all year round. There, for example, it's always cyclone season, but we have already scheduled training missions for prevention. It doesn't stop. As I see it, it's really constant; prevention never stops. It's a shame that the people who provide the responses don't deal with prevention. I think it would actually be the ideal time. The response, it's the ideal time because everything's still fresh.

[6]The capital of Madagascar, Antananarivo, is popularly referred to as Tana.

Along the same lines, we were frequently told about elements of prevention that are activated once there is an alert. This is one description, given by an actor from the BNGRC:

> (...) when the warning is given that there's a cyclone coming, the population in the lower-lying areas should move if these areas are at risk, they should go somewhere higher. That does happen. All the schools are closed while the cyclone passes. Except in the areas not at risk. Putting sandbags on the roofs, reinforcing roofs and not only with sandbags but strengthening them with nails. Reinforcing the walls of traditional constructions. There are tree branches and planks that we use to reinforce the corners. We create storerooms higher up, in the areas that aren't at risk. And then we have to work out how much accommodation will be available when the water rises. We do all of that. Even following the warning in the media, whether it's on the radio, on television or in the papers. So the whole population is listening to the radio, watching television or reading the papers, etc.

Finally, forecast and warning often go hand in hand:

> As I told you, our task/mission is to monitor tropical cyclones. By giving weather forecasts it is possible to detect drought as well as floods, for example. We are very involved in predicting and announcing these natural disasters. So it's up to us to put out the warnings.

Some people say that they are not comfortable with this delineation:

> But I'm working on all the aspects of the emergency-development continuum. So that means (...) on preparation and prevention as well. I don't really like the word prevention because in many cases we can't prevent the disasters, we can only protect the population.

3.1.5 Definitions of and Approaches to Risks

The risks vary and are directly linked to the topography and climate, which are very different in the north and the south of the country. In the north, the population is at risk of cyclones and floods. In the south, they are extremely vulnerable to drought. They are therefore facing recurrent problems of food security. All the actors interviewed agreed that these were the greatest threats facing Madagascar. In parallel, the deterioration of the environment was also mentioned a lot, in particular with regard to the coastal areas, bush fires and deforestation. The risks of a tsunami (Madagascar was one of the countries affected by the tsunami in 2004), earthquakes and invasions of locusts were also mentioned by some interviewees.

However, it became apparent that there exist different approaches to these risks. The examples below give an indication of their diversity and also of their cohesion. Indeed, these definitions – although expressed differently – form a logistic entity that contributes to illustrating the way in which the actors interviewed perceive the existing risks listed above.

The first approach, which demonstrates a probabilistic attitude, focuses on the combination of a hazard and a vulnerability. It is the approach most commonly adopted by experts in risk and disaster management:

> (...) a risk – as an expert in risk and disaster management, risks are the combination or the association of hazards, vulnerability and the resilience of the population. So those three components. (...) All of that, that forms a whole.

Others stress the anticipation needed in order to be able to identify risks, while still using the same probabilistic vocabulary. In their view,

> (. . .) risks, that means anticipating an event (. . .). There are environmental risks, structural risks and economic risks. It's the anticipation of an event that might create a certain vulnerability. As far as I'm concerned, I would always want to link risk to vulnerability.

One NGO also defines the risk in terms of vulnerability:

> A risk? A risk exists as soon as there is a hazard that may arise and a certain degree of vulnerability. Property may be lost. The risk appears where the level of vulnerability is significant and the probability of a hazard is high. That's an academic definition . . .

Others describe risk as a deviation from a normal situation:

> Risk is a disruption that will alter the situation of a community from the usual state. That's what we think of as risk.

A deviation which is hard to predict and which people attempt to quantify:

> A risk, that's probably an unpredictable or random event – actually, probably more random than unpredictable. (. . .) I think that a risk is an event that occurs randomly. It's a statistical concept. In general risk is disruptive, otherwise it wouldn't really pose much of a problem.

For some people, the definition of risk depends on the identification process emanating from the field:

> Yes, it is essentially to know the location. Of course there's a scientific basis behind it, but it's essentially the analysis of the capacities of the population in the field. With this outline, which remains theoretical, determining the risk is based on what we observe in the field. What is their level of production? Do they have the ability to adapt? That is what will determine the risks for the different municipalities and regions. Afterwards we can group the regions according to the main type of hazard or risk.

Some opt for a more anthropological definition. For them a risk is

> (. . .) something harmful, something inevitable. (. . .) Risk is like death. Death is something brief; you don't know the time or the date or the place where death will get you. That's the way I define risk.

A risk may also mean learning:

> I think that a risk is something that comes from nature, that arrives just like that, and then we learn what this thing is and we get used to things like that. Yes, for example, we're already used to cyclones because cyclones are always causing destruction . . . as soon as there's a cyclone there's a risk. So, everyone is worried about the wind first of all, then everyone worries about the rain, and after that they worry about the rising waters. Even though they know it's going to happen, risk makes people fearful, that's certainly true.

A risk situation is not definitive; it may worsen, in which case the identification processes become very important and make it possible to introduce some nuances into the concept of risk:

> For us, a risk, it's like having a population in a state of increased vulnerability, and with an external event, well, that could lead to a disaster. That's what risk is for us: just having elements that mean that a situation which isn't necessarily very good to start with could be tipped over the edge and become even more negative. For example, if there's no access to

> drinking water, that's already very bad and a cyclone could turn that into a disaster,(with the risk) of cholera even. That's the main sort of thing we deal with. And this risk is always there, and that's exactly what we're trying to avoid; we're trying to avoid this vulnerability plus the external event turning the risk into a disaster, which can happen very quickly here, especially when it involves water or sanitation. That's what we're working on.

This clearly defines and identifies the risks present in Madagascar. However, in order to study the crisis management situation, it is important to know how these risks are managed and the contexts in which these interventions take place.

3.2 The Circulation of Risk Information in Madagascar

Having set out the risks and the approaches adopted, as well as the main actors involved in risk and disaster management in Madagascar and their fields of action, in this section we now offer a synthesis of the ways in which information related to risks, disasters and crises circulates. These are the models we came across during our investigation. The interviews with the actors in the field enabled us to identify a number of scenarios and a range of 'information circulation profiles'. To complement this initial analysis, we also wanted to identify 'actor profiles'. The aim here was to distinguish groups of actors according to their methods and their position in relation to the streams of information they are called upon to process, produce, receive and/or transmit.

Carrying out this analysis does not mean that we believe we have seen or indeed understood everything. We conducted 30 interviews and transcribed around 350 pages, which is both a lot and a little. The intention in the rest of this chapter is to present an organised interpretation of the material. Our analysis is confined to, and focuses on, the content that came out of these interviews and to what the individual interviewees wished to tell us about their 'reality'. We have intentionally left out the cultural and/or ethnographic aspects that were not directly mentioned to us.

In the analysis presented below, we have focussed on the transfer of information. Following a short description of the source of the information, the two main questions we wanted to answer are:

- How does the information circulate? In what direction does it circulate and what are the preferred channels?
- What does the recipient do with the information received? Does he pass it on immediately or does he take ownership of it and transform it before passing it on further?

3.2.1 The Information Circulation Profiles

During the interviews, we tried to understand what each of the interviewees 'did with' the information, by attempting to identify the salient features of their descriptions and, at a later stage, comparing the different ways this information was used.

The information circulation profiles are a function of the context, the position and the perception that the actors have of their role. The models set out here are presented as an ideal standard, and the quotations have been selected to provide an explanation of the different situations. It should be noted that, depending on the context, the same actor may fall into a number of categories and thus be quoted in different profiles.

3.2.1.1 Vertical Communication

By vertical communication we mean top-down communication of information, where the circulation models are primarily technical (what), operational (who) or organisational (how). There are also cases of bottom-up circulation which, depending on their timing in relation to the information coming down, may relate to information gathering in the field (before), a discussion (during) or feedback (after).

Information Flow: Cascade Model

This description is applied to a flow of information moving down towards the recipients, who are categorised as a whole rather on the basis of their individual characteristics. In this case, the quality (clarity, absence of interference, etc.) is not of primary importance to the transmitter; rather, her/his principal concern is to maximise the transfer (and its usefulness). The information cascade describes the phenomenon of bulk information transfer, which requires a substantial amount of data to be gathered, usually from a priority source – which then forms a frame of reference – as well as from additional sources, some of which may feed into the primary source. In most cases, the information is technical. In the examples given, the majority of those transmitting information are state organs.

This category includes the risk and disaster management training sessions which have been organised across the country in the last few years by the BNGRC. These involved:

> About 120 people taking part in a workshop. There were a lot of us – around 900 to 1000 people trained to local manager level. As we gradually gained more experience of the training sessions, we were able to increase the number of participants, especially during simulation exercises. The aim was to have an impact on the participation in the simulation exercises, like the memory of the tsunami, for example. In that case it was the television pictures and the unforgettable memories every individual has of that time. That was our aim. During the simulation exercises there were about 2000 or 3000 people taking part. The whole village was there.

The aim of the training sessions is to 'spread' the information as widely as possible by creating a chain of knowledge between the different levels of action. At administrative levels, the participants had:

> (...) training sessions including raising awareness at regional level. This also involved those in charge at district level, municipality level and neighbourhood level. We also had

> simulation exercises at neighbourhood level. That allows everyone to benefit from the contents and to 'fix' the image. Why? Well, because we organise a meeting in a region, in the capital of the region, for example. We then invite three other regions to participate. Representatives come from the other regions and we study a specific scenario, such as flooding (...). This enables us to cover about 20 % of the total geographical area in one go. In turn, when they get back home, they do more or less the same thing. This is better than repeating it. It's a very practical solution.

This functionalist vision of information is a response to a centralised vision of the production and organisation of information, which is itself the corollary to the coordination of risk and disaster management operations:

> Since the BNGRC has to be the leader – the coordinator – we wrote to every actor requesting information, to be centralised here at the BNGRC. (...) The presence of international experts also helps to create an aura of trust. Once the sponsors are convinced, the help can be available.

This information confirms the utility of a single top-down transmission system, flowing from the BNGRC, the governmental reference agency, down to the lowest administrative level in the country. Although this desire for centralisation and distribution encounters structural difficulties in terms of facilities, it seems to be backed up by a strong political will:

> This is why we set up early warning systems. Here, at the BNGRC, we are going to establish an information base, in which there will be a proper place for the early warning. This is because our information sources are really going to be centred and focussed there. It will be based on the information systems from municipality level up to regional level.

Alongside the BNGRC is the Madagascan meteorological service, whose role in the early warning system is absolutely key, as we have seen. It is also working to improve the performance of its information system:

> We are very much involved in forecasting and announcing these natural disasters. So it is up to us to issue the warnings. It's the Madagascan meteorological service that issues warnings in cases of flooding, tropical cyclones and even drought.

This information is then distributed to the actors concerned, according to a list drawn up in advance in collaboration with the BNGRC.

This top-down information system follows the administrative organisation of the Madagascan risk and disaster management agencies, especially with regard to the type of information and the technical and financial means required to produce it. However, some actors seem to be critical of its unilateral nature, which they see as typical of the chronic inability of the governmental institutions and their decentralised regional representatives to pass information up the chain:

> There is a lack of consultation and of information emanating from those in charge at regional level. Possibly because they want to respond to the most immediate needs, they neglect the information aspect. They don't know that it's only once they have given us the information that we can offer a response specific to their region.

In the actors' day to day work in periods of prevention and response to cyclones, the top-down flow of information can be observed during the BNGRC information sessions. Originally, it was decided to split these sessions into two parts: an initial 'plenary' part during which the BNGRC would pass on information to its partners and a second part consisting of informal exchanges among the participants. At the time we carried out our study, the sessions were primarily plenary, with the informal exchanges taking place at the end, usually in somewhat of a rush as everyone prepared to leave.

This does not stop the BNGRC being proud that these 'partners' are attending, using their presence to justify its actions and organise the levels of intervention of the international actors, with their considerable resources and technical skills, and the national actors, who in most cases have little. The aim of this communication operation is therefore to maintain a symbolic balance between the different actors:

> Up to now we have received a lot of good help and I hope that will continue. There may of course be some gaps in the information relating to the actions undertaken by the various units, but I think it is essentially a question of organisation and I'm in the process of getting that sorted. I have seen that everyone is prepared to play their part in organising things. In the meetings, everyone is present or represented. The other day, there was even someone from the World Bank ....

Information Flow: Elevator Model

This information circulation profile refers to a situation in which those involved organise the circulation themselves on a vertical axis and according to their needs.

The information may flow in either direction, from the field (bottom) to the levels where decisions are made (top). This vertical structure is partially explained by the fact that decisions are taken in Antananarivo and implemented in a location that may be very far removed from the capital, in terms of both the actual number of kilometres and the cultural environment.

This type of information was mentioned on numerous occasions by our interviewees, who frequently brought up the cultural diversity of the island and the problems this causes in establishing action plans. The notion of a vertical structure is also rooted in the hierarchical operation of a number of organisations, whose structure more or less mirrors the administrative divisions of the country. It can also be explained by the way the actors view their action, which can be as a vector transmitting knowledge, skills and 'development' in general.

In this model, the actors go into the field to look for information, which they then transform and use for their actions. In a context where information is a rare commodity, there are many actors who are keen to describe themselves as 'information finders':

> We are the ones who go and look for the information; we don't wait for it to come to us. So we have no actual sources of information. If we need to know something, whether we are talking about preparation or intervention, or if we are looking for information about a disaster, which we can use as a basis for our work ... I don't go and talk to our financial backers and ask for money to do something if I'm not certain, if I haven't been there and had a look myself so I know what I'm talking about. (...) I can't use information from the Ministry of Agriculture that is five years old, or from the Ministry of the Interior which is incomplete. Our information sources are always the same: ourselves.

These actors, who often belong to NGOs, have developed the skills, the methodology and the internal organisation needed to gather their information. Depending on their requirements, they turn to a variety of sources, which may be administrative or documentation:

> [Our sources are] the authorities, at all levels, be it national or local, and national and international organisations. We exchange information, we discuss and consult with them and then sometimes, when we can, we talk to the beneficiaries, but that tends to be only in theory. It's difficult to get access to them ... We are trying: for the post-cyclonic situation there are websites which keep us informed about the evolution of the cyclone, reports that come in, etc.

Other information comes directly from the field. In this case the NGOs set up a proper information gathering system, which means mobilising personnel and financial and logistic resources:

> We are essentially information producers. Our information comes from the municipalities themselves, from the people we have trained there. (...) Let's say that we drew up our questionnaires and our information matrices precisely because there was no information available in the system, in the administration. Our aim was to gather the missing information so that we could carry out a vulnerability analysis. However, we have only limited resources, and we try not to duplicate other activities. We try to get some of our information form health or education authorities. But there is a lot of information that is either missing or difficult to get hold of.

In this category, the actors choose their own sources, schedules and contacts in order to get the information they need when they need it. Yet again, considerable resources are needed to do this:

> The problem is this: when a cyclone hits – BOOM – all communications are cut off; you have no phone, nothing. (...) Then everyone turns to the CNS for information: we meet every two days at the CNS to get information. But it is also hard for the CNS to collect the information and to find the financial resources to send out a helicopter or a plane. Even when you get there it's still difficult to get the information. Later, it is up to the municipalities to record the situation where they are, and to send that information to the district administration, which passes it on to the CNS, which then makes the information public.

All those we spoke to were of the opinion that information gathering is the initial – and indispensable – phase of correctly fulfilling their task of responding to disasters:

> We spent the first two days investigating the situation, before starting any form of distribution, and on the third day we began the distribution. The initial investigation – at group level – was to determine which villages and population groups needed help with water and sanitation. That took us two days and the further investigations, which lasted one or two weeks, were carried out once distribution had started.

As was stated earlier, this information circulation model is typical of, though not exclusive to, NGOs which like to stress to both their backers and the governmental agencies that rely heavily on them that their ability to produce information guarantees their capacity to undertake relevant action in the field. The NGOs' autonomous ability to produce information is without doubt one of the distinguishing characteristics of the information circulation system. In this way, international organisations are able to complete the task of compiling this information into a report.

Information Flow: Staircase Model

This model describes a circulation profile in which information travels both up and down. It is characterised by a wide range of actors and intermediaries, as well as a degree of discontinuity in the flow of information from transmitter to receiver. We encountered this profile in organisations with formalised and hierarchical communication methods, or where information did not flow smoothly between the different actors. It can be observed, for example, in the workings of the military and civilian authorities in Maroantsetra district and can also be adapted to the communication system used by the Madagascan meteorological services.

This information circulation situation is typical of the operation of the Civil Protection Corps. We encountered a number of representatives of the CPC who were seconded to Maroantsetra:

> For distribution we have two channels: one goes through the army and the other through the BNGRC. The Ministry of the Interior and Administrative Reform is the ministry that oversees the work of the BNGRC, which is part of it. The information comes to us through the CRIC, which we belong to, and the local aid committee. In Madagascar, whenever there is a crisis, or even to prevent crises, the solution is always to set up a committee. I mean an ad hoc committee. (. . .) Everything is centralised in Tana and then Tana sends the information on to us.

The BNGRC, with its local and regional structures, functions in the same way. The information has to pass through every level of the administrative chain before reaching its final destination:

> For example, in the municipalities and the small villages, there are actors who belong to the NGOs. They are the ones who have their antennae out all the time, who are actually on site. At district level we also have the NGOs. The BNGRC has its administrative structure: regions, districts, municipalities, etc. Then we have the CDGRC. And then there are our various actors, in other words our partners (. . .) We have connections at all levels and, in the BNGRC, we coordinate all the actions. Now, what we would like to see in parallel to our warning system is information coming back to us. We need a reliable information system at municipality level, so that the information reaches us. Once that happens, we can respond.

Here, we see both the need and the problems encountered by government agencies trying to pass back the information we mentioned in the section describing the cascade information flow. These difficulties can be rendered even greater by the staircase model, where we often see that the steps are too high.

This type of profile often also highlights the difficulties faced by the actors as they try to work with different types of information, which needs to be organised and prioritised. This situation is particularly noticeable in the case of the meteorological service, which seems to have problems collating information from different sources to produce the appropriate coherent and complete information:

> With the equipment we have, we can detect the (cyclone) system when it is 4,000 kilometres from Madagascar. Should we announce it immediately we detect it, even when it is still 4,000 kilometres away? Almost all our stations are coastal. There is a risk and when a cyclone passes, the stations are usually destroyed. The data doesn't reflect the reality any more: we would have to rebuild the stations, which is not always possible given our financial situation. We get documents from the WMO and automatically we have to pass on

> the information to the meteorological stations affected by the cyclone first. Because what follows, are the warnings. If the cyclone is not going to affect the other stations, there is no point in alerting them. And that is the structure of the meteorological service, which is divided into regions: North, South and Centre. It is their responsibility to transmit the information to the local authorities, from where it will eventually reach the local population.

Family and informal information networks can also be included in this category. Although no specific research has been done into their actual role in risk and disaster management, they clearly play a significant part in the circulation of information, in a way that can be easily integrated into the more formal structures:

> When it comes to sources of information, there are some that are fundamental. There are the BNGRC office, the television and the people in the field. (...) The military, in other words. In Madagascar they come from all over the country, so there's always someone who has friends or family in the area. For example, I can call my aunt and she can tell me 'The water has reached us, or whatever'. Then it's up to me to interpret the information in the light of what she's telling me, and then to pass this on to my bosses.

This style of circulation is a good illustration of how difficult it can be to pass the information back following a cyclone, as well as of the gap between the theoretical models which have been tested and the far more complex reality in the field:

> Usually, I would say 72 hours; in fact, this has been tested, and all the information from the initial damage assessments arrived within 72 hours.[7] That was fine. However, there is a lot to do because there is also the matter of accessibility: it is always the most vulnerable communities that are hit. And vulnerable here means inaccessible. They can't pass on the level of damage until the water level has dropped because they can't get around.

As we have seen, a vertical information flow causes problems with information transfer and access to information. This is one of the reasons why a number of actors believe that the way information circulates in the Madagascan system is inadequate or inappropriate[8]:

> The information I consider to be inadequate is usually that which comes from the base. Not only does it take a long time to reach us, it is also insufficient: sometimes it doesn't even correspond to reality. For example, we have always asked for the actual number of victims to be communicated to the BNGRC, yet they tend to send percentage figures, such as the percentage of villages flooded or the percentage of victims ... As a result, responses may be delayed or not suited to the qualitative and quantitative needs of the victims.

[7]Other sources mention that it often takes two months for the assessments to be completed.

[8]Buffet (2011) observed the same thing in his comparative study of the DIPECHO programmes related to Cyclone Bingiza: Doctors of the World taking 'on board' the Chief Medical Officer of Maroantsetra for the post-cyclonic evaluation; CARE being more involved in replacement through the collection of the EIMA forms the centralisation and compilation of the data and the direct transmission to the BNGRC rather than the CDGRC (for an explanation of the EIMA forms, see point 3.3 where these are discussed at length).

3.2.1.2 Horizontal Communication

The exchanges of information between those actors in the development field who are not part of governmental institutions form the basis of horizontal communication. We have observed that this communication between actors is the starting point for establishing communications networks. Based on the personal relationships between actors engaged in similar projects, they also include local actors and a number of actors from outside the international development field.

Information Flow: Satellite Model

This term is used to describe a nodal structure in which information is gathered from the sources, integrated into a system of ideas or reference, then distributed to the recipients, whose specific characteristics are taken into account. In this model, information flows in a large number of directions and requires those acting as transmitters to deploy a range of strategies when selecting the information to be sent and the addressees. It reflects information transfer models found, for example, in certain UN agencies or in NGOs. One could also include the local employees in the field, as well as the Mayor and Member of Parliament for Maroantsetra, whose functions require them to work with a range of actors.

In addition, this sideways flow requires the various actors to have a greater autonomy in their ability to gather and distribute information which, in this context, is on an individual rather than an institutional basis:

> The actors in the field don't always have time to acquire knowledge they don't yet possess. But teaching myself is also part of my job. I make the effort to read information and to integrate it. In our positions we have to integrate a vast range of different items of information, relating to a number of subject areas. It is up to us to make the effort.

This 'networking' ability can also be seen in centralised institutions:

> A cyclone is coming: first the meteorological service lets us know, then we tell the districts that will be affected, so are at risk, and the districts tell the leaders in the municipalities. At the same time we get information from them, from the people who have been affected. They tell us 'Our house has been blown away' or 'A dyke has collapsed'. The head of the district passes information on to the CNS, by phone. (...) There is a secretary whose job it is to answer the phone. All the information is put into the computer data base. We try and check our facts. We don't simply accept one report of a house blowing away; we phone someone else. For example, the head of the school district or the representative of Madagascar national radio. (...) This can all be done very quickly; these days we know everything within an hour.

Where it is incorporated into existing structures, the organisation of the information can be considerably decentralised and established in a multipolar form:

> In the event of an emergency there is also the Inter-Agency Standing Committee. This is a committee composed of UN agencies and expanded to include a number of NGOs involved in the post-cyclone activities. This is where our actions are coordinated and exchanges take place. For example, setting up the 'Flash Appeal' and the tools we use. This is also where

> we plan the support that we can provide to the BNGRC. (...) There is also the specific group, the emergency, the disasters. (...) But since disaster management involves a range of sectors, at various levels, it must be integrated into action and development programmes. We must – it is a duty, which we are keen to uphold – be in contact with other development actors from the various ministerial departments and the scientific community, as well as from various financial development projects.

Some actors have, from the outset, opted for a satellite modelling of the information flow, which makes it possible to establish a system of levels for the collaboration between the various actors present on site:

> If we are asked who we are collaborating with, the satellite seems like a good idea because we are in the centre, though without being the leader, since the question is aimed at us. (...) The distance from the centre reflects the relationship. I would put the BNGRC there. The international NGOs, well we tend to work together so it's a sort of community, but that's good. The UN agencies are sometimes a bit far removed from us. I think it's a good tool, although it could do with some reworking, but it does become a bit cumbersome. (...) And maybe we could get the ministries responsible for this involved. I think they are a very long way from us; the Ministry of Health and so on seem completely disconnected.

In this system, the actors' ability to form a network for cooperation and information is also a factor. The information can circulate because the modalities for exchanging information among partners have been established and are put into practice:

> Last week I was in the prime minister's office. (...) We work with all the ministries because the emergency has an impact on every area: agriculture, roads, education, and health. All sectors are affected by the crises, so we are in contact with, and work in close collaboration with, our partners in the ministries. Not necessarily with the ministers, of course, but with all the ministries. And especially with the BNGRC, which I have been working for years to set up, establish and consolidate.

Organising the information into a network like this takes place over a period of time and so offers our interviewees the opportunity to discuss the history of the relationship between the actors involved in risk and disaster management in Madagascar. A clearer picture of the 'archaeology' of these relationships allows a clearer understanding of the present situation:

> There are a number of levels involved in disaster management. There is the CNS or BNGRC level, which is an official level. It's a platform which brings together the government and its networks, the ministries and the NGOs present in the field. But a few years ago, another platform was set up. This was the CRIC, and it brought the government, the NGOs and the financial backers to the discussion table. In practice, since 2002, this communication forum and platform has disappeared and things have become more one-sided. A guy with a mike gets up and speaks, we listen, we make notes, we take in information and when it's finished we all say 'See you next time' and head off home. There is no dialogue. I'm not happy with this way of doing things: it's too top-down, too one-sided. We are there to listen and just sit passively. It's hard to intervene as there is so little opportunity to exchange ideas. That's not the way to get things done. So we decided to invite the partners we work with to spend two days with us here. The NGOs have been meeting each other. We are talking, trying to divide up the tasks and the geographical areas between us, working out how to deal with the shortcomings and seeing how we can intervene together and at what level.

The informal response to communication situations deemed inadequate is also creating an information flow at various levels.

This horizontal information situation, which seemed to suit the majority of our interviewees, nevertheless does create certain problems, particularly when it intersects with vertical information flow systems:

> You see, when we draw a diagram, it's the horizontal and sideways relationships that are important. The information and feedback are important. [In other cases] it's very much a downward flow: they give but are not interested in receiving. Especially the elected representatives.

Information Flow: Bridging Model

This information circulation profile uses a different channel, which does not fit into a classification which systematically contrasts vertical and horizontal profiles. This bridging model uses elements from different profiles simultaneously: from the cascade, through its tendency to pass on information with only an incomplete knowledge of how it will be received; from the elevator because it first gathers information from various levels, and from the networks because it allows the previous categories to be crossed. However, the key characteristic is its detachment from the geographical scales on which the other categories depend, making use instead of the socio-technical elements we will discuss later. Information circulating according to this transitional profile may encounter receivers who can be close or distant and who choose and/or have the capacity to access the information or not. This information has been processed by the transmitter, who has adapted it to the norms of a given medium and the target population. There is not a single form of bridging but a range of possibilities.

This category could have been specially created for the Mayor of Maroantsetra who, in addition to his municipal activities has, for several years, run a local radio station which he uses as an information and prevention tool in the event of cyclone warnings. This radio prevention work is the product of his experience as a 'media man', his close collaboration with the risk and disaster management 'partners and, most importantly, his personal network, his skills as an engineer and the personal financial resources he invests in the project.

In order to gain a better insight into this atypical figure in the field of risk and disaster management in Madagascar, we spoke to him at greater length. Here follow some extracts from our conversation:

> I have a good source of information because they are going to bring Internet to Maroantsetra. (. . .) We phone directly, we don't really listen to the radio: there is a delay and the weather is only mentioned at fixed times. We take the weather information directly from Tana and they are happy to give us this information. They send us faxes to let us know about the conditions here. Friends and I have a fax. I started the radio station in 1996, when I got a subscription to satellite TV and I found the weather channel that gives information about cyclones. I started broadcasting on this subject. I work hard to get lots of information. I get a lot because I don't just sit at my desk with my arms folded . . . I call them; if it's a question of money and I have to pay for the phone calls myself, I don't mind. Ordinarily, the prime minister is the head of the district and he should be the one making everyone aware, but he doesn't do it so I have to do it myself. He isn't on top of the problem: at home he doesn't

> watch the satellite channel, he has no information and he doesn't listen to the radio. When the cyclone arrives he isn't concerned about it. He doesn't have the equipment. As we all know, broadcasting ethics mean we should let the people know about approaching cyclones so that they can protect themselves. I do what I can. I work in conjunction with Medair,[9] and we exchange information, which works very well and is a great help. Medair receives the information, but that's as far as it goes, and to pass the information on to the population they turn to the radio. (. . .) At the radio station we have journalists, we discuss things, we try to disseminate information and we form small groups to try to interpret what is going on and what will happen in the future.

This radio communication also happens across the country, through the national radio and television channels, though its impact has never actually been measured:

> I see that people are made aware of the situation through the radio. When the cyclone arrives, the national radio and television channels try to warn people, telling them not to go out to sea, to shut themselves in at home, to put sandbags in place, etc. But that's all. There's no real awareness raising, with people being told how to deal with the risks, if they exist. Sometimes people just ignore the warnings; they carry on with their daily lives to get enough rice for the day. Risk management is the last thing on their minds. When they are in their vanilla plantation, they stay there and it's impossible to get them away. If we tried to take two hours to talk to them about risk prevention, they would probably ask if we'd gone mad.

In addition to the economic and cultural factors, and behaviour often described as 'fatalistic' (together with the traditional representations of natural disasters), in the field it has often been noted that there seems to be a direct correlation between recent experiences and the receptiveness of the population to risk and disaster warnings. For example, in Maroantsetra the population is much more receptive since they suffered the cyclone (Buffet 2010).

In this context, the Madagascan meteorological service is, officially, the only institution producing information:

> We have to broadcast bulletins through the official channels: national radio and television. We also have individuals who ask us for information: we give it to them, we have grouped them together. Then there is the whole official side of things: the authorities, the president's office, the prime minister's office and the Ministry of Public Works, Transport and Meteorology, which is the ministry responsible for us. But at the moment it is only the Ministry of Public works and Transport: transport. For the other ministries, we also have to provide information if they request it. We also have the NGOs and the other users, most of which are members of the BNGRC CRIC.

We see here that the information produced needs to be able to be adapted to suit several types of partners.

In these cases of information flowing according to the bridging model, no impact study has been carried out to see whether the messages reach their target. The only indication we have is the success of the local radio station run by the Mayor of Maroantsetra, which was mentioned frequently during our interviews with the inhabitants of Ankofa. In this very isolated village – a day's journey from Maroantsetra by motorised pirogue (dugout), which most of the inhabitants

[9]Medair is an NGO that has been working in Madagascar since 2001.

would be unable to afford – where there are no newspapers or television, and where only one NGO is operating, the information source the inhabitants considered most reliable was indeed the radio. However, the radio does require 'intermediaries' who, as we shall see later, often made it difficult to use. For this reason, the inhabitants also make use of their knowledge of the sky and their beliefs, while also relying on cyclone warnings issued by the members of the NGO present in the village. When we visited, the Mayor of Ankofa pointed out that they had suffered relatively little damage this year as a result of following the safety warnings. He did tell us that a number of houses had been destroyed, stocks had been lost and livestock scattered, without however being able to give precise figures.

3.2.2 Actor Profiles

In addition to our analysis of the way information circulates, we also tried to get a better understanding of the position of the actors with regard to the flow of information exchanged in their daily practice. In this context, the task of the major players involved in risk and disaster management is to find the correct register of action to enable them to achieve the goals set by their organisation.

We have defined a number of actor profiles, which are characterised by their practices, methods, the register of language used and their objectives. Once again, these profiles are standardised ideal solutions, based on the information obtained from several interviews, and in no way represent any actual individual. Nor does this attempt at classification include any intent to create a hierarchy; rather, it seeks to understand the construction of the situation we observed.

The actors we encountered can be seen as 'translators' (according to the terminology used in the work of Callon 1986 and Akrich et al. 2006) since, on a daily basis, they all perform translation operations involving establishing connections, tools, discourse and personal relations, whether they are 'actors', acting or 'actants'.[10]

Depending on their aims and needs, our interviewees receive, analyse, adapt and transmit information. In doing this they play a role in creating what could be called 'a chain of actors'.

3.2.2.1 The Coordinator

The people we encountered who held coordination posts – where the actor is placed at the heart of the system in which he is functioning – have to be adaptable in order to enable the project to make progress across all sectors:

> My role was primarily to ensure the coordination of all forms of intervention.

[10]An actant is defined by its ability *to act, to form a weight, an intensity in the process of the action.* An actant may be an actor, an organisation, an object or a metaphysical entity (cf Akrich 1992).

or by following the vertical structure of the national administrative organisations:

> As a Member of Parliament, my task is to listen to what people say because I have to act as a link between the population, the State and the government. A Member of Parliament collects the grievances of his constituents, then passes on the information to the government. It is then up to the government, where available, to revise legislation which falls within its competence. That is the primary function of a Member of Parliament.

This information transfer role is the keystone of the organisation of the majority of the institutions active in the field. These functions require a comprehensive understanding of the stakes involved – at all levels, political, economic, ecological, social, ethnographic, etc. – and of the needs of the actors:

> We are working to reduce risks and vulnerability, by trying to work with the communities to improve access to drinking water all year round. In this way, in the event of a cyclone, they will be less vulnerable.

In the example below, it is clear that this position of a translator is rooted in the need for continuous learning:

> One element of the consultant's role is the ability to increase his own knowledge. In other words, to be aware of everything that is going on and of the lessons learned, and to be able to assimilate it all. This knowledge then has to be "redistributed" to others, by guiding them and helping them to understand it, so that they, in their turn, can also pass it on. At one time it was difficult to follow these steps because we didn't have the necessary reference material. But I think that this is pretty readily available now. [...] One of my roles is to contribute to learning and to developing human resources in the field of disaster reduction and crisis management in general.

This is a role played by many expatriates working in international organisations whose mission is to establish a cohesive situation across the territory covered by the organisation, from the headquarters (which is often in Europe) to the area in which they operate in Madagascar. This 'chain of operations' includes the numerous instances of 'consultation' or 'petitions' that we have come across repeatedly. This profile corresponds to a role that can be described as follows:

> My role is that of a motivator or a facilitator. I act as the secretariat to working groups, ensure that information circulates, produce information, bring people into contact, create opportunities for reflection, organise the exchange and sharing of ideas, enable certain institutions to establish a base and assist with requests. I am, in fact, the only person whose sole task is to support the risk and disaster management organisation. The others who work with the organisation in Madagascar all have other duties as well.

3.2.2.2 The Producer

The producer is someone who has assembled the resources needed to go and find for herself or himself the information he requires in order to achieve the objectives set by his organisation. In Madagascar, where information is as scarce as it is essential, information producers have this ability to go out into the field to gather information.

To do so, they sometimes make use of intermediaries. These may be tools – such as the EIMA[11] forms – or people they have trained to gather information:

> You've got ECHO,[12] or a couple of guys like that. They have representatives who turn up and ask you what's going on. And they don't just want a photo of a flooded area: they want exact figures. The problem is that if you wait for the figures from the CNS it takes too long! So, the way we usually cooperate is to provide logistic resources and we go and evaluate the situation together. We look at what's going on, they look too and then, together, we come up with figures that we can both use.

Like the other actors, the producers have to deal with a dense, multipolar and heterogeneous network of contacts, leading to a constant need for translation processes:

> The aim of the SIRSA project, at the government's request, was to extend the geographical area covered by the early warning system and to include an additional dimension so that it can be used as a decision-making tool in the implementation of the national rural development plan. In other words, a means of tracking the implementation including impact indicators. It is funded by the European Commission and at the moment they are working on the two southern provinces (…). Our involvement consists of providing the partners with an assessment methodology which considers the impact of external factors on both the availability and accessibility of food. In addition, we provide the partners with an early detection and warning system, for those population groups who are unable to meet their own needs throughout the year.

The Madagascan meteorological service is also part of the technical production of information translated in order to reach the various targets of weather warnings, as discussed previously.

3.2.2.3 The Transmitter

In this category too, the actors cannot manage without a translation process. They are characterised by the fact that part of their mandate is linked to the quality of the transmission of the information they pass on. As mentioned earlier, one actor may wear several 'hats'. For example, the meteorological service not only produces information, it also transmits it in the form of warnings:

> We really have to get the message across. We need to find a suitable form of words, that people will be able to understand, without things being over-dramatized, and in a way that will make them aware of the danger threatening them. As far as the others are concerned, we simply transmit.

The other major 'actor-transmitter' is the BNGRC which, although claiming this role, is unable to respond to all the requests it receives. The quality of a transmission

---

[11]These forms for the *Enquête Initiale Multi-Aléas* [Initial Survey of Multiple Disasters] are used to send information back from the local BNGRC agents to the headquarters. (See point 3.3. where these are discussed at length and Appendix for an example of these forms.)

[12]European Commission Humanitarian Aid and Civil Protection organisation.

cannot be improvised and may depend on the organisation. 'I think that the reason I've been sent here is firstly to get things organised and to dispatch as quickly as possible. This is a question of organisation and restructuring'. This organisation is sometimes left up to the professionals:

> We were looking at information that came to the CNS from all over Madagascar. It was my job to sort the information, to examine it and, if it is correct, to pass it on. I discuss with an associate about the map, what we're going to do, whether we're going to transmit the information, or whether it's a state secret, or whether we need more time.

Here, we see that the decision to pass on information does not always depend solely on the wishes of the transmitting body.

There are also transmitters within the international organisations. In many cases, it is more the function of the person interviewed in the organisation which gives him the role of a transmitter. Here, the person in charge of the mission for an NGO explains how he extracts the key facts from the information supplied to him, enabling him to communicate with his teams and his partners. While the NGO for which he works has no actual terms of reference relating to the circulation of information, his position within the organisation means that he has to do this:

> [...] I am also in charge of all the 'macro' management, by which I mean human resources, financial resources and material resources. I am supported by the teams working alongside me, be it here in Tana or out in the field. [...] Analysing the epidemiological data allows us to measure the risk. When faced with the spread of HIV in prisons or the indicators of severe malnutrition, monitoring the data closely allows us to assess the risks. [...] To prevent risks in the current crisis, we follow developments in the weather situation etc., simply using the tools we have available.

3.2.2.4 The Forwarder

We referred above to the Mayor of Maroantsetra, an atypical case among those interviewed. A true 'media man', self-taught, he is one of the people most actively concerned with protection in Maroantsetra. His various functions (mayor, businessman, director of a radio station), coupled with his background as a former student of the Faculty of Engineering in Geneva and his financial resources, enable him to monitor the information in a way that is unique among the actors we encountered. For his role as a producer of information, he has procured the software needed to calculate the speed at which cyclones move. An excellent networker, he works in cooperation with the actors of the Madagascan risk and disaster management organisations but also with a personal network which allows him to get information from Europe or Antananarivo if the need arises. As the director of a radio station, he works together with foreign media, NGOs and international organisations to transmit educational messages. As a journalist, he keeps his listeners informed with 'non-stop' updates on the behaviour and risks of the cyclones. As a mayor, he knows his community and the situation in his district:

> Usually, since I have the radio, I am the first to get involved and to inform the population. For example, if I see that a cyclone is forming, I start letting all the people know. I try to

> follow how it's developing. Usually I have to do this on the satellite TV channel (...). They give the exact location, with the longitude details and everything – I use my computer to calculate the distance from the centre to where it will hit our coast. I try to say that at a certain time it will be at a certain distance, and as soon as I see that that is what's happening I start telling everyone. [...] Sometimes I also ask my son, who is in France and who has Internet, because on Internet you can find much more detailed information.

This remains an exceptional case. In the rest of the country, relations between the media and the risk and disaster management authorities are, like all information, under the direct control of the relevant minister. Information is only released by the BNGRC communication service:

> At that time I was supposed to be a press attaché. In other words, it was me that got the information from the CNS, not the journalists.

As part of their attempts to retain a certain degree of independence from their sources, the media look for information wherever seems most appropriate. This can sometimes lead to inconsistencies between the various sources of information:

> Some channels have three different sources. There is one that works with the national meteorological office, while two others surf the Internet and another uses MétéoFrance. Sometimes the warnings issued by these three channels differ. The danger is that there are districts who are not alerted, even though there is a warning out for their area.

3.2.2.5 The Operator

Operators use the information they receive from elsewhere to carry out their actions. Generally speaking, they are at the end of the information chain and implement the instructions received. In our study, this category was represented in particular by the members of the fire and rescue service of the Civil Protection Corps working in Maroantsetra:

> The BNGRC is the only one, [...] the authority directly above us, who asks the Ministry of Defence what we should be doing, how we should be used. So, once we're in the field our boss is the BNGRC.

To a certain extent, this situation also applies to the NGO personnel present in the field who are themselves dependent on decisions taken at other levels:

> With regard to Tana, and the crisis they had in Tana with the disaster victims, the problem was that for a very long time the state thought it would be able to manage the situation. They waited before officially declaring a crisis, and the rain just kept on falling. Then, when they launched their appeal, ECHO pulled out of the funding and we lost another week because we had to discuss everything again with UNICEF. Our action was delayed by a week: we arrived 5 or 6 weeks after the camps had been set up.

It is clear that at the end of the chain, there are also numerous operations taking place to achieve the goals.

In summary, these actor profiles highlight the different ways in which information circulates among those involved in risk and disaster management in Madagascar. This diversity shows that there are no fixed profiles as certain actors fit into a number of profiles.

3.3 The Socio-technical Intermediaries

In accordance with our theoretical framework, we observed events as 'a set of practices linked to actors and supported by material arrangements', as sociologists of sciences and techniques would express it. The two previous sections identify the ways in which information circulates and the actors responsible for risk management, at local and national levels. We now need to consider the intermediaries that circulate information among the actors and to see how the various points of view can be linked.

During our field study, we noted that the protagonists are connected through 'intermediaries' and that the circulation (or non-circulation) of the information is closely linked to these material aspects. The intermediaries reflect the ongoing translation process. As John Law and Michel Callon (1995) explain it,

> When we follow a scientist in action, or even more so the conception and production of a scientific statement or a technical artefact, what we observe is the multiplicity of elements involved, of which they are, to a certain extent, a synthesis. We have called this process of association 'translation'. The entities that surround us, be they human beings, objects or texts, are composite realities because they are the result of a process of composition

Nor should it be forgotten that 'any entity has a variable geometry as it changes as the configuration of actions that it prolongs and transmits is altered'.

During our stay in Madagascar, we frequently heard the phrase: 'It often doesn't take much for this type of project to succeed …'. This led us to search our interviews for the elements that get things going, because they make them possible, or those that are missing and which would have been essential to ensure that the information did circulate.

There are four key intermediaries: batteries, fuel, books and figures. We will look in detail at each and their respective roles in the circulation of information. Their presence allows different actors and levels to be connected and information to be carried and transmitted. We examined both the presence and the absence of these intermediaries: what they do, what they could do and what they do not do.

3.3.1 *Batteries*

As we know, in Madagascar the radio is an essential form of connection, particularly in remote rural areas which have no mains electricity, where it is the only means of receiving information (Francken et al. 2008). According to figures supplied by the National Office of Statistics, in 1997, 45 % of households had a radio (Francken et al. 2009). As the meteorologist we spoke to put it:

> Everyone should have a radio. This was the advice given during the awareness campaign for tropical cyclones. During a cyclone you need a radio because once the cyclone arrives the electricity is cut off to avoid accidents. It's cut off automatically. You need to have a radio that uses batteries. As far as the national radio station is concerned, I think that there

> was a campaign at some point, explaining that everyone should have a radio in the house, or even a TV. Except for the really isolated areas – they don't have TV. This was at the same time as the awareness raising campaign for radios.

Batteries are a crucial intermediary in the circulation of information. According to the Mayor of Maroantsetra, a town situated on the annual 'cyclone highway', people in rural communities are used to using battery-powered radios. However, those who live in towns tend not to have battery-powered radios, preferring to use the ones that run on mains electricity. In the event of a power cut, a frequent occurrence during the cyclone season, batteries are essential for radios and are very closely linked to the use made of them:

> I think we should make everyone aware of the need to buy a radio, so that they have at least got a little battery-powered radio.

> They keep calling me, and I can't answer all those phone calls, so I tell everyone to buy battery-powered radios so they can hear what the cyclone is doing. I don't know whether they actually do buy them or not. This doesn't only apply to the urban population, it's for the whole district of Maroantsetra because we cover the whole area and when there's a power cut it's always me who has to pass on information.

The radio is the medium that is brought to life by the battery, once it has been inserted. It is a connector providing essential information, and in the remotest regions, it is one of only two ways of receiving information. The other is sending volunteers into the field, as mentioned by some NGOs.

However, while almost half of the population has a radio, a member of an NGO who has been based in Madagascar for a long time told us that

> They don't necessarily have batteries all year round. At some times of the year they can afford batteries and at some times they can't. In the lean season, which is also the hurricane season, there are plenty of people who don't have the money to buy batteries. Since there aren't yet many wind-up radios, there are people who don't listen to the radio ... but there are some who have a TV, out in the bush. It's amazing, you see villages with really high TV antennas. [...] They have the batteries in cars or trucks to charge the radio batteries. But that's in the rich areas, the areas where they have cash crops, such as vanilla, coffee or cloves. That brings in a lot of money at once, and when they have money they buy radio-cassette players. They do it mostly so that they have music, but it does mean that they have the radio too.

The wind-up radio is seen as an interesting alternative to radios that use batteries or mains electricity. The European Commission representative mentioned that they had funded procurement programmes for wind-up radios in other countries but not in Madagascar.[13]

The radio is also very closely linked in to the range of prevention strategies deployed in Madagascar. The university professor interviewed believes that

---

[13]Since that time, CARE has distributed wind-up radios to villagers, giving them some responsibility during periods of alert. However, results would seem to be mixed, as indicated by the evaluation carried out by Doctors of the World following Cyclone Bingiza (Buffet 2011).

> Local radio stations, and local media, are the most urgent area. First of all, radio presenters need to be trained [...] because people listen to the radio. Secondly, those in charge in these areas need to be made aware of the situation. Thirdly, the idea needs to be spread among the religious and village communities. All of this needs to be part of the system. If not there will be no point. And there should be lots of exercises organised, regularly, so that people can remember what to do if the risk materialises.

The radio also links different scales of action – albeit sometimes with difficulty – and acts as a 'bridge':

> Warnings and things like that are issued at national level. But since people there don't always listen to national radio, they should also be broadcast on local radio. Mind you, relations between national and local radio are not always as good as they should be. So they have to sort it out themselves.

However, one radio communication device has been put in place: the single sideband (SSB) network. This device is primarily used by actors involved in prevention and assistance. According to our interviewees, this new system has greatly improved communication, despite a lack of stability and the antennas being vulnerable to high winds:

> When we got the SSBs, the collaboration worked well because we could exchange information. Before, we went down there every six months or so. But now we can be in touch every day. The communication has become much closer. That is a definite improvement.

One interviewee working for an NGO confirmed that most information is passed on orally in Madagascar:

> We talk, we're in a society where people talk, where information is passed on orally. So the SSB works well and the telephone works well, but reports don't work, and as for books ....

Batteries are an intermediary which connects technology. (On the one hand, there is the battery-powered radio and, on the other, the wind-up, as a non-polluting, sustainable alternative.) Batteries also link actors (those who transmit the information during the cyclone season and those who receive it, as well as those who do not receive the information because they have no batteries). In this way, where used, batteries enable information to circulate, at various levels: international, national and local.

3.3.2 Fuel

Just as batteries and radios play a useful and effective role in preventing disasters and coordinating the response to them, fuel also acts as a crucial socio-technical intermediary. Indeed, the last means of communication mentioned by some NGOs is sending volunteers out into the field.

As one NGO manager explained, when disaster strikes, fuel makes it possible to carry out reconnaissance quickly, using all available modes of transport, in order to assess the scale and seriousness of the damage:

> We made resources available, we arrived and we flew over the affected area. We identified the villages with the worst flooding, we held meetings with everybody, we provided boats and we sent teams off in all directions to fill in the forms (EIMA). We collected the forms, collated them and passed them on to the District and to the CNS.

A former BNGRC manager confirmed that fuel makes it possible to tackle unusual or extraordinary situations using unusual or extraordinary vehicles:

> There are some communities so remote that we would be unable to do anything without major equipment, such as helicopters.

It also enables aid, equipment and people to be transported to the affected areas. As a member of the BNGRC explained:

> For example, X[14] is a place that is inaccessible by road or river, so the WFP and UNICEF had to use a helicopter to get to those in need.

In the chain of action, fuel also allows information to circulate. Specifically, it supports the link between manpower and aid at all levels (international, national, regional and local).

However, as in the case of batteries, there is often a shortage of fuel, which hampers the circulation process:

> The fire brigade are very happy to have a bit of fuel to run their engines on operations, because in the other six brigades in Madagascar, they've have got virtually no fuel available to take out the engines. The towns can't afford to put fuel in a fire truck.

> It's too expensive to fly, or even to drive. You need fuel. And there's never enough money, so we have to stay where we are ....

This shortage of fuel, coupled with the lack of transport, complicates and slows down operations:

> The Head of the District has a pirogue. How can you visit 15 villages in 2 weeks in a dugout? When we work with these people, they almost always ask for fuel. Because they've got an engine but they can't run it.

> They don't have any specific equipment to cope with the flooding. They don't have any boats, so when a dyke gave way to the south of Tana one Saturday night, they called out the Civil Protection Corps, who could only come out with one boat. It took all night to carry out an emergency evacuation of the people who were stranded on a small islet that had formed.

These shortages also mean that actions have to be cut back:

> Instead of rations of rice of 400 gm per head, we can only send half as much because there aren't the means to transport them.

In order to be able to keep functioning, the actors prepare, anticipate and find a way to manage:

[14] This location preferred to remain anonymous.

> In a flood, we keep an eye on the speed of the current and the state of the roads to see whether we need four or five trucks or, for the boats, whether we need an outboard motor, etc.

They come up with inventive solutions:

> The buckets that we have distributed – we really have to give people new, clean buckets so that they can disinfect them with bleach and use them to store water – it's unbelievably awkward to transport water by plane. So we're going to order some folding jerry cans, because we've seen that you can get them. So now, we'll be able to include folding jerry cans in our emergency measures. We'll be able to get lots more in a plane and we'll be able to reach more people, more quickly.

Some, but not all, NGOs try to anticipate the shortage of fuel:

> For example, we take precautions, such as having 600 litres stored here as a reserve. We do that so in case there is a problem at the petrol station, with no fuel available for the pirogues or the vehicles. We also keep emergency food stocks here.

However, the question of fuel is also very closely linked to the state of the infrastructure. Can it be used or not? One NGO explained that

> Another limiting factor was that the landing strip was still flooded in some places, so only small aircraft could use it.

Finally, the question of fuel is connected to that of oil fires, a danger seemingly ignored by both the Madagascan authorities and all other agencies. However, as one of our interviewees explained:

> If there were to be an oil fire, either on highway 7 going south or, more importantly, on the fuel route we wouldn't be able to do anything. Really, nothing at all because the Civil Protection Corps isn't equipped to deal with fires – not forest fires, and not this type of fire. So that would be a real problem and the fire would be only be extinguished when there was no more fuel left to burn ....

To summarise, fuel – this 'seemingly unimportant item' – connects a chain of actors and allows both the circulation of information and actual movements and actions to take place. In contrast, a lack of fuel can lead to the physical and psychological isolation of those who have none. This forces them to develop alternative strategies using the means at their disposal. Just like the battery, if used incorrectly, fuel also poses a risk to the environment and the population.

3.3.3 Books, Forms and Reports

As part of this study, we discussed the question of written information at length with our interviewees. This was partly because our work forms part of a project promoting the creation of a 'field library'. In addition, as academics, the written word is our preferred medium (e.g. more so than radio, television or live performances). Finally, it was because the question of written material is not a neutral one and, in the context of risk and disaster management in Madagascar, it embodies a certain number of concerns.

It is important to realise that there is no single form of written material but rather a range, corresponding to the different stages of the emergency described above: before, during and after. We have therefore decided to deal with these phases separately, looking for each case at the 'type' of written format that an analysis of the interviews indicated was best suited to the phase. We will see how those involved classify these different tools according to criteria of usefulness, on which there seems to be more or less general agreement.

3.3.3.1 Before: Books

The interviews contained a number of questions relating to the training and role of the interviewee, the systems for transferring information in Madagascar and also the field library project.

Mention of books as a means of passing on knowledge often came up during the first part of the interviews, when discussing the education and training our interviewees had been given for the purposes of their professional practice. Firstly, books are seen as an important element of primary education. They are deemed to meet the needs of teachers (teachers' guides) and pupils (textbooks). Secondly, they are seen as playing an important role in university education:[15]

> When I was a student in Cape Town, it was through the books belonging to the risk and disaster lecturer that I discovered what risk actually is.

Thirdly, books may play a role at a later stage in the interviewee's life, such as during professional training, or similar. This is a more operational case:

> When I started in this field, my reference books were books published by the United Nations.

For many people, books are in direct competition with – and are often losing out to – other written or audio-visual media or sources of information:

> I have to confess that some of my knowledge of natural disasters comes from films, news coverage or information gleaned from other media. 30 years ago Haroun Tazieff was making that sort of film report.

Internet was also mentioned quite a lot, at least by those in Antananarivo who have Internet access: 'It might be because there is so much information on the Internet that people don't use books'.

Books seem to be strictly linked to acquiring knowledge and to education. They are seen primarily as a useful tool for a certain sector of the population: intellectual and academic circles. The interviewees believed that, exceptionally, and subject to a range of reservations, books could also be used as part of prevention actions to train and inform the public. While this is a valuable use of books, it is nevertheless countered by the need to target the recipients very carefully: 'For every category, a list of suitable types of books could be drawn up'. The list would need to include

[15]The interviewees quoted in this paragraph all have a university education at postgraduate level.

'books which set out measures that the community, or an individual, can take at their own level', books which could be used to give readers often very practical information 'on how to coordinate preventive actions'.

In the context of Madagascar, books are also of a certain 'practical' value: 'Today, the people here would be lost if they had computers. A book will always get you there', provided they meet certain criteria of 'usefulness' and 'ease of use'. 'Not big books, but ones that are easy to read and easy to take with you' is what we were told.

Nevertheless, the target group for information in book form is difficult to define:

> … I believe children and adolescents are very important because if we want to pass on the notion of risk, the quickest way will be via the children. It is easy to persuade them and they can then act as messengers, to their parents and to everyone. Sometimes adults are no longer receptive to messages. And decision-makers, leaders – including the traditional ones, such as doctors – teachers, senior technical representatives from the Ministries, important citizens, NGO representatives and all the rest who are concerned with development in the field often get started on development activities without taking proper account of the risks involved.

While the need for risk-related information and training, at all levels actively involved in disaster prevention or response, is universally recognised, most of our interviewees expressed a degree of resistance, either individually or collectively, to the use of books. As the interviews progressed, it became clear that books were actually more of an embarrassment 'because only 60 % of the population of Madagascar can read and write', leading to the question: 'If we bring books, who is going to read them?' Some people suggested a range of categories: 'the vulnerable population, who could be given strip cartoons and films. Political decision-makers could have books. Schools could have DVDs, CDs, books and magazines. Scientists could use books and reports'.

This situation is seen as …

> a national problem! Here, in Madagascar, people are not all that keen on reading. To give you an example: there are plenty of books in the library, but getting people to read them is really hard work! People are forced to read, that's the problem.

This opinion is shared by others but more in relation to the accessibility of books:

> I would have liked to ask how we could get access to the books. (…) I would think it would be better if the books were available in every province.

Questions of language and the complexity of the content were also raised regularly:

> Books in French, in a trunk – and I bet they are long books – being sent off out into the bush somewhere; I don't give that much of a chance.

Interviewees also referred to the lack of time, as well as of interest:

> Reading a book takes time, and people don't have much time, apart from intellectuals perhaps.

> Books … there are people who don't really like reading books. I'm much more of a computer person, myself, but I do read in bed from time to time to help me get to sleep.

For many of our interviewees, the lack of enthusiasm for books is based mainly on cultural reasons:

> I don't think we've got much of a book culture here; you very rarely see anyone reading.

3.3.3.2 During: Forms

Another socio-technical intermediary mentioned frequently during the interviews is the EIMA (Enquête Initiale Multi-Aléas [Initial Survey of Multiple Disasters]) assessment form. This form has a far more operational objective and acts as a liaison agent between the different actors. While our interviewees were wary of the ability of books to create a connection between the various actors or to transfer information, these forms, despite being mentioned less often, seem to have unanimous approval.

Unlike books, forms are indeed seen as a useful tool that everyone can understand:

> As the person in charge of BNGRC operations in the field, I am interested in the content of the forms and the procedures.

> We all have to have the same reading of the situation, with a common frame of reference; some sort of summary sheet that states that in such and such a region a particular person has done this, that the future needs are this, this and this and what we need to meet these needs is this, this and this.

These forms make it easier to coordinate the activities of the various participants involved in the management of risks and disasters, both in Antananarivo and in the field, i.e. on the coast. The ideal situation in this context would be for forms to be used alongside books:

> It would be really good if the head of a fokontany could have something like a small evaluation committee, which could start work immediately after the cyclone. They should already have the forms and have developed some working methods. They could analyse the damage within 48 hours, and from there the chain of communication is clear: the information is sent to the Mayor, from there to the head of the district and from there to Tana. The aim would be to eliminate the need for external NGOs because they would be able to manage things themselves, so that might be a small book.

Assessment forms are seen as a means of increasing the autonomy of the local populations. However, even though it is recognised to be efficient, this system also seems to be dependent on the local circumstances:

> This form was never finished! That is because, firstly, the partners didn't have time to fill in their stock and, secondly, we didn't have the figures for the number of victims. When it gets to three or four weeks after the event it's too late. By then each NGO has started its own organisation, with no coordination. I think that that's the sort of form we should have. And the BNGRC should tell us who the partners are, what they are prepared to do, and what their stocks are and where.

The apparent simplicity of the system based on assessment forms means it is not possible to circumvent the local constraints (time and distance) which slow down the process:

People have to walk here with the forms, which takes them a week, so we have already lost a week while waiting for the information. [...] But we have made resources available, we came, we flew over the area, we identified the places with the worst flooding, we held meetings with all sorts of people, we provided boats and sent teams off in all directions to get the forms filled in, we got the forms back, we consolidated them and we gave them to the district and the CNS. But all that takes two weeks, and during the cyclone period two weeks is, well, ...

It is clear from this that these forms, while seen as a light and effective instrument, require complex and heavy logistics.

In addition, as with all tools, these forms have to be adapted to suit the needs of the users, or they are likely to remain unused or filled in unreliably[16]:

At the CNS we spent 3 hours working on forms for streamlining and evaluation. Because the EIMA forms are a good tool, but for us, if we want to plan an intervention, they are useless ... well, maybe not useless, but definitely inadequate.

3.3.3.3 After: Reports

Reports are without question the tools most widely used in the practices of participants. They are the result of actions carried out to evaluate, identify, manage, etc. Everyone produces reports, for funding agencies, partners, relevant authorities and NGO headquarters, in the form of monthly reports:

As part of monitoring XX, we produce a report on the annual survey. (...) And we ask our managers to lead a meeting every month with the participating partners in the regions by saying 'Here are the reports'.

I came last Friday and I'll be back again next Monday with my report.

This also demonstrates that reports owe their existence to the involvement of large numbers of individuals and intermediaries. They are the sort of documents that one should be familiar with. For example, we were often asked whether we had heard of a particular report.

The consequences – direct or indirect – can also be very important:

When things are going well, we talk about them, we produce reports and these reports are read by some of the agencies that have funded our work, who then speak to other NGOs, who then try it in their own way in a different area. [...] Then an expert in something or other chances upon it, he puts it in his report and it becomes a United Nations or a World Bank programme involving millions of dollars.

But at the moment, the experts from X[17] have had to carry out an assessment. They've produced a report which says that it is an unnecessary expense. So they've forced the result.

[16]Following an awareness raising campaign among local actors, one NGO noted that the figures given were much more reliable.

[17]This organisation preferred to remain anonymous.

Reports are thus seen as reliable sources of information:

> I would definitely opt for the 'lessons learned' in the field by the UN or regional institutes and NGOs, because when they write reports they include the things they have actually encountered in the field.

This notion of reliability stemming from a knowledge of the 'field' also appears in other interviews:

> I prefer the documents issued by the NGOs. You have to read the NGO websites and reports because they know much more about things than anyone else.

For actors involved in aid and development, reports are by far the best way of transferring and validating information which, thanks to the way it is collected through forms, is seen as a precious commodity, which can be further developed:

> If X[18] has been working for three or six months then there is a lot of information in their final report. The question that then arises is what then happens to that information. In other words, X has learnt a lot of things, they have made good use of what they have learnt and they have included this information in a report made available to others. But afterwards, will what is in the report be used to prevent crises in the future? Will it be of use to other operators and the local authorities? In my opinion that is something we don't yet do enough of.

Books, forms and reports are the means of communication used among the agencies involved in risk and disaster management in Madagascar. They allow communication – mainly vertical – between the actors in line with a model which permits the accumulation of knowledge: top-down in the training phase and bottom-up in the phase of information gathering and the preparation of reports, for example, reports aimed at passing the information 'up' to funding agencies. In the rare cases where knowledge is transferred, this communication may also be horizontal. The 'written' tool, as a formalised representation of reality, or socio-technical intermediary, is able to establish a link between the facts and the people involved – here in relation to a disaster and the response to it – while at the same time marking out the limits of a territory between those who use it and the others. It means clearly defined norms – traceability, centralisation, organisation, validation of information and justification of the correct use of funds[19] – and is a key factor in reconnaissance. It allows certain actors to complete their missions satisfactorily, and at the same time, it forms the border between two sections of Madagascan society: those who act and those who endure.[20] It would be possible to map out the written information which connects just as much as it excludes. This raises the question of understanding and accessibility, as well as of the effectiveness of the means of communication chosen:

---

[18]This organisation preferred to remain anonymous.

[19]This justification is required both by the headquarters, when the organisation's own money is involved, and even more so by financial backers.

[20]There is also a separation between those who manage to find the time to read the various reports and those who concentrate on their operational tasks. For example, an international NGO may have its own pool of experts on climate change, but the field coordinators are unfamiliar with their work.... Thanks to C. Buffet for drawing my attention to this.

> Books, and other forms of written information, are not the way information is passed on here. That's one of the reasons why it is so difficult to get hold of written reports. No, not written information. (...) We talk, we're in a oral culture, where information is passed on orally. That's why the SSBs and the telephone work well, but reports don't, and nor do books. Forget the books!

3.3.4 Figures

Establishing facts and having 'figures' is another key socio-technical intermediary. Figures are one of the basic ingredients of the most sought after information on the island. There is a constant demand for figures to be communicated:

> ... that's the problem with figures. Every time they keep asking us for figures. That really makes things difficult for us because we have to justify everything with figures. We do things on a rough basis, but .... but with figures we need to note everything down because we are forever being asked 'how much?' or 'how many?'

The problems that arise when actors are trying to put together figures were mentioned in several interviews. The figures alone are not enough; they need to be qualified in order to be seen as reliable and credible. One of the criteria is rapid evaluation, but it is difficult to achieve this speed in the field:

> They want figures straight after [the disaster] and we can't provide them. That's because the cyclone has just happened, in remote areas where there are no figures available. We can give percentages. But we can't say how exactly many people have been affected; sometimes we don't know where people have gone and we have to wait about a week, (...) But after a week the information is already out of date. There are people who return to their homes and we don't know exactly who the victims are. Where are the people who were in the centres or who has no food left – we don't know who has been affected. That's the problem.

Another indication of quality is whether there is enough information. This is another difficult criterion:

> (...) there's always some information missing. That's because you can always get more details. And the information has to be correct if we want to respond effectively. There's always something missing. One example, for this area: even though we've spent several hours here, we're still missing some information. That's a bit of a handicap for the action.

For this reason, some NGOs develop their own evaluation system, allowing them to produce usable information:

> Let's say that we devised our own questionnaires and information matrices precisely because in the system, in the administration, some information was incomplete. So, the aim was to gather the missing information in order to be able to carry out the vulnerability assessment. But our resources are still somewhat restricted. We want to avoid duplication. We try to get some information from health or education facilities. But there's still a lot of information about health care or the level of malnutrition, for example, that we can't get hold of, or only with great difficulty. The same goes for weather information too. It's hard to get hold of it. There are very few functioning rain gauges. There is a network, but it isn't good enough for our needs.

Acquiring the detailed figures requires an evaluation consisting of several stages:

> [After a disaster] everyone comes to the CNS asking for information, so we meet every two days at the CNS to get some information. The CNS also has problems gathering information and getting the money together to enable a helicopter or a plane to be sent to the area. Even when they reach the affected area, gathering information is still complicated. Afterwards, it's the responsibility of the municipalities to survey the situation and to send the information to the district, from where it is then sent to the CNS, who make it publicly available.

However, the information gathered does not always meet the needs, as illustrated by the two following extracts from interviews:

> I think the information is inadequate; I'm thinking especially of the information that comes from the base, which takes ages and is inadequate as well. Sometimes this information bears little relation to reality. For example, we have always asked the local authorities to give the BNGRC the actual numbers of victims. But they tend to send percentages, such as the percentage of villages flooded and the percentage of victims.

> We always try to get as much information as we can before leaving so that we can assess what type of equipment and what sort of personnel we need to take. In the field there isn't really a very good evaluation system here. Take the recording of the number of victims, for example. If we don't have people on the ground to tell us what the real situation is with regard to the victims, we have to ask the leaders in the region, who are likely to bump up the numbers of victims, knowing that that's the criterion the bureau (BNGRC) uses to allocate aid. If they say there are 30,000 victims, they will probably get 30 tonnes of rice and dried vegetables, but if they say 80,000 then they'll get that much more.

Getting the figures is also made more difficult by the local geography and the fact that some areas are less well known than others:

> (...) there are some areas we know quite well because we have development projects there and others that we know less well and where there are not as many operators. [...] Very few projects, very few operators and we all found ourselves in a situation where we have little information about what is actually happening because there are no links and the administrative chain didn't work properly. So, a big gap suddenly opened up and we had to fly over the area to try see what was happening and to try and understand it.

These are the very figures that are needed to instigate all forms of aid in the event of a disaster:

> As you are aware, for NGOs, once the numbers start rising it is much easier to get donations etc. We base our efforts on official information. It really is the official figures that we take as the basis for our work.

And for a figure to become official and to be considered reliable, it has to be double-checked:

> Yes, we double check the figures, but it's not just us involved. We share the task with the NGOs, and we also share the sectors with them so that we can respond quickly. We carry out a survey for one or two days and then on the third day we can start the real intervention.

In other words, reaching a figure involves a complex process of agreement and negotiation:

> Representatives from the IGOs come here. They ask us what's going on. And they don't want just a photo of a flooded area, they want precise figures... But the problem is that if we wait for the figures from the CNS it's too slow. So the sort of collaboration we normally do is to provide logistic support. Then we carry out the assessment together. We observe what's happening, and so do they and at the end of the day we agree some figures that both sides can accept.

The figures may indeed vary considerably:

> Well, yes, we had figures for the victims and the damage that were much higher than the figures they were giving in Tana for the first two weeks. This meant that the international funding agencies, who aren't usually present on the ground but who get the official figures from the BNGRC, were saying that there was no real urgency and for two weeks people were talking about 300 victims. In fact, it was 300 victims in the town of Maroantsetra, in the urban area, but 150,000 in the district. And we came to an agreement with the mayors: there were 60,000 people actually in the water.

Having figures (percentages, statistics, etc.) seems to be an essential element of producing information of practical use for the action to be undertaken. Figures are at the heart of the evaluation and counting processes, as well as of negotiations and consensus. Figures are socio-technical intermediaries which are subjected to verification processes, until all the actors involved agree that they are reliable. Once that stage has been reached, the figures can be used to direct the actions to be undertaken and to determine the level of intervention (numbers of trucks, tonnes of soap, kilos of rice, etc.).

An analysis of the socio-technical intermediaries reveals the considerable number of operations required for the action to get underway, as illustrated by the detailed description above. Once these operations have begun, the socio-technical intermediary becomes extremely powerful and active: we have seen the important work – essential but fraught with difficulties – that has to be carried out before information can be seen as credible and a useful reference. This is true of figures but even more so of the EIMA forms and of reports.

3.4 Conclusion

At the end of this case study of the circulation of information in the event of risk or crisis in Madagascar, it is important to produce a clear and detailed summary. We have identified three key areas which we believe should be taken into consideration when developing a guide to best practices.[21]

[21] Among other things, this research has led to the development of a guide to good practices for risk and crisis management in Madagascar.

3.4.1 Continuity Between Categories and Reference Points for Action

It became clear to us that many of the predetermined categories were not suited to the practices followed in the field by the actors we interviewed. This applied particularly to prevention and response. While these are clearly seen as two distinct moments in specialist literature, and by UN agencies, this differentiation does not seem relevant to the practices of the actors in the field. During the interviews, we were often told that prevention and response should go hand in hand, and we saw that many NGOs operate simultaneously in both domains. Within the BNGRC, these categories are also seen as simultaneous actions even though, during our visit, it was clear that priority was being given to urgent matters, with little time being available for reflection and preventive actions.

It also appears that it is the events that have been experienced – the major disasters – that act as reference points, rather than the categories. For example, Cyclone Gafilo, which devastated Madagascar in 2004, is an important reference point for all the actors we spoke to. We realised that it contributed to establishing a dynamic which led to improving prevention and actions to be undertaken. The lessons learned and the various evaluations carried out following the major cyclones (what worked well and what needs improving) should perhaps be seen as the new starting points since, on the one hand, they reflect the actors' practices and, on the other hand, they increase the flexibility of the categories, which some find difficult to implement in the field.

3.4.2 Structure Linking the Levels of Information

We have seen that vertical information flow is the most common profile encountered in Madagascar. This is because of the situation in the country and the highly centralised administrative structure, as well as the existence of a strong presidential power, the sole decision-maker with regard to a number of actions in the field which are coordinated by the BNGRC.

The interviews highlighted the tensions that exist between the different levels of information and the problems in creating a link between these levels. As illustrated by the following extract, the tension is greatest in the field and with regard to gathering information from the municipalities:

> Gradually we have to work in the municipalities, to identify people, to train them, to teach them how to gather and transmit the information and to provide the equipment they would need. It's not really very difficult. There is no information gathering system. It's not that people have the information but are unwilling to pass it on! The information just isn't collected. No-one is actually paid to do that, apart from the agents who work for the big NGOs. In the field there are agents working for the development projects, whom we have trained to do prevention work, and who know without waiting for instructions from me that, if there is a cyclone, then when things have calmed down they need to grab their rucksacks, with enough food for three days and a stack of EIMA forms. Then they need to go and get the forms filled in. There need to be agents like that in every community, but we pay ours.

It is also very frustrating in cases where the content of the message is not always compatible with the level of information. There has been no translation. Many actors insist on the crucial need to harmonise the content of the message – 'Let us decide on the actual wording' – with the way it is transmitted and the target audience:

> We have to make sure that the actors realise that they need to know how to talk [to the inhabitants]. So far, those who have been trying to carry out this awareness campaign haven't known how to speak to people. You have to select the right person to teach them; in some places if you use certain people, everyone will listen. But if the vazaha,[22] the foreigners, come here trying to teach people, then no-one will understand. There's always someone who knows and we have to make sure this person really understands that it's important.

The question of means of communication came up frequently. What would make the translation process easier: communication on a face-to-face basis, as suggested by the previous interviewee, or using a more high-tech solution, as suggested by the interviewee quoted below?

> I would concentrate on the communication system. We need a really efficient system, covering the whole country – that would be telecommunication, using a simple language that could be adapted to suit all levels. A language which would really get across the subject being discussed and the frequency of the information. In Madagascar, we would call that making 'a big noise': making maximum use of telecommunications and the media to make sure that people hear, repeating it as often as necessary. We keep repeating to make sure that people understand, using words that really get the message across.

Finally, it appears that for information to be understood by the people it is aimed at, it must be suited to the situation. This extract offers a good example of the sort of translation needed:

> The important thing is always to define the target at the outset. What do we expect from that target in terms of change or as a result of the action? Then we have to define the appropriate method for the target group. And, finally, it is very important to identify the knowledge to be transferred and to ensure that there is neither too much nor too little and that it uses simple language. That's important, even for people who already have a certain level of training. Sometimes it is difficult to understand the terms used in risk and disaster management. It needs to be simple and pragmatic. One should always start by presenting a bit of the theoretical aspect, just a bit, and then cover the practical aspect. [...] There needs to be someone monitoring the exercise, firstly whether the information has been understood, to be sure that the target group has grasped the information, been able to interpret it correctly, assimilate it and integrate it. Then there need to be s a strategy in place for the next stages because we don't keep giving out information, just like that. We always expect there to be something backing it up. We need to try and direct the follow-on processes: to try to have some to provide support, to ensure that information has been passed on and that it will be put into practice.

[22]Malagasy word for white people. However, in contrast, the presence of a *vazaha* can also have a positive effect: 'It's good that a *vazaha* went to see them.' And in some cases, a *vazaha* who is aware of cultural differences and has a respectful attitude can achieve better results than an educated 'local' from the city, with a different ethnic background, etc.

This translation mechanism can also operate through other elements, which can be seen as various forms of appropriation and 'co-production' of messages, such as traditional singing competitions.

In terms of understanding information, the crucial questions are therefore not only 'who said what to whom?' and 'what are the groups targeted, with what sort of information and for which type of action?', or even 'what information do we need to improve the understanding of the situation and the quality of the response, in relation to both the prevention of and the response to the disaster?', but most importantly 'who can pass on the information?' and 'what means do we have available for passing on the information?'

Indeed, it is clear that the tensions are a significant factor in choosing the relevant scale of analysis to consider. The choice will be seen as legitimate if the translation processes have functioned correctly. The following extract is a good illustration of the translation work, a task which is difficult yet necessary if the information is to be considered relevant:

> One of the problems we face is the level of analysis. Most of the communications we see here relate to households. But we can't deal with households because if we want to cover the whole country we have to establish a base unit. We need to define something that is logistically feasible. The base unit we work with is the municipality. That is already quite big and diverse. But when we discuss things with our partners, like the WFP or an NGO that wants to intervene in the area, we tell them that a particular municipality has such and such a problem and is facing such and such a risk. But that's not always enough for them. They want to know more about the place: the type of households, the social classes, who are the most vulnerable people, which element of the town is most exposed to a risk, etc. We always have to make a compromise on the level of analysis.

3.4.3 *Connexity and Contiguity*

Isolation, distances, response time as well as how close the affected areas were are among the other topics mentioned frequently in our interviews. As we have made clear, a range of socio-technical intermediaries (batteries/radios, fuel, written material (forms, reports, books and figures)) make it possible to compensate for distance and to form connections. We have seen that in risk and crisis management in Madagascar, prevention is viewed primarily in terms of proximity. However, the people we spoke to stated on numerous occasions that an element that appears physically close may not actually be so in reality. A short distance does not necessarily mean that communication will be easy. For this reason, we can say that, as well as relationships of proximity (which we can also call 'contiguity'), there are relationships of connexity.[23] It would seem that information based primarily on this type of relationship is the most useful. However, as we have seen, the socio-technical intermediaries are a key requirement.

[23]For more information on contiguity and connexity, see Lévy (1999) and November (2004).

Since 2010, these ideas have been gradually put into practice. For example, the BNGRC, in partnership with a local telephone company, has established a mass SMS message system to alert the populations at risk from an imminent threat. This partnership also allows users to call either the Madagascan meteorological service or the BNGRC directly for additional information, using a toll-free number. (National follow-up report on the implementation of the Hyogo Framework for Action, interim report, 2010.)

References

Akrich, M. (1992). The de-scription of technical objects. In W. Bijker & J. Law (Eds.), *Shaping technology/building society: Studies in sociotechnical change* (pp. 205–224). Cambridge, MA: MIT Press.

Akrich, M., Callon, M., & Latour, B. (Eds.). (2006). *Sociologie de la traduction: textes fondateurs* (Sciences sociales). Paris: Mines Paris.

Buffet, C. (2010). *Rapport de capitalisation. Madagascar. Programme Réduction des Risques de Catastrophes 2008–2010.* Médecins du Monde-France (p. 52).

Buffet, C. (2011). *Réduction des risques de catastrophes à Madagascar. Étude comparative des programmes DIPECHO au regard du cyclone Bingiza.* Médecins du Monde-France and European Commission (Humanitarian Aid Program) (p. 61).

Callon, M. (1986). Some elements of a sociology of translation: Domestication of the scallops and the fishermen of St Brieuc Bay. In J. Law (Ed.), *Power, action and belief: A new sociology of knowledge?* (pp. 196–223). London: Routledge.

Callon, M., & Law, J. (1995). Agency and the Hybrid Collectif. *The South Atlantic Quarterly, 94*(2), 481–505.

Francken, N., Minten, B., & Swinnen, J. F. M. (2008). Media, monitoring, and capture of public funds: Evidence from Madagascar. *World Development, 37*(1), 242–255.

Francken, N., Minten, B., & Swinnen, J. F. M. (2009). *The Political Economy of Relief Aid Allocation: Evidence from Madagascar.* LICOS Discussion Paper Series (Number 237-2009) University of Leuven: LICOS Centre for Institutions and Economic Performance.

Guha-Sapir, D., Vos, F., Below, R., & Ponserre, S. (2011). *Annual Disaster Statistical Review 2010. Numbers and trends.* Centre for Research on the Epidemiology of Disasters (CRED). Brussels, Belgium: Université catholique de Louvain.

Lévy, J. (1999). *Le tournant géographique. Penser l'espace pour lire le monde.* Paris: Belin.

Maplecroft. (2011). *Climate change risk atlas 2011.* http://maplecroft.com/about/news/ccvi.html. Accessed 3 May 2014.

Morisset, J. (Ed.). (2010). *Madagascar: vers un agenda de relance économique.* Madagascar: World Bank.

November, V. (2004). Being close to risk. From proximity to connexity. *International Journal of Sustainable Development, 7*(3), 273–286.

Revet, S. (2009). *Les organisations internationales et la gestion des risques et des catastrophes « naturels ». Les Études du CERI* (Vol. 157 – septembre 2009). CERI, Sciences Po: Paris.

Rodriguez, F. K. (2010). *Stratégie Nationale de Gestion des Risques et des Catastrophes. Antananarivo, Madagascar* (Project MAG/99/005/A/07/31-05/31). Madagascar: UNDP/CNS.

United Nations. (2011). *Implementation of the International Strategy for Disaster Reduction. Report of the Secretary-General* (Vol. 12 – August 2011). Geneva: United Nations.

Vos, F., Rodriguez, J., Below, R., & Guha-Sapir, D. (2010). *Annual Disaster Statistical Review 2009. The numbers and trends* (Centre of Research on the Epidemiology of Disasters (CRED)). Brussels/Belgium: Université catholique de Louvain.

Chapter 4
Using and Communicating Information: Practices Adopted by Two NGOs in Cameroon

4.1 Introduction

4.1.1 The National Context with Regard to Health and Environmental Problems

Cameroon is a country in Central Africa. It is often said to be a condensed version of Africa as it brings together all the representative elements of the continent. Its wide range of climates, cultures, demographic data, peoples and languages have earned it the nickname of 'Africa in miniature'.

Cameroon has been in turn a German colony (1884–1918); a British colony, covering an area to the west of the present country; and a French colony (1918–1960). Prior to that, contacts between Europe and Africa were established in 1472 by the Portuguese explorer Fernando Pó. He explored part of the Wouri estuary, which he called the 'Rio dos Camaroes' (Shrimp River), leading later to the name of Cameroon. Throughout the centuries, various European religious missions and trading posts were established, until eventually a treaty of assistance was signed between Germany and the Douala. From the time of this agreement and the permanent arrival of European settlers, the consequences for the peoples of Cameroon were the same as in other colonies across the world: the deconstruction of the local social structures and their replacement by western institutions. One effect of this was a 'reform' of the health-care system.

A sociohistoric evaluation of the colonial presence in Cameroon shows that, overall, it was characterised by clear discriminatory intentions between the health-care policies applied to the local population and the colonisers. Priority was given to the health of the Europeans and medical services were provided for the local population, without any involvement on their part in the way their health-care system was set up. Following independence in 1960, the national health-care policy, continuing the practices of the colonial period, was based exclusively on the

V. November, Y. Leanza, *Risk, Disaster and Crisis Reduction*,
DOI 10.1007/978-3-319-08542-5_4

development of European biomedicine.[1] Various institutions for medical training were founded in 1969, including the University Centre for Health Sciences (CUSS). This centre, which in 1993 was renamed the Faculty of Medicine and Biomedical Sciences (FMSB), is concerned exclusively with training health professionals with responsibility for public health (Okalla and Le Vigouroux 2006).

However, Cameroon has a number of medical traditions, not only that which was imported by the Europeans. Today, as well as the doctors, there are at least two groups of 'caregivers' providing health care. The doctors are trained in medical schools (in Cameroon or elsewhere) and have a biomedical view of illness. They are recognised as official medical practitioners by the Ministry of Health. The two other groups of caregivers providing health care are the traditional therapists and the faith healers (Wamba 2005). According to the WHO, a traditional therapist is 'a person recognized by his community as being competent to dispense health care through the use of animal, vegetable and mineral substances or through other methods based on a socio-cultural and religious foundation, as well as on the knowledge, behaviour and beliefs associated with physical and mental welfare and on the etiology of the diseases and disorders prevalent in the community' (World Health Organisation 1976). In many African countries the term traditional therapist is often used as a synonym for nganga (De Rosny 1992). In this study, the term nganga refers to a 'seer' or someone who has been given the gift of second sight. His role is purely diagnostic, while a traditional therapist offers treatment. There are, however, some nganga who combine the two roles. They are known as traditional therapists-seers. The faith healers believe they have received a divine gift for healing. They are often to be found at the heart of religious organisations (or churches) and offer no medication other than prayer or the laying on of hands during religious ceremonies, which may be attended by several hundred people (Wamba 2005). For the purposes of this research, we have focussed solely on traditional therapists.

Until very recently there were no links between the health authorities and the numerous urban or rural traditional therapists even though, for some illnesses, their contribution was widely recognised by the population. The imposition of biomedicine as the sole reference for medical care and understanding of the illness also implied a relationship of power between the exponents of the different forms of medicine, rendering any collaboration between local medicine and biomedicine virtually impossible (Wamba 2005). Only the priests maintained good relations with the doctors because they often had a dual role, religious and medical. (However, priests should not be confused with faith healers, who often have no religious training.) The need to bring together the traditional therapists and the health services did not become important until the collapse of the public health structures caused by the advent of the African economic crisis of 1980 (Hours 1990). Other events, such as the failure of the structural adjustment programmes and the emergence of certain

[1] 'Biomedicine' is a term used to refer to traditional western medicine, where the principal characteristic is the focus on biology, to the detriment of other dimensions of human health, hence the prefix 'bio'. In this work practitioners of this type of medicine are referred to as doctors.

diseases, such as AIDS, for which the public health system was unable to provide any satisfactory solution, drove the State towards the decentralisation of health-care services.

The movement towards decentralisation can also be seen as the State distancing itself from its responsibilities (Hours 1986). It resulted in the power of the State being called into question (Eboko 2000) and the intervention of national and international organisations in an effort to reduce the risk factors and to combat endemo-epidemic diseases. In the context of Cameroon, as in most African countries, the principal risk factors are environmental, socio-economic and human. Each risk factor creates a specific type of health problem, most of which are considered to be endemic (Baudon et al. 1999).

In terms of the environment, the risk factors are linked to difficult geographic, climatic and ecological conditions. These factors lead to the proliferation and transmission of a large number of diseases borne by mosquitoes or other insects. These include malaria, yellow fever, filariasis, onchocerciasis, sleeping sickness and plague. Furthermore, harsh climatic conditions, such as drought, are the cause of airborne diseases, such as acute respiratory infections, tuberculosis and measles. The same applies to cerebrospinal and meningococcal meningitis, which is particularly prevalent in areas with a Sudano-Sahelian climate. Meningitis epidemics occur in the cold and dry season: the dryness combined with the sandstorms weakens the nasal mucus membranes, making the population more vulnerable to these infections.

From the socio-economic point of view, underdevelopment, poverty and poor living conditions are considered to be high risk factors for disease. For example, a lack of personal and collective hygiene, difficult access to drinking water and malnutrition favour the transmission and spread of bacteria. These risk factors contribute to diseases caused by faecal contamination, such as cholera, diarrhoeas, viral hepatitis, poliomyelitis as well as diseases spread by cutaneous transmission, such as leprosy.

In terms of human factors, the behaviour of individuals is seen as a factor in the transmission of major endemic diseases, such as sexually transmitted diseases, in particular HIV/AIDS. It also appears that human dietary patterns are also the cause of health problems, such as obesity. However, of all the endemic diseases rife in Cameroon, malaria and AIDS are the two that most affect the population.

Malaria is the most widely spread endemic disease in the world. According to Youmba and Barrère (2005), it affects almost two billion people. Sub-Saharan Africa alone has the highest rate of infection: 80–90 %. Every year malaria kills between 1.1 and 2.7 million people across the world, including 1 million children aged under 5 in Sub-Saharan Africa. In Cameroon malaria is the most common cause of morbidity (35–40 %) and death (50 %) among under-fives and pregnant women (Youmba and Barrère 2005).

The Joint United Nations Programme on HIV/AIDS (2008) estimates that the total number of people living with HIV/AIDS is between 30 and 36 million. Of these, 23 million – 67 % – live in sub-Saharan Africa. The same UN programme estimates that in Cameroon 3.9–6.2 % of the population carry the virus.

Today there is a range of organisations available to support the state of Cameroon and its minister of health in their endeavours to reduce the risk factors and combat the major endemic diseases (Eboko 1999). These include UN bodies (WHO, World Bank, UNICEF, UNAIDS, WFP, etc.); international organisations such as bilateral and multilateral cooperation agencies (European Union, ACDI,[2] GTZ[3] etc.) and, finally, NGOs, both international (Care International, MSF, etc.) and local (WESDE, PROSENAT etc.). This study is concerned with the professionals active within WESDE and PROSENAT.[4]

4.1.2 Objectives of the Research Carried Out in Cameroon

For this part of the study, we have looked in depth at the questions relating to how information is collected and communicated to the target population groups. The problem of the prevention of health risks opens up a very wide field, which goes far beyond the capabilities of the public health service. In most cases, the task of preventing inappropriate behaviour and risk factors which contribute to the spread of disease are restricted solely to limiting the spread of the disease among population groups already affected. This is not enough. Nowadays, the State, in Cameroon as elsewhere, finds it increasingly difficult to communicate preventive messages using only official health-care specialists, in other words, those recognised by government bodies (such as the Ministry of Health). For example, in campaigns intended to raise awareness of sexually transmitted diseases, when the preventive talk is given by an expert, there is a distinct feeling of passive resistance among the population. People are less likely to make an effort and interpret the educational health statements passed on by the experts as, for example, measures aimed at controlling or reducing the number of births.

Paradoxically, when the preventive action is led by non-official health professionals, the population groups are more likely to pick up on the message and to improve their high risk social behaviour. This is because these groups pay far greater attention to the religious authorities (imams, priests, religious leaders from other faiths); the community leaders, such as the traditional authorities; and the practitioners of traditional medicine (traditional therapists, marabouts, etc.) than the health-care professionals. The lack of attention paid to the messages delivered by these experts demonstrates the need to involve the community structures in the fight against health risks. This is the way in which, like many other structures, WESDE and PROSENAT, the two organisations selected for this research project, are involved in health education and disease prevention. However, as we will see, this was not always easy.

---

[2]Canadian Development Agency.

[3]German technical cooperation.

[4]WESDE (Water Energy and Sanitation for Development); PROSENAT (*Progrès Santé par Espèce Naturelle,* [Health Progress through Natural Means]); these two NGOs are at the centre of the research presented here. More information on these organisations follows later in this chapter.

WESDE and PROSENAT act as relay centres for health care and the communication of information. Thus, if a member of PROSENAT is asked a difficult question, it can be transferred and put to someone else, such as a doctor or an exorcist priest. The same applies to WESDE, which works closely with organisations which are specialised in dealing with children, social assistants or hospitals. It would therefore appear that these two structures are the first place in which a 'therapeutic path' (Janzen 1995) is determined as they guide the communities in their search for care and advice. The health action messages pass through these different structures. We can assume that they play a role in passing on the health education messages devised by the officially approved health-care agencies, such as the ministry and the WHO. This thus enables them to act as intermediaries between the communities and the other players in the health field.

In addition, their field of action is growing as that of the public health services declines. Hours (1986) and, more recently, Okalla and Le Vigouroux (2006) have highlighted the process by which the state of Cameroon is distancing itself from its responsibilities. The role played by local NGOs in the fight to reduce health risks is seen as an essential contribution to the programme to improve development through promoting good health, incorporating both individual responsibility and the collective responsibility of the population groups. However, the lack of state resources makes this contribution essential, leading to the following paradoxical situation: a state which has little inclination to recognise the benefits of traditional medicine is, by default, partly obliged to make use of the networks established by the practitioners of such medicine to spread the message of prevention.

As indicated above in the general outline of this research project, our interest in these NGOs stems from the fact that, like the public health services, they occupy a prime position in the use and communication of health education messages. Thus, we first explored how the caregivers in these structures define the risks: this is our first research question. We also looked at the source of their knowledge and information pertaining to these risks. In order to answer this second research question, we studied their training (basic and ongoing) and other sources of information available to the caregivers in the two organisations. Finally, we examined the means favoured by these caregivers to transmit the information to the target groups (their clients, patients or communities). The first two questions (definition of the risk and source of information) enabled us to explore the representations or ethnotheories and the third question their practices.

4.1.3 Presentation of Two NGOs, Local Contexts and Populations

4.1.3.1 WESDE

WESDE (Water Energy and Sanitation for Development) is a non-governmental organisation (NGO) established in January 2004 in Maroua, capital of the Extreme

North region[5] of Cameroon. This region has a population of approximately three million and covers just under 35,000 km^2, which is 7.2 % of the national territory. To the west the region borders Niger, to the north and east Chad. The inhabitants live mainly from agriculture, livestock and fishing. Over the past few decades, agriculture has changed radically, partly because of demographic pressure (the rural population of the Extreme North region has more than doubled in 50 years Roupsard 1987) and partly because some of the agricultural land previously devoted to food production is now used to grow cotton. A farming system known as 'cotton-cereals' has been introduced whereby farmers grow cotton followed by cereals (mainly sorghum), alternating with the seasons (Devèze 2006). However, this system is very dependent on the world cotton price, which has collapsed since the beginning of the century. Moreover, soil fertility has been drastically reduced by the fact that this system does not include a fallow period (Njomaha 2003). These conditions, together with other social problems such as internal migration, corruption and an increasing lack of interest shown by central government in this distant region, are the ingredients of a cocktail which could well prove explosive in the long term (Courade 2000; Devèze 2006).

This part of Cameroon suffers from a very harsh Sahelian, desert climate. Such conditions undoubtedly have devastating consequences on life in general as they are accompanied by dryness which, in turn, leads to a lack of water. A lack or shortage of water, or poor water management, causes considerable problems for both livestock and arable farming, as well as for the health of the population.

Both livestock and arable farming are highly dependent on climatic conditions. Thus, a long dry season leads to a lack of food grown in the fields or obtained from the animals. In such circumstances, the population is at great risk of famine. The principal effect of this – malnutrition – can weaken the immune system among children, thereby rendering them very vulnerable to disease.

It should however be noted that the risks to which the people of Cameroon, and especially those in Maroua, are constantly exposed do not stem entirely from the lack or shortage of water caused by the severe climate. Poor use of water or the agricultural produce, or inadequate management, can also constitute a source of disease. Similarly behaviour patterns, notably risky food practices such as all eating from the same dish, also present real dangers to human health. In their own way, each of these factors is the cause of serious health problems.

The ways in which the arable and livestock produce are used have an indirect effect on health. Apart from the fact that malnutrition caused by famine reduces the immune defence system, poor management or treatment of agricultural, animal (or fish) produce can also expose the population to major risk of disease. Thus, most of the inhabitants of Maroua suffer from the secondary effects of the pollution caused

[5]Since 2008 Cameroon has been divided into regions rather than the former provinces.

by the waste products from SODECOTON[6] and NOTACAM.[7] In addition to the pollution caused by industry, people often share their living quarters with animals, which exposes them to the risk of contamination.

With regard to eating habits, the custom of several people sharing the same plate or using the same water bowl presents a major risk for the transmission of contagious diseases, such as tuberculosis or measles. With regard to health problems related to water, its management and use raise the problem of inadequate hygiene. In most cases, the villages make no provision latrines or toilets when building houses. The rural population therefore defecates upstream in rivers where the water is used for a range of purposes: laundry, drinking, horticultural irrigation, etc. People collect their water supplies from the place where animals drink. Wells, where they exist, are badly maintained. All these factors combine to cause diseases, the most common of which are the diarrhoeal diseases and cholera. There are also the cyclical diseases, which are related to specific climatic variations. These include meningitis and certain respiratory afflictions (such as asthma).

In addition, certain behaviour patterns and ways of life, reinforced by customs and practices, are also partly responsible for the health risks to which the population are regularly exposed. This is true of traditional practices such as scarification, female genital cutting and certain traditional hairdressing practices. These are carried out on young children, in some cases soon after birth. It should be noted that it is not the scarification or female circumcision itself that cause the danger, but the way they are carried out. In most cases, those who officiate at the female circumcision or scarification ceremonies use the same instrument – a non-disinfected knife or razor blade – for several people.

Certain customs, reinforced by religious beliefs, are also a factor in the transmission of sexually transmitted infections (STI)[8] and HIV/AIDS. This completes the general clinical summary of situations liable to lead to health problems among the population groups of Maroua, in particular in rural areas. Gubry has compiled an inventory and notes that

> The morbidity rate, which has a direct bearing on the mortality rate, is in all cases linked to the standard of living in general, the ecological environment, food, access to drinking water, health care infrastructures and personnel, communication facilities, education and the customs of the population … There is no denying the fact that in almost all these areas northern Cameroon has disadvantages and is lagging behind the rest of the country; this is a significant discrepancy which the publicly stated or implicit policy of regional balance has thus far been unable to resolve. (Gubry 1996: 120)

For the purposes of this research project and for the population of Maroua, we have selected two areas from this long list of health problems: STIs and HIV/AIDS and disease linked to water. This choice is explained by the fact that they constitute the

[6] A cotton processing company; the products are used in the manufacture of textiles.

[7] A company processing animal skins; the products are used in the manufacture of shoes and leather bags.

[8] STIs are also referred to as sexually transmitted diseases (STD).

main health problems faced by the population of Maroua and are those for which the staff of WESDE are endeavouring to communicate a preventive message.

Although the health problems arising from the environmental pollution caused by industrial toxic waste have been mentioned, they are not covered by this research project. This is because as yet WESDE has not made them a priority area, though not because they do not represent a danger to health. Rather, the heads of these industries are unwilling to discuss solutions which would protect the population from the health risks caused by their products. It should be pointed out that these health problems are not confined to the Maroua region. In other regions in Cameroon, such as Yaoundé, the site of our second research project, the health-care situation is equally difficult.

In this context, WESDE's aim is to promote the better management of resources and to stimulate local potential for sustainable development. The NGO's activities cover three main sectors:

1. The integrated management of water resources
2. The promotion and wider use of renewable sources of energy
3. Multi-sector sanitation – health and education

Four main themes, which cut across these three sectors, have been developed simultaneously: (1) education and environmental information, (2) research applied to development, (3) strengthening capabilities and (4) type and development. WESDE is working towards the following goals:

1. Increasing the percentage of the population with permanent access to drinking water
2. Improving sanitation and living conditions among the poorer sectors of the population
3. Educating and training population groups to ensure sustainable management of water resources and to protect the environment
4. Reducing the spread of HIV/AIDS and sexually transmitted infections (STI)

To achieve these aims, WESDE has recruited staff with a wide range of skills and knowledge. The NGO employs a total of 23 people, comprising five coordinators, five health-care trainers, four social workers, three environmental experts, two nurses, a lawyer, a secretary, a driver, an accountant and a janitor. Of these, seven are paid employees and 16 are volunteers. Seven have attended university, including one with a specialist diploma and one at Masters level. Seven have completed secondary education and the remaining nine have completed primary education.

The research focussed on two of WESDE's activities: multi-sector sanitation and environmental education and information. To facilitate the work, all of the WESDE staff were approached individually and nine were selected for the actual interview process. This selection was based on two main criteria: the ability to speak French and the knowledge of an area of activity related to health or environmental education. The activities considered were those related to community health education and environmental health education.

4.1.3.2 PROSENAT

PROSENAT (Progrès Santé par Espèce Naturelle, [Health Progress through Natural Means]) is an organisation which brings together therapists using various medical traditions. It is a Common Initiative Group (CIG) in the sense of Cameroon law (law no. 92/006 of 14 August 1992 and the corresponding enabling legislation no. 92/455/PM of 23 November 1992). The creation of CIGs is part of the government strategy to reduce poverty. Unlike WESDE, which is a non-profit-making organisation, PROSENAT can be seen as a group of economic interests, since the ultimate aim of CIGs is economic development. The flexibility of the legal provisions which apply to these 'groups' enables each organisation to find its place in the economic and social environment, taking account of the specific problems it encounters or is seeking to resolve. The CIGs, together with other types of associations, such as cooperatives, development committees and of course the traditional local associations (tontines, manjong, chii, sourga, etc.), are seen as a key driving force in the economy of Cameroon, thanks to the effect of solidarity and consolidation of resources they create. As in the case of agriculture, they counter the failings, or even the disengagement, of the State, however without the rural communities in which they have been established being able to achieve a significant level of development (Moupou and Akei Mbanga 2008).

PROSENAT was established in March 2003 in Yaoundé, the administrative and political capital of Cameroon, located in the Centre region. The Cameroon National Institute of Statistics estimates its population to be around 1,250,000 (figure for 2006 available on www.statistics-cameroon.org). However, this figure is a projection based on the 1987 census, and the figure of two million inhabitants is sometimes given (Wamba, personal communication). The city has grown up round a trading post established by the Germans. Under the French protectorate, this trading station became the capital of Cameroon. The population growth is phenomenal, since in 1926 there were only 5,500 inhabitants. This growth is the result of internal migration, caused mainly by the rural exodus. The city has a multi-ethnic population. The Béti and Bamiléké appear to be the largest groups, though there are many others from all regions of Cameroon (Socpa 2003). The ethnic diversity is the cause of tension in Cameroon internal politics (Yenshu Vubo 2006).

Yaoundé is one of the largest metropolitan areas in Cameroon, others being Douala and Bafoussam. The climate here is much milder than in the Maroua region; temperatures often drop below 15° and rarely exceed 40° in the shade. This type of climate has the advantage of being suited to lush vegetation and thus favourable to dense agricultural practices which, at least in part, avoids health problems caused by malnutrition.

Although the climate in this part of Cameroon would appear to make it a pleasant place to live, the inhabitants of Yaoundé are nevertheless not spared from the health problems found in the Maroua region. So it is that the HIV/AIDS pandemic is a scourge common to both areas. Yaoundé, being much more part of the modern, globalised world, also has some incidence of health problems such as hyper-/hypotension, cardiovascular disease, diabetes and obesity, which the population itself refers to as 'diseases caused by civilisation'. There are many others, such as malaria and tuberculosis, which as a result of the availability of medical services equipped with new medical technology seem to have been brought under control by the public health-care system. However, HIV/AIDS and the long list of cardiovascular diseases claim new victims every day and are a focus for health-care professionals in both the biomedicine and the traditional medicine sectors. Nowadays these illnesses are seen in Cameroon as public health problems, with society as a whole striving to find ways of limiting their spread.

This explains the gradual emergence of health-care structures being set up almost in competition with the public health system. These structures, mostly run by non-specialised staff, offer patients health care at affordable prices. There are many indications that patients no longer automatically turn to the hospital. Studies of the route taken by patients seeking treatment reveal that they use hospitals for very precise services using the latest technology, such as X-rays or screening tests, for example, for STIs or AIDS. The actual care is increasingly being provided by less specialised health-care structures. In other words, medical care strategies go far beyond the care offered solely by public health services. These days, many agencies, both national and international, are involved in the fight against these diseases. PROSENAT is one of them.

It is a group of therapists, made up of both doctors and traditional therapists who are concerned with various health problems, including STI and AIDS and cardiovascular disease. These two categories of disease were chosen not only because they are particularly dramatic but also because they came up regularly in discussions among the therapists who are members of PROSENAT. With regard to cardiovascular diseases, the focus in this research project is on obesity, a condition which currently affects a large number of people in Yaoundé. They are highly likely to turn to this group of therapists to seek some form of relief.

When it was founded, PROSENAT was made up solely of traditional therapists. Today the organisation has diversified and the membership includes doctors and exorcist priests. Its aim is to carry out activities promoting primary health care in Cameroon. To this end, PROSENAT has defined the following goals:

1. To set up 'health-care posts' and promote training in and research into the use of medicinal plants
2. To fight poverty and squalor by improving health through means easily accessible to the population
3. To be part of the fight against endemics and pandemics in collaboration with the Ministry of Health, non-governmental organisations (NGO) and international institutions (WHO)

PROSENAT is run by a coordinator, known as a Delegate. At the time the research was carried out, the organisation had 25 active members, including six doctors, four exorcist priests, two faith healers (seers) and 13 traditional therapists. To ensure that our work proceeded smoothly, we met all the members of

PROSENAT during a General Assembly in February 2007. On that occasion, we were able to present the aims of the research. To select participants for the study, we held individual discussions with every member, following which ten people were chosen: four doctors and six traditional therapists. The choice of participants was based on two criteria: a knowledge of French and familiarity with the treatments for illnesses for which a preventive discourse exists.

4.1.4 Research Methods

We used two research methods to collect data: personal interviews (PI) and direct observation (DO). Ws carried out PIs in Yaoundé and Maroua and DO only in Yaoundé. The decision to undertake DO in Yaoundé was based on the characteristics of the participants. For example, when studying traditional therapies, certain aspects of the healing procedure are not easily expressed in words. Furthermore, it is not always straightforward to differentiate between a discourse relating to prevention and one relating to therapy. We therefore decided to follow a number of healing sessions with the traditional therapists in order to be able to distinguish the preventive messages from the therapeutic discourse.

4.1.4.1 Field Studies

The PIs were of a semi-directive nature. All interviews were recorded using a camera and a dictaphone (two recordings for greater security). The consultations we observed were filmed. The collection of data from the traditional therapists in Yaoundé took place in three stages: the initial interviews, the DO and the actual PI. In the case of bio-doctors and the WESDE caregivers, PIs were the only method used to collect data.

1. The initial interviews
   These took place in two stages. The aim was to gather information on the professional training and/or initiation route followed by the therapists. We also tried to identify in the professional training the information relating to (disease) risk prevention and the diseases for which such information was given. Following the preliminary interviews, we arranged DO sessions with six traditional therapists.[9]

[9] Some examples of questions discussed during the preliminary interviews: how does one become a traditional therapist/seer? Is there someone with whom you follow an apprenticeship or who initiates you into the function of traditional therapist/seer? How is the power to heal transmitted from one person to another? Is there a path to follow or stages to go through in order to become a traditional therapist/seer? If so, could you describe the details of these stages? What is a pupil expected to know at the end of each stage? If you have received a gift, how is it passed on? How did you learn about the use of traditional medicinal plants?

2. Direct observation
   The DO related to the consultations with the traditional therapists. We attended four consultations with traditional therapists, three of which concerned obesity and one illnesses brought on by witchcraft. All the DO sessions were filmed. During the sessions we did not ask questions, but rather tried to pinpoint the aspects which linked to the way in which the therapists use and transmit educational and preventive messages. To this end we watched again the video footage of each therapist and analysed the videos to reveal the messages. The purpose of this phase was not to gather data, but to prepare for the personal interviews (which is why this paper contains no analysis of these observations).
3. The personal interviews
   In the case of the traditional therapists, the DO sequences provided a starting point for the PIs. These PIs focused on two topics:

   (a) How the information is transmitted; is the therapist's preventive message communicated to the patients orally, in writing, using pictures or in some other way? Also, the words and metaphors used by the traditional therapists when talking about sensitive or taboo subjects, such as condoms, sexual intercourse or relationships.
   (b) Where the traditional therapists' knowledge comes from: what are their references? Where do they find the information they pass on?

In the case of the doctors and the WESDE caregivers, the interviews focused on topics related to waterborne diseases and on STI/AIDS. We looked at the same areas as for the traditional therapists: training, information sources and communication methods. STI/AIDS and malaria were common to both fields.

The data recorded for the two fields were transcribed immediately following the interviews. The thematic analyses of the interviews were carried out according to Bardin's recommendations (1993). The analyses are presented in the next three sections. The first two sections (Sect. 4.2 and 4.3) relate to the members of PROSENAT, first the doctors then the traditional therapists. The next section (Sect. 4.4) contains the analyses of the interviews and observation sessions carried out with WESDE. The fifth section is a concluding summary.

4.2 The Doctors Working with PROSENAT

Four doctors agreed to take part in the research, three men and woman. They are aged between 35 and 50 and have been practising medicine for at least 10 years.

4.2.1 Definition of Risk and of Prevention

The doctors have a common definition of risk which, in the somewhat ironic words of one of them[10] can be summarised as 'all the factors which give rise to particular danger'.

The doctors agree that to maintain good health, it is essential to 'use all possible methods to prevent the transmission of disease'. In other words, if an individual is aware of the factors that increase the risk, but ignores them, he is exhibiting irresponsible behaviour, which may lead to illness. These practitioners note that the factors which increase the danger to health vary in the level of risk. They give examples of behaviour which may increase the danger, such as the use of tobacco, drugs or alcohol, which may increase the harmful consequences caused by dependence and abuse. Further, polygamy and prostitution are practices which increase the danger of transmitting HIV/AIDS or STIs. The risks can also be increased indirectly by environmental factors. Poverty and squalor are the examples given by the practitioners to illustrate such factors. One doctor added that several risk factors exist within Cameroon society as a result of the 'overall lack of knowledge about health' among the population. Their definition of health risk, even in the context of their situation, is based on the idea of individual responsibility: 'risk derives from the wrong attitude or an inadequate response to the danger, which involves ignoring the fatal consequences that could ensue'.

In their interviews, the doctors generally divide risk into two categories: 'professional risk' and 'non-professional risk'. Professional risk is seen as 'the factors that increase danger in the medical environment'. By this, the doctors mean risks to which health professionals are exposed in their working environment, such as contaminants (infected material) and communicable diseases. 'Universal protective measures and appropriate procedures for contagious equipment', implemented constantly, were cited as means of limiting the risk factors in this environment. It is interesting to note that this particular doctor believes that there are universal preventive methods applicable in all contexts. Another of the doctors questioned emphasised how important it is for the health-care system to recognise the need to eliminate professional risks by developing universal measures (sic) to prevent contamination.

Non-professional risks are all the other risks that 'increase a particular danger'. One doctor states, with regard to non-professional risks, that the biggest challenge facing him and his colleagues is to ensure that 'practices aimed at limiting the risk are followed and monitored'. The health risks mentioned systematically in the interviews were failing to use condoms, or using them incorrectly, sharing needles and drinking contaminated water.

---

[10]In order to preserve the anonymity of all those who took part in the research project, who are easily identifiable because of the small numbers involved and their connection with PROSENAT and WESDE, the text makes no mention, not even in coded form, of the name of the participant when quoting from the interviews.

Two diseases were regularly mentioned in the interviews with doctors as prototypical examples: HIV/AIDS and tuberculosis. The doctors' main concern, in both the professional and non-professional environment, is the risk of HIV/AIDS being passed on. Again, the doctors see this specific risk facing their patients as being dependent on individual practices and the knowledge – individual and collective – of the preventive messages and instruments available.

Tuberculosis is used as a classic example by the doctors to illustrate their definition of levels of risk or different risks linked to the same disease: 'The first risk is not in treating tuberculosis once it has been identified, but rather in treating it as something else. The second risk arises when patients do not take the medication intended to cure the disease. The third risk relates to sexual relations with someone who is not treating their tuberculosis'. This doctor adds that the hospital's lack of personnel and resources to evaluate the disease is a significant factor in the spread of tuberculosis. Another doctor voiced the criticism that the medical monitoring of tuberculosis is only one facet in reducing the risk: 'The other facet is improving the standard of living. For example, not having ten people living in the same room would lessen the risk of transmission ... If people lived in better conditions, they would not be as ill'.

Although the definitions put forward by the doctors include a degree of context, the key aspect of what makes up the risk lies with the individual and individual behaviour. It is clear that from the different and underlying levels of risk, a 'before, during, after' model is emerging: detect the disease (before), treat the disease (during) and ensure that the disease does not spread (after).

With regard to prevention, the following definition represents the ideas voiced by all the doctors: 'Stopping the disease. To halt the spread one should use all available methods to prevent infection'. In addition, prevention is described as an 'action. It comprises the means on hand and a general focussed attitude to prevent a consequence. There is awareness raising, which is collective prevention, individual prevention, which asks individuals to use different methods to avoid becoming infected or infecting others, medical prevention, which is the prevention of opportunistic infection through giving treatment, and the prevention of accidents through the implementation of measures to avoid infection'. The choices made by a young person not to indulge in sexual relations before marriage or by a parent to have their children vaccinated are (frequently recurring) examples of responsible preventive behaviour given by the practitioners.

One of the doctors questioned described his view of the different stages of prevention, taking HIV/AIDS as his example. He described three levels of prevention: (1) primary prevention, (2) secondary prevention and (3) tertiary prevention. Each stage of prevention has its own timeframe, tools and methods, and challenges. The three types of prevention are set out below, illustrated by examples from the words of the doctors.

1. 'As we see it, primary prevention means avoiding any exposure. For example a consultation on abstinence can be divided into three parts. It starts with 'Sir or Madam, you are a virgin' then you explain that they can remain virgins and

thus protect themselves from exposure'. The doctors believe that exposure can be reduced through the use of educational tools, such as the dialogue shown in the example, and also by providing information about, for example, the risks involved in sharing razor blades or the need for medical staff and drug users to use single-use hypodermic needles rather than sharing them. The participants have identified the challenges posed by primary prevention as being the widespread social factors, such as poverty, illiteracy, restricted or severe cultural/moral views and irresponsible individual actions.

2. Secondary prevention consists of actions intended to avoid 'aggravating a (risk) situation'. An example of an instrument required for prevention is HIV screening at least 1 month after unprotected sexual relations. If the test results are positive, the doctor encourages the infected to person to always use a condom. The major problem with secondary prevention identified by the doctors is the 'fear of reality' when individuals are faced with the possibility that they may have contracted HIV. This fear 'which is recognised as being increased by poverty and social stigma' is likely to lead to behaviour which runs counter to the need for prevention, as a form of denial of the awful reality.
3. Tertiary prevention is aimed at individuals who have already contracted HIV/AIDS or indeed any other disease. The aim is to reduce the risk of complications caused by further infection. The doctor explained that 'the third stage of prevention is treatment. We invite the patient to take the medication, which will allow the course of the disease to be stabilised'. This type of prevention attempts to preclude opportunistic infections by providing treatment, antibiotics and other therapies. The doctor is of the opinion that the greatest problem for tertiary protection is its cost, as most infected patients are very poor and unable to afford medication.

The doctors recognise that preventive measures (and the definition of prevention) are regularly reviewed and revised. One doctor speaks of the prevention models having evolved from mass educational campaigns to more personal, individual consultations. The reason given for this change of approach is the need to adapt the preventive messages to individual requirements and life styles. 'Prevention will have been achieved when each individual tries to shape his behaviour, leading to new behaviour patterns. If everyone can exert control at an individual level, the behaviour will spread to others'. Thus, 'I hold very few mass events, but lots of individual consultations'. In addition, the doctors stressed the importance, for both the medical profession and the awareness raising programmes, of 'curbing the liberalisation of the media' in order to help the public to distinguish between the good messages and those which encourage risky behaviour, such as advertising promoting foodstuffs high in fat and sugar.

Again, the pattern of 'before, during, after' underlies the doctors' thoughts on prevention. Moreover, the emphasis is again on the characteristics of individual behaviour, although the role of contextual factors is greater than in the discussions on risk. However, this interest in contextual factors leads to the adoption of a political, or even moral, stance, whether it be as doctor confronting society or as a doctor facing a patient in an individual consultation.

4.2.2 Sources of Information and Professional Training Routes

The doctors taking part in the research are practitioners with a range of specialisations, who trained either at the University of Yaoundé or another academic institution outside Cameroon. Their training varied from a minimum of 4 years of medical school to 12 years, depending on the medical specialisation and the length of certain programmes. Most of the doctors specialise in a specific area, such as mental health, tuberculosis, HIV/AIDS or infectious diseases. Some doctors have also obtained additional qualifications in public health or other health-related areas.

According to the participating doctors, the training they received in their medical institutions was a combination of theory and practice, involving classes, laboratory work and 'field work' with patients. The theoretical subjects taught included physiology, anatomy and physiopathology. In the beginning, the academic medical training focussed on human biology, the classification of diseases and diagnostic procedures. One of the doctors referred to the general training as 'medicine without borders' because the knowledge passed on covered all medical departments, such as obstetrics, general medicine, surgery and infectious diseases. For all participants, the teaching was mainly along traditional lines, with lectures, seminars, textbooks and independent research. Some also had access to alternative teaching methods, such as exchanging information using Internet or interactive computer programs.

The internship period was described by the doctors as an opportunity for medical students to apply their theoretical knowledge in a practical setting. The practical training took place in a hospital, in both rural and urban environments. These work placements enabled the doctors to observe how experienced practitioners interact with patients, to practise diagnostic procedures and to use medical equipment. Working as a doctor in a rural environment allowed the doctors to understand what it means to work in areas with limited resources. Whether the training took place in Cameroon or elsewhere, it appears that the doctors all received similar training, of a type considered standard for their profession, at least until recently.[11]

4.2.3 Communicating Knowledge

The doctors identified three areas in the circulation of knowledge related to health and prevention:

1. The relationship between a doctor and a patient
2. The relationship between an individual and an educator
3. The relationship between a community and an educator

[11]Over the past 10 years or so, problem-based learning has become the norm in most medical schools in North America and Europe.

The doctors are primarily interested in the relationship between a doctor and a patient as all the other channels are outside their direct control. In addition, the doctors explained the importance for them of identifying the individual/collective attitudes to the disease, the ways in which it is transmitted and the means whereby it can be prevented. Knowing this enables the doctors to improve their relationship with their patients or any other target group. One of the doctors felt that in order to be able to pass on the information about prevention, 'it is up to doctors to deconstruct the false beliefs' held in the community on health matters, to warn of the consequences of irresponsible behaviour and to condemn practices which stigmatise others while at the same time encouraging the acceptance of new ideas.

The doctors deal with a very varied clientele. Education in matters of prevention targets everyone who consults them, irrespective of age, gender or social standing. The doctors talk of using educational tools during their consultations in order to teach their patients about health, disease and prevention. One doctor described the tools used in his attempts at health education, 'How do we teach an illiterate population? It is sometimes very difficult to put certain things into words and we have to use objects such as bananas or models of the sexual organs to demonstrate how to put on a condom'. The doctors believe their role as educators to be important since they are the primary providers of health care for the community. Therefore, individuals who need information about health matters come to them directly. This is particularly true in places with limited access to television, radio, Internet or written health information.

Before information can be transmitted, it is important that the consultation be tailored to the patients' needs and level of education. Thus, doctors start a consultation with asking questions and trying to instigate a discussion. They listen to the concerns of the patient and plan a means of transmitting the information in a way that can be easily understood and which is likely to produce a positive response. Doctors encourage patients to take an active part in consultations, in order to help with the diagnosis of the problems, thereby enabling individuals to participate in planning the prevention.

It is important for doctors to 'be aware' of the language they use, using an interpreter if they do not speak the patient's dialect. The doctors say that they choose their terminology carefully, often using simple words rather than scientific descriptions. They are also wary of raising taboo subjects directly with certain patients who might have a negative reaction. They add that the approach they use is to introduce delicate subjects, such as the prevention of HIV/AIDS, as subcategories of wider discussions. Other devices are to make use of metaphors or humour in order to create a more relaxed atmosphere.

During the consultations the doctors also make use of visual materials to help get the information over. Leaflets and other forms of written information dealing with subjects such as health, disease and prevention are provided to the patients at the clinic. There is a certain degree of embarrassment attached to health-related communications in the communities. Posters are used to display non-verbal information in picture form. These posters, showing grotesque images representing the consequences of risky behaviour, are a means of eliminating fear among the population so that they adopt the recommended preventive measures. Condoms are distributed and the doctors use models of penises to demonstrate their correct use as well as to explain how condoms can act to prevent the transmission of STI/HIV or pregnancy.

From time to time the practitioners also take part in awareness raising and educational activities in the hospitals. Their involvement depends on their availability, interest and specialisation. Usually, the doctors are invited to present awareness raising programmes organised by religious organisations or community groups. When raising the subject of religious beliefs, the doctor, acting here in the role of educator, must respect the Church's ideas and avoid any conflict of interests. This means concentrating on the prevention techniques which are more social or moral than medical, such as fidelity and abstinence. Meetings are also held, where doctors can talk to women infected with HIV/AIDS or in schools which organise awareness raising days devoted to specific areas.

An initial analysis of the statements relating to the transmission of information indicates that the doctors say they follow the recommendations set out in the scientific literature: using a range of approaches, taking account of the patients' requirements, ensuring that patients are involved in decisions made about their health and using visual or other material to assist in communicating the message. However, a recent study into patient-doctor communication in Cameroon shows that patients do not always understand the diagnosis and the proposed treatment. The patient's understanding of his condition is rarely, or only superficially, discussed (Labhardt et al. 2009). This study was not carried out in Yaoundé, but in a rural area in the Centre region and it is clear that the doctors working with PROSENAT have a particular interest in offering various form of explanations for a disease (cf preparatory work Wamba 2005) or they would not be collaborating with a network of traditional therapists. At the same time, applying the results of Western medicine and academic research carried out in the north, with no consideration for the nature of local communication, is perhaps a restriction inherent in the approach adopted by the doctors questioned and thus also a restriction in the medical training given outside of 'Western' contexts.

4.2.4 Circulation of Information

The doctors are involved in health education awareness raising programmes intended to reduce the spread of disease, to prevent negligence and to change individuals' habits and behaviour. Education in a hospital context covers areas such as the recognition of symptoms, the ways a disease is spread and methods of prevention. The doctors talk to the patient's family in order to break the taboos surrounding the condition and thus to ensure that the patient receives the required care and support on leaving hospital. The services and resources promised in the awareness raising campaign are delivered by the medical clinics, which provide condoms, vaccines and documents.

The doctors also work with community organisations to develop education and prevention programmes. One of the doctors describes his participation in the development of health education awareness raising programmes as follows:

> At the beginning of the year we draw up a plan of action. A plan of action lasts around three months. We get involved in health education because, first and foremost, we want people to understand their health problems. Many individuals are incapable of recognising the health problems which require a visit to a doctor. People need to know when they are ill. The programmes are devised to focus on specific diseases, such as combatting malaria, combatting typhoid, combatting HIV/AIDS and combatting digestive diseases. We try to set up events, for example bringing together women to enable them to talk about problems linked to the menopause so that the bodily changes they undergo don't hit them like a bolt from the blue.

The first stage in creating a plan for the doctor is to listen to the needs of the community. The prevention and awareness raising messages sent out need to be tailored to the health problems and social difficulties encountered by the target group. One participant explains:

> When you (as a doctor) realise that there is a health concern, for example a problem related to the purity of the water, the cause of the trouble must first be investigated. The problem may not arise solely from the consumption of contaminated water, but also from the way someone stores or treats the water. For example, the other day I treated a baby who was crying and in great distress. I found that he had health problems because his mother was washing his bottle with contaminated water before filling it with milk.

Those in charge of organising these actions have to ensure that the community has access to the services and materials being promoted by the event, whether it be HIV screening facilities, condom dispensers or water purification tablets. As explained in the interviews, from the doctors' point of view, the transfer of information is usually the follow-up to a process of integration: they do not bombard the community with new information for no reason. For example, one practitioner stated that during consultations with his patients, he 'works to establish a relationship with them, rather than criticising the habits which have caused their complaints, which would upset them, thereby delaying their recovery'.

When it comes to intervening in a community, the participating doctors adopt a 'softly softly' approach. On arrival in the community, they must first greet the Chief or some other influential individual in order to obtain his approval. Then the first information meeting can be organised. Since not all members of the community feel comfortable attending this sort of meeting, the hope is that the first group will pass on the information to the rest of the community. The second meeting usually has a far higher attendance rate, which is a good indication that the information has been passed on and interest has been aroused. If a very delicate subject is to be raised, such as HIV, the purpose of the meeting is usually camouflaged in a wider topic and accompanied by a more general discussion. This can be a challenge because the community may become resistant and annoyed as the discussion homes in on the modern methods of prevention of HIV.

The doctors have identified several obstacles to the development of prevention and awareness raising programmes. Two of these represent a major challenge: the social stigma and the low level of literacy. A third relates to the use of impersonal scientific or academic language, far removed from their everyday speech. Taboo subjects also form a significant obstacle. One doctor recalled his experiences with this problem:

> Taboos are particularly bound up with HIV/AIDS. It is quite a challenge to introduce the subject of protection into a conversation when working with a population which sees sex as a taboo area. I think one has to talk about the sexual organs, while respecting people's sensitivity, but at the same time, I do need to be able to do my job. I have discussed sex with students, but I realised that they were aware of the health and prevention messages. It is important to research the target population before going there or before preparing the presentation of the messages to be communicated so that the communication is tailored to their level of understanding.

During the interviews conducted with the doctors, we identified some metaphors used when discussing taboo subjects. Some referred to sex as 'making a baby' or 'thinking of the devil', which are expressions used by the community. Some doctors used the term 'third leg' to represent the penis and the female sexual organ is referred to symbolically as the 'palace'. This terminology makes for a more comfortable atmosphere during the awareness raising discussions. It is important to note that several doctors indicated that they were not willing to use metaphors, preferring to be frank and direct.

Experience has taught the participating doctors that there is a high risk of psychological repercussions for patients who are told that they are seropositive, because of the fear that surrounds the diagnosis, the stigma, the disease and death. The doctors stressed the need for health-care professionals to manage the consultation procedures with great caution in order to reduce the risk of devastating consequences. The diagnostic approach suggested by the doctors is as follows:

> Before undertaking the HIV screening procedure, the doctor should talk to the patient and explain the potential risks associated with the transmission of HIV. If the test results are positive for HIV, there should be a post-test consultation to remind the patient of the important points discussed before the test. Once the patients have been given their test results they should be monitored in order to assess the risks they may pose to themselves.

One of the doctors put forward a possible explanation for the effects of an HIV infection on mental health: a widely held belief in Cameroon society is that AIDS is a disease that destroys. 'I often hear patients declaring that AIDS will exterminate us all'. The fact that patients with AIDS believe that their death is imminent creates a state of mind which can produce neurotic or suicidal tendencies. Many feel guilty for having contracted AIDS through sexual relations. The doctor emphasised the crucial need for patients to have professional help in their mental struggle against the consequences of the disease. If the patient agrees, the doctor can pass on the positive test results to the family so that the patient has an additional support network.

Managing tuberculosis requires the doctors to be able to convince families of the importance of vaccinating their children as a preventive measure. In order to reduce the number of cases of tuberculosis, the doctors need to establish living standards through awareness raising campaigns. The tuberculosis prevention programmes in the hospitals have identified two aims for the preventive measures: to contain an epidemic and to improve living conditions. One example of unsafe living conditions is overcrowding in rural housing. Improving these conditions requires an economic strategy, which is why several of the doctors interviewed believe that this is outside their remit. The doctors note people's need to have access to sources of drinking water, healthy food and sanitary homes in order to be able to tackle the increase in epidemics. However, yet again they can only take note of the needs and shortcomings, but it is not in their power to change the economic situation of their patients.

Promoting water purification measures is one area where doctors can exercise considerable influence on the living standards of the community. They identified the problem here as being a 'storage problem'. Discussions of preventive measures to avoid the water becoming contaminated should cover a range of aspects, such as not only how to make the water suitable for drinking but also how to 'cover water, to treat or dispose of water that has been used and how to separate it for different uses such as washing oneself and washing clothes'. Doctors work together with the patients to develop a plan for saving water. To do this they also work together with community environmental groups. One of the participating doctors described his role in the following way: 'Cooperation among caregivers is important in order to pinpoint the sources of contaminated water and to make recommendations on the most suitable purification methods. As a rule, an outbreak of an epidemic of diarrhoea, dysentery or typhoid fever in a community is a good indicator that the water is contaminated. Ever since the doctors observed the first epidemics, based on the diagnoses of their patients, they have worked in conjunction with the public health sector and environmental organisations to make their concerns known. An epidemic requires a rapid response. Thus, the doctors see themselves as the 'watchdogs' of both the community and governmental and non-governmental organisations. Their consultations allow the doctors to get an indication of any rise or fall in the incidence of a particular disease'.

Once again the doctors are showing, at least in their discussions, their sensitivity to the contextual conditions surrounding their activities. In contrast to what was revealed by the analysis of their definitions of risk and prevention, the way they work seems to take account of social factors. Of course, we refer here to activities involving groups working with NGOs, such as PROSENAT, or religious organisations. In these circumstances it would be difficult not to take account of the obstacles that must be overcome if the message is to be transmitted. Although these obstacles, which include illiteracy, taboos and social stigma, may appear insurmountable, leading to a feeling of powerlessness, the participating doctors feel a commitment to the fight against disease.

Taking tuberculosis and HIV/AIDS as prototypes, the participating doctors showed that the different tasks they have to carry out in their work as doctors are, more or less implicitly, divided into three stages: before, during and after the risk. They also demonstrated, at least in their discourse, that the knowledge they hold must be converted if their clients are to be able to understand it. This conversion is conditioned by the circumstances of the context, but also by those of the patient, be it an individual or a group. The doctors' 'classic' biomedical training offers insufficient preparation for the exercise of tailoring the situation to suit the circumstances.

4.3 The PROSENAT Traditional Therapists

Seven traditional therapists took part in the research. They were all men and their ages range from 41 to 55. They have a lengthy experience of medicine based on plants having, in most cases, been initiated at a very early age.

4.3.1 Definition of Risk and of Prevention

For the traditional therapists the very notion of formulating a definition of prevention or risk was a strange request, which they found very difficult to fulfil. Traditional therapists are not used to answering questions about their own interpretations of the concepts of risk and prevention. In their eyes, the answer is based on common sense. As one of the traditional therapists replied clearly: 'Rather than treating the devil, it is better to avoid him'. Initially there was a misunderstanding regarding the aim of our question about risk and prevention: it was seen as a way of testing knowledge. Several of the therapists asked for advice on how to reply and found it difficult to provide examples from everyday life to support their definition. They also asked for the question to be reworded to make it easier to understand. After giving their final reply, they were keen to seek approval. However, after a slow start, the dialogue with the traditional therapists enabled them to express a view which illustrates their unique perspective, bringing together risk and disease in a context geared to the understanding of disease and health and specific to these traditional experts.

The definitions of risk and prevention given by the traditional therapists express a holistic view of healing. The replies indicated the importance of health in a general sense, encompassing physical health, the environment, the spirit and the networks within these different levels. The traditional therapists see health and healing as a continuous process situated between the symptoms experienced and the specific ailments. In this sense, healing is a continuous process involving supporting and preventive measures.

Risk has generally been associated with a body of knowledge or rather of ignorance. An inadequate knowledge of the risk factors is linked to a higher rate of illness and infection. In detail, the risk as described by the traditional therapists covers two distinct areas:

1. Public risk, identified as an individual risk
2. Collective risk

'Risk is that to which a person exposes himself, with good or bad consequences, by acting in a certain way either alone, with someone else or in a specific environment'. According to the traditional therapists, individual risk in particular is related to the fear of suffering or dying. This fear derives from the known (or in some cases, imagined) effects of the diseases and the limited possibility of access to the health care required. A disease such as HIV/AIDS immediately suggests suffering and death and, thus, the traditional therapists explain that 'if you put yourself into a dangerous situation by contracting a disease that is difficult to treat, you run the risk of not being able to turn to traditional medicine to treat the disease'. However, the consequences of individual risk are seen as an individual responsibility to the community, thus justifying the notion of 'public risk': all individual behaviour has implications for both the individual and the community. 'Protecting the individual allows you to protect the community by maintaining a healthy environment'. Collective risks are increased as a result of a lack of action to tackle the widespread health problems of the community. One of the traditional therapists explained that 'the collective risk emerges when individuals do not act sufficiently rapidly to grasp a problem and find a solution; they may all die'.

Prevention is a dominant feature of traditional medicine. Continued healing is achieved when 'individuals are aware of the measures they should take to remain healthy'. Traditional therapists are taught preventive medicine as part of the holistic context of their formal studies. Causality is a branch of preventive medicine practised by many healers. The concept of causality is to 'treat the disease by concentrating on what causes it and alerting individuals to these causes so they can avoid the disease'. For example, communities with a high obesity rate are made aware of dietary regimes, of food considered healthy and of the importance of purifying one's body. One participant recalled the words of his mentor: 'Tell me what you eat and I will tell you what you are suffering from'. He continued:

> ... food is a source of several forms of illness, if not all. If we talk of food, we are also talking about the digestive system, meaning that the stomach is the home of our illnesses ... In order to help the population better, I must teach them about food hygiene and about how to maintain a healthy digestive system. I tell the patients which plants they can use to help purify their intestines, liver, kidneys and blood because these are the organs in which the illnesses we suffer from reside.

Knowledge of prevention in holistic treatments differs from that in biomedical treatments, in terms of the results they hope to achieve. In traditional medicine, prevention is an indirect process. Keeping the body in a good state of health in order to reinforce its internal resistance to illness is a constant goal for traditional therapists, who do not limit themselves to the symptoms presented by the patient. Biomedical preventive measures focus on an immediate response as a means of restricting cases of a disease, for example, using condoms or purifying water. Not all these methods are recommended by traditional therapists; while they recognise their importance, they prefer to combine these tools with a holistic approach. Traditional therapists represent the health of their patients as a series of links with the mind, diet and the environment. They thus prefer to create structures which directly increase the immunity of the body and the spirit by means of dietary regimes, purging and prayers.

Prevention was defined as 'the different measures available to us or surrounding us, which enable us to prepare for potential dangers'. The communities are warned that to ignore the messages about the prevention of disease is to put themselves at risk. 'The risk run by individuals who refuse to take preventive measures is that they will fall ill. They say that if you take a risk, you will meet a problem or fire and fire will burn you'. The preventive methods used must respect individuals' cultural norms while at the same time tackling social behaviour patterns in order to reduce the obstacles to preventing disease. The traditional therapists believe that prevention should focus on the health of the whole body and not just on a disease. They say that when providing care and advice, it is important 'for the discussion not to concentrate only on the disease, but to include the body and its component parts. If the various parts of the body function correctly, this will destroy the disease [before it even appears], thus we are engaged in prevention'.

In the light of these views on prevention, we believe that traditional therapists are able to participate in programmes where the aim is to draw attention to the concerns related to public health. According to one of the participants, 'When we speak of prevention and risks we are talking about public health problems. Talking of public health is talking about health at national level'. For example, stagnant water becomes a public health concern when it causes an outbreak of waterborne disease. The traditional therapists, who have a strong social role (these are people often recognised by the community), can help by exerting pressure on local authorities and promoting the need for a water purification system since, if the water remains untreated, it will continue to infect their population. In this sense, they are a valuable asset for the public health system because of the respect accorded to them within their society. Their familiarity with the community enables them to introduce public health messages in ways that are more acceptable and more appropriate.

4.3.2 Training and Sources of Information

Our analysis of the training routes for traditional therapists highlighted how these specialists see their role within the medical profession. The primary aim of traditional therapists is to 'help people suffering from illness'. However, some traditional therapists accept that their expertise does not cover all diseases or ailments. According to the traditional therapists, traditional remedies can treat a range of ailments, such as sexually transmitted infections, staphylococcal infections, gynaecological problems, the symptoms of HIV and AIDS, malaria and diarrhoea. These natural remedies are mixtures of local plants and roots.

The effectiveness of traditional medicines is first trialled by the healers themselves, before advocating their powers and effects on the patients. The public are made aware of the natural remedies and of prevention through group discussions and, occasionally, also through the organisation of awareness raising programmes and conferences. Their advice means that they are often the first to be involved in spreading knowledge about the disease. They are also the first to be consulted by those who are ill, before they turn to hospital doctors (Ryan 1998).

One of the aspects of the traditional therapists' training which distinguishes it very clearly from biomedical training is the gift of healing passed down through the family line. This inherited traditional medical knowledge usually passes through the paternal side of the family. For traditional therapists training starts at birth. The parent or the elder transmits his knowledge of disease and treatment using informal educational methods. If, as sometimes happens, the student also acquires an academic education, this is with a view to developing and enhancing the knowledge obtained from parents and elders. This type of family education places a great deal of responsibility on the shoulders of the child destined to follow the traditional healing practices of his ancestors.

For the child selected, training 'starts at birth and is continuous'. There are three differing forms of education which progressively transform the child into traditional professional practitioner. The first is the gift that the individual has received from God. This gift is explained as, 'Knowledge, not witchcraft; respect and the willingness to increase understanding in order to be able to use the medicinal plants that God has created to take care of us'. Such knowledge intensifies the 'individual respect for nature and thus for God, as he created nature'. Traditional therapists believe that the gift of healing comes from God and thus their practices should respect all that God provides and this knowledge should be used to extend his power and his grace. The second form of education is the dream. Knowledge is communicated by experiences in dreams. The symbolic representations in the dreams are used to transmit the ancestral learning and to inspire the traditional therapist in his future search. The third form is the initiation rites, which are a series of steps to initiate the child into the field of traditional medicine so that he can harness the power of the gift of healing.

Before this knowledge is passed on from parent to child, the family needs to be certain that the child is socially and psychologically ready to work as a healer. The traditional therapist therefore teaches the child how to behave correctly and how to advise a patient, so that he does not build up a bad reputation within the community. The parents and elders pass on all their knowledge and skills connected with traditional medicine, rituals and recognition of illness.

The children chosen start their training by studying the cures for a number of 'minor' illnesses, such as fever or diarrhoea. Learning about medicinal plants is done orally. At school they are taught botany, which complements their traditional education and allows them to expand their knowledge of the plants and to learn their scientific names. The 'apprentices' are also taken into the forest, where their mentor shows them how the remedies are prepared. One of the participants recalled how his parents taught him to use plants to treat cataracts. Even after the child has been initiated, the transfer of knowledge continues as part of the journey to acquire the power of healing.

Another set of knowledge and skills passed on to traditional therapists is the ability to treat supernatural illnesses linked to spiritual/invisible beings. Some illnesses, such as diabetes, are thought to be caused by evil spirits conjured up by sorcerers. The training to deal with supernatural illnesses includes learning about witchcraft. Traditional therapists are trained to chase away invisible and evil spirits by using rituals and chants, in combination with compounds of medicinal herbs. Victims who have been put under a spell are treated by the traditional therapists who believe that with the power of God and the help of their ancestors (traditional therapists), they are able to break the spell. The role of the medicinal plants used is to purify the body and to chase away the invisible spirits.

Those traditional therapists who have received no formal schooling and those who wish to continue to learn are invited to take part in local seminars. These are organised by experienced traditional therapists who have had formal education, in conjunction with doctors and representatives of health authorities and various health associations, such as the Cambodian Diabetes Association (as part of the South-South development programme). Like their medical colleagues, traditional therapists need to keep their knowledge up to date. In general, the seminars focus on conventional medicine and the identification of a range of chronic conditions and serious illnesses. Living and working in Yaoundé should mean that there is relatively easy access to this type of training. However, Heinzerling (2005) noted that for the south-west region, despite the interest shown by traditional therapists in complementary medical training, such courses are very rare. These seminars usually follow the same pattern. The first stage deals with the recognition of the specific symptoms of diseases. The second stage covers the evaluation of the remedies currently offered. Thus, the traditional therapists are made aware of the importance of hygiene (cleanliness) during the preparation of a remedy. The advantage of these sessions is being able to hear what their experienced colleagues have to say and to exchange knowledge.

4.3.3 Communicating Knowledge

Traditional therapists believe that one of their main roles is to pass on knowledge related to the risks facing the community. One participant described his approach to education about HIV/AIDS, stating that, 'The awareness raising programmes should identify the additional risks, as many children die from the disease before reaching puberty, before knowing anything about any sexual practices'. It is important for the traditional therapists to talk to their patients about a range of very widespread diseases in order to improve awareness at a collective level. However, they recognise that educating people about the risks is not solely the responsibility of traditional medicine (their medicine). If risk is to be reduced across the whole community, the traditional therapists, the religious leaders and local community leaders must work together to bring about change.

Traditional therapists mainly pass on their knowledge orally. They sometimes take part – in this case as instructors – in group seminars organised by trained traditional therapists, by non-profit-making organisations or by government or religious institutions. The respect and recognition accorded to them as the first line of health care in their community (Ryan 1998) confer on them a high level of credibility when it comes to passing on information. The social position inherited from their ancestors enables them to play an active role in the local social-health care system. The members of the community trust their traditional therapists and their natural remedies because they represent ancestral beliefs and practices rooted in a familiar shared system of meaning. In the understanding of the clients, this system does not seem to be in contradiction with what is offered by the 'recently' established biomedicine. The clients are happy to consult both health-care systems for the same ailment, but to treat different symptoms and causes (Beninguisse and De Brouwere 2004). The traditional therapists live and work in the local villages, where they hold consultations in the local dialect, which is a great advantage compared with the government health-care system which is not available everywhere and is expensive. It is easy for the traditional therapists to establish links with the community as they are familiar with the cultural norms and expectations. This is very important when it comes to prevention or delicate and taboo subjects.

Traditional therapists pass on their messages about prevention during consultations with patients, during group meetings, in community organisations or by calling at people's homes. They count on the patients to spread the word on prevention to their families and neighbours. The subject of HIV/AIDS prevention is a good example of the importance of the traditional therapists being aware of the terminology they use, in order to avoid going beyond what is considered socially acceptable. They must also respect religious beliefs, which often place restrictions on what can be discussed in terms of HIV/AIDS prevention. For instance, when traditional therapists talk about sexual relations, they use metaphors such as 'beating the tamtams' (African drums) for sexual intercourse. For the female menstrual cycle, they talk of 'seeing a person's flowers'. They refer to condoms as 'robes' and the 'naked body' for the penis. The traditional therapists explain to their patients that 'It is important to cover the naked body with a robe in order to protect it from the outside'. Condoms are also referred to as rubbers or hats. Some expressions are borrowed from childish language because their words are simple and easily understood. For example, young children call the male sexual organ a 'whistle'.

Traditional therapists also use metaphors in their holistic approach to attempting to understand and explain the primary cause of certain illnesses, particularly those which have supernatural origins. When a patient arrives with an ailment, the traditional therapists are unable to refer immediately to the supernatural side of the patient's illness, even when they see quickly that something is amiss in that area. The traditional therapists explained that they first have to assess the ailment from a medical point of view. The conversation then gradually moves to explaining to the patient that his illness has a supernatural cause.

One interesting example of the use of metaphors to establish a connection between the realm of the ancestors and the world of the living is that used to identify and explain obesity and its symptoms. The supernatural signs of obesity are known as 'guisiqui' and 'night poison'. 'Guisiqui' means 'to be bloated'. The term 'night poison' refers to the nocturnal habit of 'eating one's dreams'. It is used to describe individuals whose corpulence is thought to be due to this habit. Unless this phenomenon can be stopped, it will lead to obesity. The explanation given for eating the dreams is attributed to evil spirits cast upon unfaithful individuals. Supernatural disruption is treated using traditional methods, such as praying for divine intervention. Once the patient is strong enough to defend himself against the evil spirits, medicinal plants can be used to protect him from the 'night poison'.

Not all the traditional therapists taking part feel the need to use metaphors when talking about prevention. Some traditional therapists said they were uncomfortable raising subjects considered taboo with their clients. Others said that, instead of using metaphors, they preferred not to discuss these sensitive subjects in order to avoid any conflict with public and religious leaders. Instead, they prefer to promote preventive measures, such as abstinence and fidelity. The traditional therapists recognise that the spread of HIV/AIDS cannot be ignored because of its increasing prevalence within the community. The form of prevention against AIDS recommended most frequently is fidelity since, as the traditional therapists report, even the condom is not 100 % effective. The therapists understand that AIDS is partly a social disease, and thus, they recommend to their patients to be honest in their relationships. There is also a growing belief that AIDS is a supernatural disease. In this situation condoms are totally ineffective as the disease is transmitted by supernatural means.

Where HIV/AIDS is not transmitted by supernatural means, the patients tend not to pay much heed to the medical prevention message. Many people see the use of condoms as a foreign practice which reduces pleasure during intercourse. This was the opinion of 63 % of young men and 46 % of young women questioned by Meekers and Klein (2002) in Yaoundé and Douala. The prevention message as given by traditional therapists makes use of fear and provocation. The public are constantly warned that if they do not follow the practices intended to prevent HIV/AIDS, they risk having to cope with the effects of a disease which leads to a slow and painful death. The traditional therapists also explain to their patients that contracting AIDS is far more serious than reduction in pleasure associated with wearing a condom.

Traditional therapists also use other means of transmitting information, particularly when invited to take part in the community awareness raising programmes. For example, visual aids (such as posters) are useful when addressing large groups or young children. Other methods, such as theatre and role-play, can be used to pass on messages about diseases, hygiene and prevention. These methods are a very valuable means of educating the population about sensitive issues because they entertain, involve the audience and are well suited to the indirect transmission of information on these delicate subjects. Most of these methods are used by other organisations with which PROSENAT is sometimes associated, but this is still rare.

4.3.4 Circulation of Information

PROSENAT's intention is to establish cooperation between the traditional therapists (who use traditional remedies) and other caregivers in the ways in which they tackle prevention in relation to public health. The members of the organisation meet regularly to discuss the issues related to their aim of 'maintaining health through the use of natural remedies and the recognition of traditional health care practices'. The lack of official recognition is a major obstacle encountered by traditional therapists. It limits their involvement in national prevention and awareness raising campaigns. Government disregard for the work of traditional therapists reinforces the idea that traditional medicine is inferior and ineffective in comparison with biomedicine. As a result, traditional therapists are unable to contribute their ideas and preventive methods to establishing public health policies.

The regular meetings of the members of PROSENAT are also intended to offer a forum to discuss and compare knowledge related to the about the use of natural plants in human medicine. Any dialogue needs to transcend an important – or even fundamental – rule followed by traditional therapists: the secrecy surrounding the preparation and composition of remedies. The diverse and secret nature of their healing practices is a veritable challenge when it comes to establishing a framework of regulation governing the production and distribution of natural remedies on a large scale. PROSENAT also works with colleagues from conventional medicine to seek ways to improve the structure (practices and remedies) of traditional healing.

The members of PROSENAT also collaborate among themselves, acting as mentors, according to their skills and hierarchy (the older practitioners being more respected and thus higher up in the hierarchy). The group is encountering problems in recruiting independent traditional therapists as many of them do not meet the required conditions. To become a member a therapist needs to be a Cameroon national, a traditional therapist, a person of high moral repute and a person able to assist the organisation to achieve its aims.

Before starting awareness raising campaigns, the traditional therapists inform parents (if the campaigns are directed at young people) and religious and community leaders in order to obtain their approval. Without the support of the community, the message transmitted by the group would lack authority and acceptance. One of participants noted that, 'In Europe everyone has a family doctor, but in Africa every region has its own "nganga" (healer) who is consulted when problems arise'. Persuading every nganga and traditional therapist to get involved in the awareness raising campaigns will reinforce the health-care messages because the messengers are credible and accepted by the community. For example, PROSENAT encourages the traditional therapists to try to talk to the population about HIV/AIDS.

If PROSENAT is to make significant progress in its activities, the traditional therapists believe that the government must first give official recognition to traditional practices. In their eyes, PROSENAT offers a unique opportunity to establish a regulated framework for traditional health practices and traditional medical knowledge. The members of PROSENAT encourage other independent traditional therapists to join together in a collective in order to increase their power within public health while, at the same time, maintaining the required level of professional autonomy and confidentiality. In this way this political activity – joining together to be heard more clearly – is a necessary form of aid for the circulation of information.

It is clear that the traditional therapists encountered in the course of this research, like those who participated in other research projects (Heinzerling 2005; Ryan 1998) are respected individuals, whose opinion is valued. They have a system of explaining illness which is based on local conditions and which makes sense to the population. One cannot help noticing that, like the doctors, the traditional therapists may adopt a moralising tone and that some of their practices could prove counterproductive in terms of prevention. For example, ascribing purely a supernatural cause to AIDS may lead to no form of physical protection (condom) being used. However, this in no way contradicts what has been demonstrated elsewhere, which is that any theory of the transmission of diseases and their prevention brings together ideas that are necessarily normative and moral (Bonnet 2003). This collective discourse transmits and keeps alive the need to achieve some sort of order in terms of relationships, be it between humans, between humans and environments or between humans and invisibles. These ideas are a reminder of the position everyone should occupy and the rules for achieving it, which cover sexual conduct, all forms of physical contact and social relations in general. In this sense, the traditional therapists act as the guardians of standards, in the same way as other influential people, such as the chief or the elders.

Unlike the doctors, they have no linear representation of the temporality of risk, with a before, a during and an after. Their practices are part of a holistic understanding of the illness, whereby they operate in all three phases simultaneously. Because of this ability to intervene using what we in the West would call an integrated approach and because they are consulted before any other health professional, it would be wise to involve them in the national prevention programmes.

4.4 The Members of WESDE

4.4.1 The Definition of Risk and Prevention

For WESDE, the definitions of risk and prevention are key concepts. WESDE's objective is to reduce the incidence of the environmental and social risks which lead to the spread of disease in Cameroon. WESDE is a prevention organisation which communicates information about risks through awareness raising campaigns and health projects. Without a recognised and adaptable definition of community health risks and the necessary preventive measures, it would be difficult for the organisation to achieve its aims and to complete the tasks allotted to it in order to improve living conditions.

WESDE combines holistic and biomedical health-care models to define and promote the concepts of risk and prevention. Using a multidisciplinary approach to explain risk and prevention, WESDE is able to tailor the information so that the public feel involved and are able to understand the health messages in a familiar context. In his interview, the WESDE coordinator very quickly explained that 'the message has to be adapted to suit the living conditions... There is no point in telling someone who sleeps in a straw hut to fit a metal door to stop the mosquitoes getting in; to do so would be to treat that person with contempt'. All the members[12] of WESDE stated that they were trying to set up awareness raising and hygiene programmes as a means of providing an immediate response to health problems while at the same time establishing the framework conditions for a social empowerment and health-care system. In order to do this, they need to 'find the right topic, the right words and the right target to transmit the information'.

The members of WESDE define risk as 'the consequences incurred by a person carrying out a given activity'. WESDE explains to a variety of groups the dangers inherent in the risk, in order to prevent dangerous behaviour. They encourage communities to be mindful of their risky behaviour because, as one member put it, 'a danger can arise at any moment, sometimes without one being aware of its approach'. Another WESDE member noted that the presence of risks to health increases when 'poor choices or behaviour occur on a regular basis'. Undesirable consequences or risks are the result of bad habits, such as not using protection during sexual intercourse or drinking contaminated water. The members of WESDE believe that their task of setting up awareness raising and education programmes allows the population to identify the risks and break the cycles of unsafe behaviour patterns.

Changing behaviour patterns is not the only aim of WESDE's programmes since all habits, good or bad, are the result of individual and collective attitudes. One member of WESDE sees risk as 'an attitude which exposes a person to various consequences. I could say that risk is an attitude, a behaviour pattern that exposes the individual to certain dangers and degenerations'. The attitudes adopted by certain members of a community can expose the whole community to certain dangers (in this case dangers related to health). Risk is also defined as poor choices. One WESDE participant explained that, 'Risks are errors made by individuals through ignorance'. Attitudes are shaped by customs, beliefs and experiences. On being invited to talk about his experience, one of the WESDE members stated that in some rural villages people think that HIV/AIDS is a disease 'that specifically affects those who live in towns' or that the disease was introduced by 'white people, who infected condoms with the virus'. Talking about environmental aspects, a WESDE member recalled cases where the population did not know that the presence of microorganisms in their water could cause disease. The result was that many people used their clothing to filter the water and trap the large particles, assuming that this was a satisfactory way of purifying the water. Thus, risk derives from behaviour, but also from attitudes and knowledge or rather a lack of knowledge.

Prevention was defined collectively by the members of WESDE as a system of warnings, 'a system to warn individuals to avoid the devil entering into them'. 'Prevention is a mechanism which maintains protection by promoting avoidance. Emphasis should be put on attitudes and developing risk education through training

---

[12]The members of WESDE are also referred to as facilitators, coordinators or educators and their activities encompass all these roles.

and establishing groups of watchdogs to inform the public of the need to avoid certain dangers'. WESDE's approach is to go beyond the external influences on attitude and to place the emphasis clearly on the consequences of risk and the prevention tools available to improve social conditions and the health of individuals. The participants believe that educating communities gives them 'alternative viewpoints on risk and prevention, challenging the structures of traditional wisdom'.

4.4.2 Training and Sources of Information

According to an administrator, when recruiting members the organisation has no specific expectations in terms of professional experience or academic background. The academic careers of the members vary from primary education to university degrees in areas such as the environment, health-care and social work. These people, who are now members of WESDE, explained that they had heard of it in various ways, such as by word of mouth or through adverts in the media. Whatever the previous level of education, the organisation offers additional training for all its members. Seminars have been developed to train new members and to improve their knowledge of the diseases targeted by WESDE and also of the prevention tools available.

The members of WESDE attend training courses, which usually last between 1 and 2 weeks. The main areas covered are HIV/AIDS, orphans and vulnerable children and the purification of water. The attendees also have the opportunity to learn how to plan and set up awareness raising campaigns. These courses include both theory and practice. The education programme provided for the members also covers ways of making it easier to approach the public during the awareness raising campaigns. For example, the members of WESDE receive training in educational methods suited to young children. The WESDE training sessions take the form of lectures and films presented in a classroom. The films deal with the different ways in which a disease can be transmitted and tackle the subject of prevention through the options available. For example, in the case of HIV/AIDS, these are condoms, abstinence and fidelity. Educational documents and texts are made available to those members of WESDE who are interested in learning more or for research purposes. The members also mentioned that they are offered the opportunity to learn in the field through work placements in other areas in Cameroon. They have also taken part in awareness raising programmes focussing on local health risks. This initial experience has enabled new members of WESDE to familiarise themselves with the different educational tools used by the organisation as well as to acquire the skills needed to obtain a positive response from the public.

The members have a wide range of academic and professional experience. Some are former health professional drawn from the fields of nursing care, biomedicine and natural sciences. Several have expertise in the fields of communicable diseases, neonatal care, traditional medicine and health-care systems. The members also include social workers with experience of working with sufferers of HIV/AIDS or who have been part of structures taking care of orphans. Some members have the data processing, information technology and problem solving skills that are essential if WESDE is to function efficiently. In addition, members regularly receive additional training from UNICEF, WHO and governmental and non-governmental organisations.

4.4.3 Communicating Knowledge

WESDE's activities are primarily focussed on the transmission of knowledge and thus, over the years and based on a system of trial and error, it has developed a range of effective communication tools for use in awareness raising and prevention programmes. One of the greatest challenges to WESDE in its quest to transmit knowledge is illiteracy. In order to reach illiterate groups, the members of WESDE need to pay particular attention to the way they formulate their message: they need to be descriptive, to use metaphors, to speak the local dialect and to involve the local population. 'The real problems occur in the villages because it is difficult to get the health care information across. For example, if the villagers are uneducated or don't speak French we need to use an interpreter. We have to find someone who speaks the local dialect and get him to translate and transmit the information'.

When it comes to prevention, the members of WESDE believe that they 'first need to assess their target audience'. Translators are recruited to translate the material into the local dialect, either orally or in writing, in order to make it more accessible. In many cases illustrations based on everyday behaviour are developed so that individuals can identify with the message. When dealing with an illiterate community, it is extremely important to be highly sensitive to the language used. The WESDE representatives said that they 'respect the local dialects and the level of education of the groups targeted'.

Raising awareness about HIV/AIDS is difficult in Muslim areas, particularly for female volunteers. One WESDE volunteer explained that women 'met with disapproval if they attempted to sit down or to talk with men about certain subjects, especially those related to sex or the use of condoms'. The advantage of having female volunteers is the ease with which they can talk to the other women. For this reason, WESDE usually generally organises groups where 'the women get together with the women and the men with the men'. Separating the men, women and children makes it possible to 'concentrate on subjects specific to the age or gender, with less tension and with the participants more at ease'. One female member of WESDE explained her approaching to educating women in sexual matters: 'I meet the women directly and I say that I too am a woman and that I have come to them to talk about sex. Some react by covering their faces or by laughing because they are ashamed. If at all possible I try to speak to them in their language, using their mother tongue'. Children are also encouraged to share their newly acquired knowledge with their families.

A descriptive approach is key when illustrating health risks with objects and photos. It is not enough simply to show the public an image; it must be explained and described to ensure that the message is understood correctly. One example of an illustration presented by a member of WESDE shows a picture of a healthy patient followed by a picture representing death. One of the WESDE facilitators explained that he has to elaborate on the images, concentrating on what causes the illness, how it can be transmitted and why this leads to the person's death.

Talking about sex to the communities requires the messages (educational and otherwise) to be passed on using analogies and metaphors. Various analogies are used to describe intercourse, such as 'when daddy sleeps with mommy' or 'hunting'. Metaphors are used to describe the sexual organs. For example, the penis might be referred to as 'father of the house', 'banana', 'vehicle', 'the third leg', 'the thing', 'it', 'the top' or 'the bag'. A condom is commonly known as a 'rubber', 'banana skin', 'new skin', 'protective skin' or 'sock'. Using these metaphors makes it easier to discuss these taboo areas.

Other methods of transmitting information include ads on the radio, televised reports, films, brochures, posters and plays. WESDE works together with a company called GTC to produce educational material related to HIV/AIDS. Through the medium of drama, a message can be passed on in play. Theatre productions present sketches about everyday behaviour patterns and preventive measures. These sketches tackle delicate subjects, such as alcoholism and HIV/AIDS. One production is a parody involving a man and a woman who conceal their unprotected sexual encounters. The woman falls ill. The couple goes to hospital, where the lovers are tested and told they have HIV/AIDS. The actors and presenters then talk about the importance of using a condom and show how it works. Other messages conveyed through drama include highlighting the need to support family members with HIV/AIDS, rather than avoiding or abandoning them. Women are targeted in the educational sketches to show how a mother can transmit HIV to her child during pregnancy, birth and while breastfeeding. However, this means of transmitting information can also run into problems, such as an incorrect interpretation of the message and the scepticism of the audience.

In regions where religion makes it impossible to discuss sex and sexually transmitted diseases, people rapidly reject the HIV prevention messages. To avoid stigmatising anyone, WESDE does not teach large groups, but rather addresses individually those already suffering from HIV. WESDE provides information about the use of condoms and about the dangers of sharing razors (which are used not only privately but also publicly in certain rituals). WESDE message is intended to encourage people to attend health centres if they feel that they may be HIV positive. The aim of this approach is to create a snowball effect, with one informed person passing on the message to others. Condoms are also distributed at the talks in order to promote their use and explain the consequences of unprotected sex.

At the start of this type of activity, the facilitator puts open questions to the audience in order to judge their attitude to the use of condoms. If the assembly agrees, the organisers demonstrate the use of condoms, with the help of an 'artificial penis' or a 'banana'. Such talks must include clear descriptions and demonstrations because 'any incorrect representation may lead to condoms being used incorrectly, resulting in an unwanted pregnancy or HIV being transmitted, as well as an increased unwillingness to trust the prevention messages being spread by WESDE'. In order to put an end to the lack of trust in the use of condoms which prevails in the community, the members of WESDE encourage people to 'distinguish themselves from their ancestors by adopting new methods and new knowledge which, as well as protecting them, will improve their quality of life'. To increase the number of people to whom they can distribute condoms and to ensure that the message is getting across, WESDE sometimes adopts the door-to-door technique. The members talk to the young people about the options open to them, such as abstinence and fidelity. Those who are unmarried are encouraged to use condoms if they are sexually active, as a means of avoiding the transmission of HIV or other sexually transmissible diseases as well as unwanted pregnancies. WESDE reports that 'communities which have not been targeted by an HIV/AIDS awareness raising campaign rarely use condoms and continue to follow dangerous sexual practices'.

Among the awareness raising programmes, the participative approach has had the best results in terms of attracting and interesting the public. Participation empowers individuals and enables them to be a part of the knowledge transmission process. The development of knowledge, and taking ownership of that knowledge, increases an individual's involvement in health-care strategies because this involvement gives him a greater sense of responsibility. The participative approach starts with a question and answer session. The facilitators encourage the audience to take part, asking them to share their knowledge of the subject under discussion. One member of WESDE described his strategy for encouraging the members of the community to take an active part:

> First, you take a good look at the people in front of you in order to build up a general picture of their age and level of education, which helps you to select the best way to get your message across. The approaches I use start with an introduction to the disease and a description of the consequences and dangers, in order to frighten the target audience. Then I gently start talking about a solution, but without giving them actual possible solutions. I tell them that there is a solution available for everyone, including children and old people. You don't say that it is for the next generation; you tell them it is for everybody. It is important to get the population interested and their interest can be observed in the way they respond. If they have a negative expression, you have to continue to encourage them. You start by asking whether anyone has any ideas that would solve the problem. Then you ask him to explain his idea or his information to the audience. This gives individuals a sense of ownership of the health care message.

During the participative discussions it is important to interest the group, to create a relaxed atmosphere and to share with the group as a whole. An analysis of the group's ideas and positive feedback reinforce the idea of participation.

The problem tree is another effective and interactive method used to record and organise the ideas emerging from the group. The problem tree is a visual tool designed as an aid to solving a problem through a participative approach. It is developed by the group, with the help of brainstorming problem solving techniques.

The different parts of a tree represent the different stages of a problem or a solution. The trunk represents the main problem, the roots are the known causes or origins of the problem and the branches are the consequences of the problem. In contrast, a 'tree solution' consists of similar elements. The trunk is the main solution, the roots are the resources which provide support for the solution and the branches and leaves are the consequences of the solution.

4.4.4 Sources of Knowledge and Stages of Its Transmission by WESDE

WESDE was set up to 'fill in the gaps in education, environmental communication and the management of natural resources, energy resources and water resources'. WESDE's organisational structure includes 'an integrated management team, consisting of a director, a secretary and administrative and programme delegates'.

The programmes run by WESDE focus on three major local problems:

- Managing water resources
- Managing energy supplies
- Managing natural resources

The management of natural resources covers a number of different aims, such as reforestation, reducing pollution levels and combating desertification. In addition, WESDE contributes to the health and education sectors. Activities in the health sector consist primarily of developing the educational programme for the prevention of HIV/AIDS.

WESDE is a non-profit-making organisation. Recruitment is on a volunteer basis. There are only 8 or 9 administrative staff paid as fulltime employees. The volunteers need to meet three criteria: 'Firstly, the strength of being willing to work for no pay. The second condition is effectiveness. The volunteers recruited must be able to work. The third criterion is multifunctionality and requires the volunteer to have the endurance needed to work in the field rather than in the office'. There are currently 122 volunteers working for WESDE, only nine of whom are women. This very low percentage is because very few women have attended school, they marry young and their activities are restricted to domestic tasks. WESDE wants to encourage more women to play a role in development. At present, there is a group of over twenty women training to become volunteers.

WESDE works in partnership with the Ministry of Water and Energy. Cooperative projects have also been set up with other ministries: Agricultural Development; Rural Development; Environment, Forests and Wild Life; Promotion of Women and Families; and the Ministry of Social Affairs. The organisation is keen to develop widespread cooperation networks with a view to managing resources. It has established national programmes to support orphans and vulnerable children. WESDE has worked with the agency CLEAR International and with CODEL to fight against HIV/AIDS in Mayo Sava and Logon. In order to continue to encourage such partnerships, satellite sites have been set up in Garoua, Maroua and

Ndjamena (Chad). The director is responsible for supervising and communicating with personnel and the officers working in the field, acting as a link between the main structure of WESDE, the satellite sites and the external partners.

Awareness raising programmes are developed by a team consisting of WESDE volunteers assisted by a programme manager. One of the WESDE members described how these programmes are established:

> We begin by organising meetings with the group to discuss how the plan will work, where the project will be, the target audience, the general message and who will be doing what in the project. At the first meeting the subjects are planned and the meeting usually lasts no more than an hour. When we embark on a project we need to mobilise individuals. We do this by going quietly to the location targeted, with a first approach being made to the leader of the village. Once we have spoken to him about our presentation, he will designate people to work with WESDE when they arrive.

WESDE has a network of interpreters, who make it possible to communicate in the local dialect. They receive the health-care messages and can pass them on to the community. Working with interpreters has not always been easy for WESDE since they were not always reliable members of the organisation. As one member of WESDE explained, 'Sometimes the information is not passed on accurately'. WESDE had to stop using locally recruited interpreters in order to avoid the message being transmitted incorrectly. Instead, WESDE now takes its trained interpreters to the area where they are needed.

Awareness raising campaigns face numerous problem, with the greatest obstacle being the need to change behaviour patterns within a community. The aim of the programmes is to educate and to encourage people to adopt preventive measures. These involve changing behaviour patterns in order to stop the spread of disease. The public are not very receptive to these prevention campaigns; they see them as 'foreign' and not relevant to their lives. The WESDE programmes have to demonstrate their value and their effectiveness, despite the traditional beliefs and the habits formed over generations. 'The public's priority lies with meeting essential day to day needs, such as food, clothing, work and sleeping. They are not interested in how they achieve this. For example, the women need water for their domestic activities, such as cooking and cleaning, but they give no thought to the purification of water because this is something unfamiliar to them and which is likely to disrupt their daily routine or their economic capacity. Poverty and hunger reduce the force and the effectiveness of prevention campaigns'.

The environmental programmes tackle the practice of cutting down trees for fuel, leading to deforestation and desertification. WESDE is supporting research into 'alternative sources of energy, using solar panels, wind turbines, bio-energy and more efficient ovens, which require 50 % less wood'. It is impossible to eradicate the use of firewood for energy, but the aim of the WESDE prevention campaigns is 'to reduce the percentage of firewood used and to encourage communities to plant more than they cut down'.

The water management programmes were established in the humid regions of Waza (in the centre of the Extreme North region) and Logone (an area bordering Chad, in the north and east of the Extreme North region). In this sector there are three important groups of interests: the fishermen, the arable farmers and the livestock farmers. WESDE encouraged 'collective discussions in order to identify common interests and come up with ideas for efficient water management systems'. The concerns of the various groups involved were investigated in order 'to find solutions applicable to all and to generate strategic initiatives'. One example is the migration of livestock farmers from Niger and Chad towards regions of Cameroon. The only source of water available to them is polluted rivers. These farmers are informed about the dangers linked to the consumption of contaminated water and are encouraged to seek a source of water which is safe for consumption.

In many rural communities the purification of water is not taken seriously. The wells in places that are known to be the sources of outbreaks of disease are not treated. This can have fatal consequences and it is important for the State to tackle the problem, with the help of the WESDE programmes. The WESDE programmes intended to increase the awareness of the need to treat water are usually located near popular water sources. WESDE technicians hold public sessions to show the population how the water pumps work. Local management committees, consisting of members of the local community, are set up. Their task is to take responsibility for learning how to keep water clean and to inform their communities about the health risks. However, there are limitations to this way of proceeding. According to one of the members of WESDE, these committees all suffer from 'a lack of organisation or of public interest'.

Teaching the population how to ensure that water is clean is 'the key solution to improving the general state of health'. The educational campaigns teach the communities how to 'separate the sources of water so that cooking, cleaning or washing are carried out using different receptacles. Clean water should be stored and dispensed using clean implements'. The communities are told of the risks of allowing the livestock or other animals to share the sources of drinking water. WESDE teach the families methods of purifying water, including using water filters. These preventive measures are more reliable than the local methods. For example, WESDE members have noted that it is common practice to 'try and purify water by filtering it through cotton cloths, which traps the larger particles'. This method has no effect on the lethal bacteria, which continue to wreak havoc. The families are instructed to use sterilisation products or to boil water in order to kill the microorganisms. WESDE recommends using one drop per litre of the sterilisation product. Communities are advised to purify their water regularly because 'pesticides can easily contaminate drinking water supplies'. If the wells dry up or if they need extra purification material, they are sent to the local branch of the Cameroon national water supply company (SNEC) which supplies bottled water at no, or only very low, cost.

All these preventive measures can be thwarted by a single individual refusing to implement them. WESDE recognises the importance of 'remembering that not everyone has the luxury of sleeping with a roof over their head'. A further challenge is to change the attitudes of the communities who do not accept that water is the source of these diseases. One member of WESDE explained that several members of the community reject the link because 'their family and their ancestors have drunk the same water for generations'. Thus, they doubt that these diseases can be carried by water and do not believe that this is the reason for the increased prevalence of blindness, parasitic infestations, gastric ulcers or even cases of paralysis. Many prefer to believe that supernatural phenomena are responsible for this increase. 'The people do not see that the diseases come for the water and so do not believe it is their problem. Their problem is that they are sick and they need to get better. They seldom go to hospital. Instead they go to a traditional therapist who gives them medicine or infusions. The traditional medicines are good at tackling the symptoms of diarrhoea, but less effective against viruses or parasitic diseases'. HIV/AIDS is another disease thought to have supernatural origins.

Another important role for WESDE is that of lobbyist and negotiator with the factories or organisations causing the pollution. WESDE specialises in offering mediation in conflicts between the manufacturing companies and the local population. WESDE works with companies that are known to cause pollution, such as SODECOTON (Societé pour le Développement du Coton). Most of these factories produce dangerous chemical waste products, which are discharged into the environment, where they contaminate water sources, kill wild life and generally cause harm to the population. WESDE tries to meet the directors of these factories, in order to persuade them to cooperate on developing strategies and finding solutions which will put an end to the practices which are destroying the environment. A WESDE negotiator described his objectives during this type of conflict mediation:

> During a meeting we would tell the representatives about the long term consequences for the population. We described the health risks they would run. We told the people in charge that we had to work together to resolve the problem. The greatest challenge facing WESDE is the indifference and resistance shown by the major companies, who deny that they are responsible for the problem.

At the time the research was carried out, no negotiations were taking place.

It appears from all the interviews that the members of WESDE are very aware of the contextual factors relating to the transmission of information. To ensure that 'this difference makes a difference' (to paraphrase Bateson) to the lives of the groups targeted, WESDE puts a great deal of effort into adapting its message in very creative ways. The medium, the transmitter and the receiver are all tailored to suit the context (and the subject to be dealt with). Gender, age, language, religion, participation, door-to-door actions, involvement of local leaders, etc., everything is taken into account so that the information will reach right into the homes and transform practices and behaviour patterns.

The sensitivity to the community demonstrated by WESDE is proof that WESDE, as a whole, has a representation of risk which brings together biomedical and academic learning and everyday knowledge. It is centred on the requirements and the context in which the population lives, without neglecting the input of modern technology. WESDE has been able to achieve an integration which avoids the radical oppositions of different epistemologies and which, in most cases, makes it possible to transmit information to the population groups most difficult to reach through the usual channels (biomedicine and even traditional therapy). WESDE's intention is not to be a substitute for the Cameroon social and health services, but rather to supplement the (limited) capacity offered by the public services. The work carried out by WESDE takes place primarily ahead of the risk (before), with the aim of preventing it, and also, to a certain extent, once the risk has made its presence felt (during) in that the water is already contaminated, the forests have already begun to disappear and the HIV/AIDS pandemic has been raging for many years.

4.5 Synthesis and Reflections

4.5.1 Professional Definitions of Risk and Prevention

The three groups of caregivers encountered in the course of this research share a common interest in the health of the population of Cameroon. Their professional activities focus on at least one shared objective: disease. At a more general level, and in the context of this specific research project, they have all agreed to consider this objective as a risk. However, this general definition (illness = risk) is perhaps their only common description of risk. The discourse on risk gives a brief insight into the symbolic worlds in which they work and on which their understanding of the realities that concern them is based.

The PROSENAT doctors have a technical representation and academic ideas about the risks. The risks vary greatly in their nature and in their consequences. They can be evaluated and measured and a solution can be implemented to reduce the probability of the consequences. This solution – the prevention – defined in academic terms and organised into three categories. One important point is that the risk is not exclusive to the community. The practitioners must also be aware of the risks associated with their work as health professionals. The doctors identify the need to protect themselves against the dangers they encounter while carrying out their functions. The doctors concentrate primarily on the state of health of individuals and on the preventive options. Their main concern is that a patient is at risk of passing on his illness, thereby putting others at risk of infection, and the doctors are well aware that they are working in a high risk environment.

The traditional therapists of PROSENAT attach no particular importance or specific significance to the risks in isolation or independently of relationships. These therapists have a holistic view of health which includes the environment and, to a certain extent, also the soul of the individual or rather the part of the being that links a person to the world of the invisible spirits and the ancestors. From their point of view, the risk is not a tangible concept; rather it is a question of finding a balance in the relationships between the body, spirit and environment of an individual. In the specific context of the interview for this research project, the traditional therapists were able to construct a general definition of risk, but it is not a concept which they adhere to in their practice or with which they identify. According to Bonnet (2003), in many West African societies, contact poses the principal risk. Contact with others or with the environment, that is to say, others or an environment which will have a negative effect, willingly or unwillingly. Establishing a contact means creating a relationship, even a brief one, and it is in such relationships that the risk as defined by the traditional therapists involved in the research resides. The notion of prevention is another unfamiliar concept for the traditional therapists. Prevention is included in their medicine, but not as a separate and distinct special aspect. What concerns them are the relationships between individuals and the natural (physical environments, family and community) and the supernatural worlds (the invisible spirits, ancestors): they seek the causes of illness in these two worlds. Risks and prevention acquire meaning when the traditional therapists collaborate in awareness raising programmes, such as those organised by PROSENAT. In this context these concepts become meaningful, especially if they are called upon to work with 'risk prevention organisations', such as WESDE. Risk is more of a collective notion. It acquires meaning when the knowledge is transmitted to a large group, rather than to an individual, which is not often the case.

The members of WESDE have a concrete, established definition of a risk. This is a key concept for their organisation and their primary purpose: WESDE is a risk prevention organisation. The aim of the organisation is to pass on knowledge about risky practices and behaviour patterns. It is therefore preferable to have pragmatic definitions of risk, reflecting both the holistic and the biomedical viewpoints. Unlike doctors, the members of WESDE are concerned primarily with population groups rather than individuals. Their aim is to raise awareness among the population in the widest sense, targeting the risky behaviour which can be prevented through education programmes. The prevention messages explain that behaviour is at the origin of all risks. Behaviour which leads to poor health is not only the fault of individuals, but may also be due to the behaviour patterns of a community. In the view of the traditional therapists and the members of WESDE (and sometimes also of the doctors), an individual can never be seen in isolation from his community. Changing individual behaviour requires intervention in the community as a whole.

The definition of risks varies in several ways from one group of professional to another, in accordance with how they are rooted in different symbolic worlds. In order to analyse this aspect, we first evaluated the position of the individual in these visions. There is a difference in the extent to which he is seen as connected to his community or his environment. Doctors see the individual as the primary target of the messages of risk prevention, as an autonomous and responsible being (responsible for his own health). The traditional therapists see a connection between individuals and different worlds, natural and supernatural (an invisible universe, which is nevertheless active and real for most people). The relationship between the individual and these two worlds is at the heart of the thinking of the traditional therapists. The WESDE caregivers see the individual as a member of a community and as belonging to several groups (age, gender, education, religion). When targeting the community – the WESDE approach – the various personas must be borne in mind. The second way in which the definition of risk differs relates to the primary causes of the problems (diseases). The doctor takes a biomedical approach, looking for biological malfunction and poor individual behaviour. The traditional therapist also looks at the body's response to disease, together with irresponsible behaviour, but in addition he considers supernatural factors (such as a spell). The members of WESDE seek to identify patterns of unsafe behaviour which, although not the primary cause of the problem, contribute to sustaining and propagating disease. The final dimension studied relates to illness. The concept of illness is understood and interpreted differently by these various professionals. Doctors see illness as the result of an invasion of the body by an external pathogen (virus, bacteria, toxin, etc.). The traditional therapist may opt for this explanation, but will certainly add that the illness is a sign of a clear imbalance between the client and the invisible world. WESDE believes that illness is the consequence of an imbalance in the environment (water shortage, polluted water, natural illness, etc.) and in the relationship between man and his natural environment.

The lack of similarity between the definitions of risk used by the various professionals and the implied differences between their symbolic worlds suggest that if the risk information which comes from outside these universes of meaning is to be accepted and used, it must be accompanied by an 'explanatory and appropriate translation'. Is this translation supplied and, if yes, how? The replies to these questions are considered in the following sections.

4.5.2 A Restricting Factor: The Funding Structure for the Transmission of Knowledge

Money is an important factor in the transfer of knowledge. The movement from top to bottom in the administration of funds designated for the creation or maintenance of awareness raising and prevention programmes is responsible for slowing down many an innovative initiative. The development planning milestones for awareness raising programmes cannot be implemented without the consent of the Cameroon government, international institutions and other financial associates. The funds granted correspond to the amount needed to set up a programme, but when it comes to actually distributing the money to the coordinators, there remains often only a fraction of what was originally asked for and allocated to them.

All community organisations have to follow a regulated process when applying for subsidies for their projects. A written request is submitted to the government or an international organisation, such as the WHO, for approval and allocation of funds. Once the funds have been agreed, the money is sent to the Cameroon Minister of Health for distribution. Since the money has to follow a top-down route through the hierarchy before reaching the community groups for which it is intended, a significant part is swallowed up on the way, either as administrative costs or through fraud. The result is that the awareness raising programmes have to be downsized or additional money has to be sought through other means.

The alternative methods that can be used to find additional funding, which amount to asking private companies to subsidise the programmes, can have a negative effect. Companies interested in health matters, such as pharmaceutical firms, can alter the original intention behind the programme. These companies may want to impose conditions on their gifts, in order to benefit from these low-level community programmes. In the case of pharmaceutical companies, they may request that only the latest therapeutic or preventive options be promoted. Such restrictions can obstruct or mislead the communities.

A new subsidy distribution system should be put in place to enable the community groups and the NGOs to accomplish their aims. The fact that regional health programmes are being restricted by internal regulations and policies illustrates how governments are themselves contributing to the death of their public health systems. Without adequate support from governmental institutions, it will never be possible to get to grips with the origins of disease or changing behaviour patterns within communities. The social decline and the restricted capacities of the community organisations are the consequence of this failure to act. This creates and perpetuates a lack of innovation in public health programmes and contributions by the NGOs. Without innovation, these action plans and the awareness raising programmes become repetitive and lose their meaning. The message received by the community is no longer motivational or relevant or even significant.

4.5.3 Professional Training Routes: Gaps in the Transmission of Knowledge

Another primary source of knowledge (and thus of information that can be passed on) is the training professionals undergo. The doctors and two of the members of WESDE have received international training, either in another country or from international trainers in Cameroon. In these cases, not only is information travelling from North to South, those who are in possession of the information are also travelling. Furthermore, the professionals receiving the training have also travelled in order to study. Our participants believe that international resources are key sources of knowledge (and information). The question is, does this movement of people help the 'translation' process? We are of the opinion that having those in possession of the information go to meet their students or encouraging professionals to spend time elsewhere is a useful contribution to the process as it establishes a dialogue between people who share the same concerns but have different approaches towards the health of the population. This situation can help to ensure that information is presented in a form appropriate to the different contexts, rather than simply handing out folders to professionals. Putting effort into such training opportunities can be likened to the effort the various caregivers have to invest in their professional practice. Thus, getting people to circulate and talk to each other about these subjects offers the chance to learn and can be seen as a resource in terms of translation.

The most important aspect of translation seems to be that the information has already been translated in the institutions which disseminate it. Information in the form of academic models, which is very common in the health-care field, is of limited use to traditional therapists or NGO workers. Thanks to their university studies, the doctors undoubtedly have the ability to understand and use this technical health-related information. However, they are not present throughout the country to translate this information into a message which can be easily grasped by other health professionals. Nor are they always available to take part in a community action with traditional therapists or NGOs. Our suggestion is that before being passed on to the target audience, the information should be translated into a form tailored to the existing level of knowledge and understanding. Even better would be for the information to be translated locally, for specific programmes, by local experts (such as traditional therapists, NGOs or doctors) who can be consulted to ensure that the information is presented in an appropriate and effective form.

It should be pointed out here that PROSENAT is truly an innovative organisation in the field of traditional therapists. Its first innovation is creating networks which bring together different traditional therapists and their knowledge. It is crucial for professionals to find means of collaborating in a positive and interactive way, both among themselves and with professionals from other sectors. One could suggest that this network allows information to circulate, the aim being to improve and support the practice of traditional therapists. However, membership is solely for traditional therapists and not for occasional cooperative ventures. This can perhaps be attributed to the characteristics of the field of traditional medicine, which is based on secrecy and the transmission of knowledge through the family line. Unfortunately traditional therapists, despite the being most consulted local health professionals, remain marginalised by the regulated medical structures (biomedicine and university). They are not recognised as legitimate sources of knowledge on health and disease. At least, this is what we are told by the participants in our research project, though official documents (from the Cameroon government and WHO) suggest that the practice of traditional therapists is recognised and that legislation leading to a national strategy on traditional medicine is currently being prepared (Lantum and Ekeke Monono 2005). Without wishing to call into question the efforts being made by the government of Cameroon, it is nevertheless justifiable to express regret, as does Monteillet (2005), that considerable resources are being invested in monitoring the prescription and distribution of medicines (in the health service, hospitals and dispensaries) while at the same time a wealth of pharmacotherapeutic learning that is about to be lost due to a lack of collective backing and the disappearance of the traditional methods of transmission (those described by the traditional therapists taking part in the research: initiation being passed on from father to son). The PROSENAT initiative is a contemporary response to this post-colonial breakdown of ancestral wisdom. It also provides a basis for successful collaborative efforts in the fight against disease which include traditional therapists, as is the case in other parts of the world and under the auspices of international organisations (Von Shariful and Moreau 2009).

4.5.4 *The Consequences of the Lack of Recognition for Traditional Medicine by the State*

Legal recognition of traditional therapies has been debated by a range of actors within international institutions as well as within the government and health sectors across Africa. Since 1978 the WHO has been asking for more cooperation and even for the integration of traditional therapy and biomedicine (Van der Geest 1997). There is continued support for traditional therapists playing a full role in the health system. The purpose of the collaboration between PROSENAT and the health sector is to improve the current situation regarding traditional medicine (preparation of medicines, evaluation of their effectiveness and safety, diagnosis, etc.) and to contribute to the health of the population through an inclusive health policy.

There are a number of problems surrounding the recognition of traditional therapies. The holistic approach of traditional medicine is in stark contrast to the purely biological (and occasionally psychosomatic) models of Western medicine. Traditional medicine places the emphasis on achieving continuity of body, spirit (in the sense of psyche) and the soul. Biomedical remedies deal with the immediate symptoms of illness, targeting the relationships between the multiple levels of the body and its response to its surroundings. The importance given to spiritual healing (and the beliefs associated with this) does not sit well with the biomedical sector, which sees illness as a purely physical phenomenon, a malfunctioning of the body. The practice of treating an evil spirit or carrying out a ritual to seek protection is considered unacceptable in medical institutions; however, these practices are often carried out, even in hospitals with the complicity of the nursing staff (Awah and Phillimore 2008).

A further obstacle to traditional medicine is the secrecy that surrounds it. Sharing medical knowledge with the patients or with other health-care professionals is not one of the characteristics of traditional medicine. The traditional therapists believe their knowledge to be their own personal property, acquired through their family line or as a chosen apprentice (Van der Geest 1997). This secrecy is a problem for the recognition of traditional therapies as it makes it difficult to regulate medicines (e.g. to verify the effects) or prescriptions (e.g. to verify the competence of the traditional therapist).

The sorry state of the Cameroon health system is an indication of the need for a multidisciplinary approach to health. In the current context such an approach is a necessity, not a luxury. Traditional therapists are an integral part of Cameroon society. Their contributions fit with 'the philosophy of self-sufficiency for primary health care. Where possible, dependence on external services should be replaced by dependence on local resources' (Van der Geest 1997; Monteillet 2005 makes the same case.) The members of PROSENAT are an example for those traditional therapists who are interested and willing to make their professional skills available to the primary health-care service in Cameroon or elsewhere. PROSENAT states that people first seek advice and care from traditional medicine, before consulting a doctor. Monteillet (2005) shows that the other source of primary health care is the travelling pharmaceutical salesman, a form of self-medication influenced by family wisdom and what is on sale on the street corner, usually analgesics according to Monteillet. The lack of any form of control over such sales and more especially the absence of knowledge on the part of the vendor or the buyer makes for a very high risk situation.

The presence of traditional therapists in the local communities that have no access to biomedical facilities is a crucial factor in maintaining good health in poor and isolated areas. The public respect these healers and can identify more easily with the care they provide than with the more technical biomedical care (Awah et al. 2008). Collaboration between biomedicine and traditional medicine is quite feasible and produces interesting results (Von Shariful and Moreau 2009).

The development of awareness raising campaigns will benefit from the recognition of traditional medicine by the public health system. These events will stand a much greater chance of being accepted and of their messages being taken up by individuals if they are supported and assisted by traditional therapists recognised by their community. The traditional therapists are an integral part of the community which means that their familiarity with the requirements and cultural expectations of the community can play a vital role in developing community action plans. In addition their knowledge of local languages will also help to formulate the public health messages by using the common language and suitable metaphors and by providing a correct translation of health-related information.

4.5.5 Translation and Transmission of the Information

Of the three groups of professionals encountered during this research project, only the members of WESDE explicitly identified the means they use to communicate the information on health and prevention to the population groups. As used here the term population does not refer to a homogenous group of individuals. WESDE's approach respects the diversity of the population, taking account of various aspects, such as gender, level of education, age and religion. The methods used for their interventions and to transmit information are established on the basis of the group targeted. The intervention strategies are devised to suit the group, as well as to encourage all members of the group to participate. The traditional therapists and the doctors work in a sort of 'tutorial' situation, preferring individual – one-to-one – consultations. This creates an environment in which they are identified as being the expert who provides care and information. The intervention is not designed to be interactive, which has the downside of potentially limiting the amount of information transmitted.

Information does not exist as a readily identifiable product. It is derived from the knowledge acquired during basic training, professional experience and additional training made available to some health-care professionals. This knowledge is always transmitted through a medium of some kind. Those participating in our research project mentioned a whole list of possibilities, such as Internet, DVDs, etc. However, the most important source of information available to the members of WESDE and PROSENAT remains the specialists belonging to international NGOs and occasionally, though rarely, written documents produced by these organisations. It is important to note that even the most modest programme emanating from an international organisation has to be approved by the ministry. Indeed, the process of transmitting information from the institutions in the North to one of the organisations in Cameroon follows a complex administrative route, as related by all the participants in the research project, whatever their professional origin. The information is examined in detail and then approved before reaching the target group through the various activities. As far as we are aware, this process does not involve any (symbolic) translation work to help ensuring that the information makes sense to the groups targeted.

4.5.6 Conclusions

The public health system in Cameroon is finding it extremely difficult to maintain an adequate level of service, as is the case for many such health services across Africa. At the same time, a whole range of new practices, in particular self-medication thanks to biomedical products available over the counter, are flourishing. This is not necessarily in the interests of the population who are left alone to deal with their illnesses and with the purveyors of false hope, who have no medical knowledge (Monteillet 2005). These practices are linked to complex representations of disease and its causes. The biological explanations furnished by Western medicine, far from being rejected, are joined to social and supernatural explanations. Only traditional medicine is considered capable of dealing with these causes. The risks are not only physical or Cartesian. Any form of contact, voluntary or involuntary, with people, specific places or invisible spirits becomes a risk. Thus, protection is not solely material; it must also be ritual and spiritual. If we wish to ward off pandemics, it is simply not possible to ignore this type of consideration when planning awareness raising and prevention campaigns. However, this does appear to be what happens.

At the end of this analysis, which has of necessity been incomplete and restricted by the fact that our means of investigation have not always been suitable for this type of field (e.g. only one or two interviews for each professional, little time available for presence and observation), it seems to us that those people to whom the population should turn first – the doctors – are the people whose initial training prepares them least well to communicate information in a relevant way. Indeed, the relationship with the patient and his surroundings are not included in the topics studied or for which they have been trained. In the end, it is the members of WESDE who, by gleaning any information they could and by identifying the complementary aspects between the two groups, have been able to develop some ideas on the transmission of information (relating to ways of translating knowledge into information that makes sense to the target groups). However, they are not the people to whom the population turn first. Even though their activities are necessary 'before' the risk, the main caregivers 'during' and 'after' the risk, in other words the doctors and the traditional therapists, have insufficient information and training relating to this crucial topic. Other research has shown that one of the principal failings of the Cameroon health system is the lack of consideration shown to the patient by the public health service professionals (Labhardt et al. 2009; Mbanya et al. 2001). If it is deemed important for knowledge to be transformed into relevant information in all cases, it will be necessary to think about making the health professionals aware of the relationship dimension of health care.

Without doubt the process of translating knowledge into information is a weak link in the chains of circulation we have presented. However, both WESDE and the traditional therapists manage very well, either with the help of their in-depth knowledge of the communities in which they work, or through creativity and the inevitable process of trial and error. It appears to us that the greatest difficulty lies in access to knowledge. For information to reach families and to make a difference in terms of taking risks, a professional has to have access to the knowledge relating to these risks and how to pass this on before he can transform it into information and make the difference that will make the difference – in other words, transform it into relevant information for the family (and the community). However, it is precisely this crucial access that is not available. Despite the willingness of the volunteers, they rarely have access to this knowledge. The members of WESDE confirmed that they have to 'track down' this knowledge by hunting out international NGO training courses or programmes. Only doctors have a reasonable chance of any additional training. Once again, to improve the health of the population groups, it is essential to consider access to knowledge. It must of course be in various forms in order to suit the needs of the various caregivers, not only academic products from the North, such as books or scientific articles.

References

Awah, P. K., & Phillimore, P. (2008). Diabetes, medicine and modernity in Cameroon. *Africa – Journal of the International African Institute, 78*(4), 475–495.

Awah, P. K., Unwin, N., & Phillimore, P. (2008). Cure or control: Complying with biomedical regime of diabetes in Cameroon. *BMC Health Services Research, 8*, 43. doi:10.1186/1472-6963-8-43.

Bardin, L. (1993). *L'analyse de contenu* (7e éd. corrigée. – ed.). Paris: Presses universitaires de France.

Baudon, D., Boutin, J.-P., Louis, F.-J., & Devret, D. (1999). Les grandes endémies africaines à l'aube de l'an 2000. *Médecine Tropicale, 59*, 34–38.

Beninguisse, G., & De Brouwere, V. (2004). Tradition and modernity in Cameroon: The confrontation between social demand and biomedical logics of health services. *African Journal of Reproductive Health, 8*(3), 152–175.

Bonnet, D. (2003). Transmissions, préventions et hygiènes en Afrique de l'Ouest. Une question anthropologique. In D. Bonnet & Y. Jaffré (Eds.), *Les maladies de passage* (pp. 5–26). Paris: Karthala.

Courade, G. (Ed.). (2000). *Le désarroi camerounais. L'épreuve de l'économie mondiale*. Paris: Karthala.
De Rosny, E. (1992). *L'Afrique des guérisons*. Paris: Karthala.
Devèze, J.-C. (2006). Le coton, moteur du développement et facteur de stabilité au Cameroun? *Afrique Contemporaine, 217*(1), 107–120.
Eboko, F. (1999). Logiques et contradictions internationales dans le champ du sida au Cameroun. *Autrepart, 12*, 123–140.
Eboko, F. (2000). Risque-sida, pouvoirs et sexualité. La puissance de l'Etat en question au Cameroun. In G. Courade (Ed.), *Le désarroi camerounais. L'épreuve de l'économie mondiale* (pp. 235–262). Paris: Karthala.
Gubry, P. (1996). *Le retour au village. Une solution à la crise économique au Cameroun*. Paris: L'Harmattan.
Heinzerling, L. M. (2005). Attitudes of traditional healers towards Western medicine in rural Cameroon. *Tropical Doctor, 35*(3), 161–164. doi:10.1258/0049475054620653.
Hours, B. (1986). *L'état sorcier. Santé publique et société au Cameroun*. Paris: Harmattan.
Hours, B. (1990). La santé publique entre soins de santé primaires et management. *Cahiers des Sciences Humaines, 35*(1), 123–140.
Janzen, J. M. (1995). *La quête de la thérapie au Bas-Zaïre*. Paris: Karthala.
Labhardt, N. D., Schiess, K., Manga, E., & Langewitz, W. (2009). Provider-patient interaction in rural Cameroon–how it relates to the patient's understanding of diagnosis and prescribed drugs, the patient's concept of illness, and access to therapy. *Patient Education and Counseling, 76*(2), 196–201. doi:10.1016/j.pec.2008.12.020.
Lantum, D. M., & Ekeke Monono, M. (2005). Republic of Cameroon. In G. Bodeker, C. K. Ong, C. Grundy, G. Burford, & K. Shein (Eds.), *WHO global atlas of traditional, complementary and alternative medicine* (pp. 13–18). Geneva: World Health Organisation, Center for Health Development.
Mbanya, D. N., Zebaze, R., Kengne, A. P., Minkoulou, E. M., Awah, P., & Beure. (2001). Knowledge, attitudes and practices of nursing staff in a rural hospital of Cameroon: How much does the health care provider know about the human immunodeficiency virus/acquired immune deficiency syndrome? *International Nursing Review, 48*(4), 241–249.
Meekers, D., & Klein, M. (2002). Determinants of condom use among young people in urban Cameroon. *Studies in Family Planning, 33*(4), 335–346.
Monteillet, N. (2005). *Le pluralisme thérapeutique au Cameroun: Crise hospitalière et nouvelles pratiques populaires*. Paris: Karthala.
Moupou, M., & Akei Mbanga, L. (2008). Désengagement de l'Etat et réponses paysannes au Cameroun. *Les Cahiers d'Outre-Mer, 241–242*, 163–183.
Njomaha, C. (2003). Durabilité des systèmes de culture dans l'Extrême-Nord Cameroun. In J. Y. Jamin, L. Seiny Boukar, & C. Floret (Eds.), *Savanes africaines: des espaces en mutation, des acteurs face à de nouveaux défis*. N'Djamena, Tchad & Montpellier. France: Prasac & Cirad.
Okalla, R., & Le Vigouroux, A. (2006). Cameroun : de la réorientation des soins de santé primaires au plan national au développement sanitaire. *Le bulletin de l'APAD, 21*, 79–91.
Programme commun des Nations Unies sur le VIH/sida. (2008). *Rapport sur l'épidémie mondiale de sida*. Genève: ONUSIDA.
Roupsard, M. (1987). *Nord-Cameroun. Ouverture et développement d'une région enclavée [thèse de doctorat non publiée]*. Paris: Paris X.
Ryan, G. W. (1998). What do sequential behavioral patterns suggest about the medical decision-making process?: Modeling home case management of acute illnesses in a rural Cameroonian village. *Social Science and Medicine, 46*(2), 209–225. doi:10.1016/S0277-9536(97)00151-2.
Socpa, A. (2003). *Démocratisation et autochtonie au Cameroun*. Berlin: Lit.
Van der Geest, S. (1997). Is there a role for traditional medicine in basic health services of Africa? A plea for community perspective. *Tropical Medicine and International Health, 2*(9), 903–911.

Von Shariful, I., & Moreau, A. (2009). Traditional healers in preventing HIV/AIDS: Roles and scopes. *Bulletin de Medicus Mundi Suisse,* 113. http://www.medicusmundi.ch/mms/services/bulletin/bulletin113_2009/chapter2/32.html.

Wamba, A. (2005). Entre tradition, religion et modernité: la construction d'un réseau de compétences thérapeutiques au Cameroun. *L'Autre: cliniques, cultures et sociétés, 6*(2), 227–237.

World Health Organisation (1976). *Médecine traditionnelle africaine*. Brazzaville. Congo: Afro n° 1.

Yenshu Vubo, E. (2006). Management of ethnic diversity in Cameroon against the backdrop of social crises. *Cahiers d'études africaines, 46*(1), 135–156.

Youmba, J. C., & Barrère, M. (2005). Paludisme. In Institut National de la Statistique du Cameroun, & ORC Macro (Eds.), *Cameroun: Demographic and Health Survey – 2004* (pp. 165–178). Yaoundé/Calverton: Institut National de la Statistique du Cameroun & ORC Macro.

Chapter 5
Conclusion

This brings us to the end of the analysis of our case studies. Although they will undoubtedly appear quite different – it was never the intention to carry out a comparative study – our analysis of the three situations was based on a similar approach and methodology. So, what can we conclude from this study?

The choice of three widely differing sites, in terms of their institutional context and their geographical location, reflects the team's desire to seek common elements in the circulation of information in diverse environments. The research fields were focussed on distinctive contexts in the dissemination of information in risk situations: centralisation, distribution, and the use/transmission of this information. The group[1] that came together for a seminar marking the end of the project recognised that the research carried out in three fields – the SHOC Room, the field library and the work of the two NGOs in Cameroon – showed that, in spite of the specific characteristics and the vertical diversity of each case studied (in terms of substance), considering the study from a horizontal point of view (in terms of functionality) revealed a number of elements in common.

In the light of the discussion that took place during the seminar, the two axes used in the research methodology looking at the movement of information can be seen as crucial. These were the temporality of risk (November), with its three stages – before, during and after – and the 'professional niche' (Leanza), which deals with the interface between the subject and the various components of its environment. These two axes provide complementary perspectives with regard to the essential dimensions of understanding risk: time and space/environment. By superimposing these two methodological approaches, it becomes easier to identify all the elements required to construct a complete strategy for the communication and dissemination of information.

[1]The project concluded with a seminar that brought together not only the team involved in carrying out the research but also representatives from all the organisations concerned.

V. November, Y. Leanza, *Risk, Disaster and Crisis Reduction*,
DOI 10.1007/978-3-319-08542-5_5

A number of important points merit more detailed investigation in order to gain greater insight into the characteristics of the information to be communicated to the recipients, as well as the methods of transmission. The following points were covered in depth in discussions held during the seminar.

5.1 The Definition of Risk

This study offers a number of definitions of risk, each of which is valid in the context for which it was formulated. Broadly speaking, risk can be considered as a clearly identified danger associated with the occurrence of a describable event, or series of events, for which it is impossible to say whether they will occur, although it is likely that they will. Risk could be described as a 'pre-event', the essential nature of which is to be a potential danger. Seen in conjunction with the vulnerability of communities and the transformation of the hazard (potential element) into reality (real element), risk leads to disaster. This explains the importance of managing risk and of decreasing vulnerability and thus of reducing the potential for disaster. The notions of uncertainty and probability are essential elements of the definition.

The importance of defining risk lies not in the actual wording chosen but rather in the acceptance of the definition by the people or communities concerned, thereby allowing the risk to be managed carefully, consistently and with continuity. It is therefore essential to take account of the different ways that the risk may be perceived, depending on context and culture. A doctor in Cameroon giving a definition of risk will not use the same words as a traditional therapist, even when talking about the same hazard. The culture is different and the way in which information is understood will be affected by whether or not they share a common definition. Any definition of risk must take account of the context or the 'niche'. Here, we have been able to show not only how risk is translated in different contexts, by different actors, but also how it passes from actor to actor through successive translations and reformulations. This process not only contributes to a common acceptance of the risk, it also allows appropriate action to be taken. This demonstrates clearly that risk can be the driving force for action provided the definition of risk makes sense.

5.2 Types of Information and Its Circulation

Information is available in a wide variety of forms, and the recipients of this information need to know what it represents and be prepared to consider it relevant in the context of the possibility of a risk event. The concept of 'hold' is essential here. The information must be understood and integrated by the people for whom it is intended. This 'hold', when it happens, reflects the way in which ownership is taken by the community, and the understanding of the information is incorporated into a continuum that is specific to that community, be it a restricted or wider community.

The research reveals that there are several possible types of message and that the messages can be transmitted in a range of ways, depending on the context and the timing (before, after or during the event). For example, rumours are one type of information found in many communities, where it is seen as a very valuable resource. The analysis of information carried out by the WHO includes rumours in the detection of risk when investigating an event liable to pose a threat to public health. The language and the wording used are clearly crucial elements in the validity and the scope of the information. For this reason the automatic rumour detection software is backed up by interpreters who check (in nine languages) that no valid rumour has been accidentally rejected.

With regard to the definition of information, it is important to remember that information is only useful if it is passed on. Information that is not disseminated has no value in risk management. As the indication of a potential risk is gradually transformed into reality, the success of the early warning given to a community where there is an increasing likelihood of danger depends on both the relevant information and the effective communication. It is essential to ensure a symbiosis between all the stages of information management and that the information gathered will be verified and confirmed before being disseminated.

A further valuable element in understanding the circulation of information is the reaction to the information – the feedback – which makes it possible to judge how useful it is and whether there is a need to modify either the content (the substance or the form) or the way in which it has been communicated. Those in charge of managing the risk must ask two questions: 'Has the message been received, understood and accepted?' and 'Will this message enable relevant action to be taken?'

5.3 The Targets for the Information and the Diversity of the Channels of Circulation

In order to determine how the information is to be targeted, it is important to understand the 'niche'. The people, objects or institutions in possession of the information must tailor the type of information to the context in which it will circulate and be received. Environment, culture and language are crucial elements in assessing the validity of information.

The following sequence can be seen as a form of continuum: translation, metaphor, hold. The translation is needed for the information to be transmitted from the point of origin to the recipients. The use of metaphors then ensures that the information is appropriate to the people receiving it. Finally, grasping the information demonstrates that it has been understood by the recipient. This transmission of information, from the point of origin to the destinations, takes place using a series of networks, which bring together a wide range of actors, who perform different functions according to the type of information, such as a coordinator, producer, transmitter and operator. We observed that there is no linear pattern in the circulation of information; circulation tends to be either more or less horizontal or more or less vertical. What seems to guarantee good circulation characteristics is the very variety in the modes of circulation, with several roles being performed simultaneously, as was clearly demonstrated in the study of the situation in Madagascar.

The case studies also showed that networks based on proximity, while important, are not the only means of ensuring the circulation of information. Other essential conditions, such as trust and the status of the source of the information, play a crucial role in ensuring that the information is picked up by the actors and transformed into action. We identified a number of situations in which relationships of connexity are key, rather than relationships of proximity. This observation could be extended to the use of social networks in a crisis situation, but our studies were carried out before the rise in the mass use of such forms of information technology.

Information is transmitted in different ways, depending on the context and the targets. These ways include training, simulation, reports, theatre and role play. Each individual form is recognised as being valuable in specific contexts and can be indispensable if the information is to be conveyed correctly.

Socio-technical intermediaries also play an important role in the circulation of information. The presence or absence of certain resources can have direct repercussions on the circulation of information. Examples include batteries for radios or loudhailers, fuel for vehicles or even paper for producing written information. Books are a frequently used intermediary and are the foundation of the idea behind the field library. Other resources, such as the computer network and the databases, make up the framework for information gathering within the WHO.

5.4 The Results of Disseminating Information

At the end of the seminar, a question was asked about the usefulness of this research for institutions and people involved in risk management and in the formulation and the dissemination of information in a crisis or risk situation. What can be expected to come out of the study that will improve the circulation of information? Depending on the types of situation, the stage involved and the roles played by the various actors, the results of the study may mean that the disaster can be averted, or the risk reduced, or even that there can be better preparation for the disaster (which may occur at some point in the near or distant future). To this end, rather than drafting a compendium of directives and guidelines for risk management practitioners, it would be good to develop a tool capable of preserving the memory of various experiences in which there was a satisfactory flow of information (or not, as the case may be).

It is also important to consider the links between those who provide the information and the recipients and, as far as possible, to avoid any disparity. The circulation of information should be managed with this in mind. In this context, one may also speak of information being controlled by the authority responsible for the source of the information (the power). Excessive centralisation of information can lead to an abuse of power by the authority (determining whether the information is distributed or not or even manipulation). While bringing together the information allows for easier management and dissemination – this is the principle behind the centralisation of health information in the SHOC Room, for example – it is desirable for the information to be able to follow lateral paths or networks that were not previously envisaged, but which could be integrated into the way information circulates. A resilient system is a system that allows information to circulate in a variety of ways and which pays specific attention to the socio-technical intermediaries involved.

At the end of the discussion, it was recognised that to achieve conditions suitable for the circulation of information, and so to reduce the potential for disaster represented by the risk, the points listed below should be taken into account and should figure on a 'check list' for the practitioners:

- Agree on the type of information;
- Understand the context and ensure that information is picked up;
- Define the networks and partnerships;
- Agree on the compatibility of the various communication channels and define the coordination procedures;
- Manage the communications resources;
- If required, agree whether regulations are needed.

5.5 Conclusion: A Tool for Practitioners

The ideas noted here reflect the exchanges between the project team and the representatives of the organisations concerned. Rather than a summary of the work carried out, the points below offer an overview of our observations. The value of the discussion, other than allowing the participants to express their points of view, is that it allowed us to bring together the actors from the three areas and to identify the common elements in the circulation of information in crisis and risk situations. These comments offer a series of clarifications regarding the elements on which it is desirable, necessary or even essential for those responsible for managing risk situations and ensuring an effective flow of information to focus their attention. Once the project had been completed, a number of guidelines were issued in the form of a series of points to be checked when monitoring risk situations. This document is intended to be used by practitioners involved in disaster prevention and information dissemination networks. Of course, their effectiveness remains to be assessed, but they meet the need, highlighted by our study, to organise decision-making and to put in place means of preventing and responding to hazards and risks. These guidelines, which follow the list of key elements given above, are listed below.

- Information
  - Identify the hazards, know the risk and understand the scope and the potential consequences
  - Identify and be aware of the vulnerabilities of the populations at risk
  - Identify the means of communication available to the populations living in the areas at risk (radio, television, loudspeaker, local press, Internet, etc.)
  - Define the types of information that are relevant to (and can be understood by) these populations and verify (test) whether they will be understood by those they are aimed at when disseminated
  - Set up the relays needed to produce the messages (sources of information)
  - Ensure easy access to the databases able to provide the additional information needed to understand the messages fully
  - Maintain an archive of the information disseminated
- Context
  - Be fully informed about the population at risk (culture, language(s), specific characteristics, customs, location, possible areas of resistance, etc.)
  - Define, identify and know the 'actors' (authorities, local leaders, NGOs, other organisations, scientific institutions [e.g. meteorology, volcanology, hydrology, biology, health], etc.)
  - Prepare the involvement and participation of the local communities in risk management and disaster response
  - Ensure that the messages transmitted can be grasped by the recipient (content, references, language(s), specific cultural characteristics, etc.)
  - Ensure that once grasped, the information can be understood and used to enable appropriate action to be taken; consider the type of action (relocation, evacuation, vaccination, etc.)
- Networks and partnerships
  - List, identify, record, contact and maintain collaborative links with potential partners in crisis management (institutional and individual leaders, governmental and non-governmental organisations, local and international agencies, etc.)
  - Maintain an up-to-date list of all these points of contact, with accurate contact details (telephone, fax, email, physical address, etc.)
  - Establish an effective coordination system to link the partners in an operational network, which can be easily activated when required
  - Where appropriate, establish formal partnership agreements for the circulation of information and the activation of distribution systems within partner networks
  - Maintain continuous monitoring in order to collect, format and disseminate the information as rapidly as possible (see also Regulation below)

- Communication channels and coordination systems
  - Establish communication links within the framework of well-defined networks
  - Ensure robust channels of communication and establish alternative back-up systems
  - Institute formal and informal communication systems; establish information sharing agreements within the networks; and ensure concerted and consistent distribution
- Means of communication
  - Identify the means of communication and categorise them in a manner appropriate to the characteristics of the location
  - Ensure the maintenance (physical and technical) of communications systems and the corresponding intermediaries (fuel for vehicles and generators, batteries for radios or loudhailers, etc.)
  - Ensure training for personnel responsible for maintaining for the equipment used to disseminate information
  - Arrange the funding required to cover the costs of equipment and communications personnel
  - Ensure that there is, and will continue to be, sufficient personnel to transmit and disseminate information
- Regulations
  - Contact the bodies concerned (political, administrative, technical) to ensure that information may circulate freely
  - Where the dissemination of information is restricted, establish appropriate systems to allow rapid checking by the authorities
  - Where appropriate, put in place systems to allow information to be shared at international level

Appendix

COMITE DE REFLEXION DESINTERVENANTS AUX CATACLYSMES (CRIC)	REPOBLIKAN'I MADAGASIKARA TANINDRAZANA-FAHAFAHANA-FANDROSOANA MINISTERE DE L'INTERIEUR ET DE LA REFORME ADMINISTRATIVE **ENQUETE INITIALE MULTI-ALEAS (EIMA)** **ALEAS DE SURVENANCE RAPIDE**	**CONSEIL NATIONAL DE SECOURS**

IDENTIFICATION (zone du rapport)

1. Faritany : ………………………………… 2. Région : ……………………………………………………… 3. District :……………………………
4. Commune : ……………………………… 5. Fokontany (concernés) ……………………………………

A. IMPACTS SUR LES HUMAINS

1. Nombre de décès : …………………………………………
2. Nombre de blessés :
   a. total : ……………………………………………………
3. Nombre de sinistrés :
   a. sans abri : ………………………………………………
   b. Déplacés (regroupés) : ………………………………
4. Nombre de disparus :……………………………………
5. Lieu d'hébergement des sans-abri OUI ….. NON……

B. DEGATS HABITAT, TRANSPORT ET COMMUNICATION

1. Dégâts sur les habitations :
   a. Nombre de maisons couchées : …………
   b. Nombre de maisons sans toit : …………
   c. Nombre de maisons inondées : …………
2. Accès par la route principale (préciser) :
   a. Praticable: ……………………………………
   b. Coupé : …………………………………………
3. Communication téléphone/radio (préciser) :
   a. Fonctionne: OUI…… NON……
4. Accès portuaire (préciser) :
   a. Fonctionne:OUI…… NON ……

C. DEGATS INFRASTRUCTURES EAU ET SANTE

5. Centre de santé et hôpitaux (préciser) :
   a. Nombre fonctionnels : ………………………
   b. Nombre non fonctionnel : ………………………
6. Disponibilité de médicaments de premier secours :
   a. Difficile : ……………………………………………………
   b. Pas de médicament : ………………………………
7. Personnel de santé (préciser) :
   a. Sans changement : ………………………………
   b. Réduit : …………………………………………………
8. Accès eau potable (préciser) :
   a. Existe : OUI…… NON……

D. DEGATS INFRASTRUCTURES, EDUCATION ET ADMINISTRATION

9. Dégâts sur les écoles (commenter si possible)
   a. Nombre fonctionnels : ………………………
   b. Nombre fonctionnels au ralenti : …………
   c. Nombre à l'arrêt : ……………………………………
10. Nombre d'enfants sans écoles (préciser)
   a. Primaire : ……………………………
   b. Secondaire : ………………………
11. Fonctionnement de l'administration (préciser)
   a. Fonctionne : OUI ……. NON…….

E. DEGATS PRODUCTION AGROPASTORALE ET COMMERCES

12. Dégâts sur les cultures en cours dans les champs (préciser état de la destruction des cultures) :
   a. vivrières : (léger, moyen, grave)…………
   b. rente : (léger, moyen, grave)……………
   c. fruits : (léger, moyen, grave)……………
13. Dégâts sur l'élevage (estimer pourcentage du cheptel perdu) :
   a. bovins : (léger, moyen, grave)……………………
   b. Ovins :(léger, moyen, grave)………………………
   c. Caprins : (léger, moyen, grave)…………………
   d. Animaux de traite : (léger, moyen, grave)…………

F. COMMENTAIRES (veuillez utiliser ces lignes pour fournir des commentaires, chiffres et faits supplémentaires pouvant améliorer l' évaluation des dégâts dans votre zone) :

……………………………………………………………………………
……………………………………………………………………………
……………………………………………………………………………
……………………………………………………………………………
……………………………………………………………………………
……………………………………………………………………………
……………………………………………………………………………
……………………………………………………………………………

Nom, organisme et signature de la personne ayant rempli ce questionnaire

……………………………………………………………………………
……………………………………………………………………………
……………………………………………………………………………
……………………………………………………………………………
……………………………………………………………………………
……………………………………………………………………………

V. November, Y. Leanza, *Risk, Disaster and Crisis Reduction*,
DOI 10.1007/978-3-319-08542-5

Index

V. November, Y. Leanza, *Risk, Disaster and Crisis Reduction*,
DOI 10.1007/978-3-319-08542-5

MIX
Papier aus verantwortungsvollen Quellen
Paper from responsible sources
FSC® C105338

If you have any concerns about our products,
you can contact us on
ProductSafety@springernature.com

In case Publisher is established outside the EU,
the EU authorized representative is:
Springer Nature Customer Service Center GmbH
Europaplatz 3, 69115 Heidelberg, Germany

Printed by Libri Plureos GmbH
in Hamburg, Germany